TQM
A Primer for Implementation

TQM
A Primer for Implementation

Lesley Munro-Faure

Malcolm Munro-Faure

IRWIN
Professional Publishing

Burr Ridge, Illinois
New York, New York

British Library Cataloging in Publication Data
A CIP catalog record for this book can be obtained from the British Library.

© RICHARD D. IRWIN, INC., 1994

Originally published as *Implementing Total Quality Management* by
Pitman Publishing, a division of Longman U.K. Ltd., copyright 1992.

This edition of *TQM: A Primer for Implementation* is published by
arrangement with Pitman Publishing, London. The Financial Times
and FT are trademarks of the Financial Times, Ltd., London.

Senior sponsoring editor:	Jean Marie Geracie
Project editor:	Beth Yates
Production manager:	Jon Christopher
Interior designer:	Jeanne M. Rivera
Cover designer:	Tim Kaage
Art coordinator:	Heather Burbridge
Compositor:	Northern Phototypesetting Co. Ltd.
Typeface:	11/13 Palatino
Printer:	Book Press, Inc.

Library of Congress Cataloging-in-Publication Data

Munro-Faure, Lesley.
    TQM: a primer for implementation / Lesley & Malcolm Munro-Faure.
        p.   cm.—(Financial times)
    Earlier ed. published under title: Implementing total quality
management. 1992
    Includes index.
    ISBN 0–7863–0138–4
    1. Total quality management.   I. Munro-Faure, Malcolm. II. Munro-
Faure, Lesley,   Implementing total quality management.   III. Title.
    IV. Series: Financial times series.
    HD62.15.M86   1994
    658.5′62—dc20   93–38863

Printed in the United States of America

1 2 3 4 5 6 7 8 9 0   BP   1 0 9 8 7 6 5 4

Preface

TQM can seem confusing because of all the jargon plus the apparent difficulty of finding hard evidence of the benefits of implementing a program of continuous quality improvement. But actually the broad concepts are quite straightforward and logical.

The objective of Total Quality Management (TQM) is to satisfy customer requirements as efficiently and profitably as possible. This requires the continuous improvement of performance as fast as developments allow. This is why the commitment to TQM must be both absolute and ongoing.

In a total quality environment all employees must strive to

1. Do the right things. This means that only activities that help a business to satisfy its customers' requirements are acceptable. Other activities should be analyzed and, if they're unnecessary, be discontinued.

2. Do things right. This means that all activities should be performed correctly, so that the output from the activity conforms to the customer's requirements.

3. Do things right first time, every time. If this can be achieved, then no more money should be wasted on checking and scrapping output or correcting errors. This type of environment is based on the concept of preventing errors from arising in the first place.

These three requirements are captured in the expression,

Do the right things right the first time, every time.

But how can you introduce a TQM environment?

Many, but not all, organizations operate procedures to ensure that the quality of their output will be acceptable to their customers. This is the starting point for a Total Quality environment.

The next steps involve ensuring that errors are prevented and the business focuses only on activities that satisfy their customers' requirements.

Introducing a TQM environment is hard work. It takes the

v

absolute commitment of everyone—especially senior management—to achieve. It also takes a considerable amount of planning.

We've written this book to help managers understand the concepts underlying TQM and the significant benefits it can bring; and to enable them to implement continuous quality improvement in any organization that's determined to succeed.

We're very grateful to the many friends and colleagues who've helped us make this book come to life. In particular, we thank the following for enthusiastically contributing time and effort to explain their experiences in implementing TQM: Joe Goasdoué of ICL, Karen Evans and Neil Clackett of the Doncaster Royal Infirmary and Montagu Hospital National Health Service Trust, David Owen and Roger Cliffe of the TSB Bank and Raj Nadarajah and Lance Arrington of Philip Crosby Associates, Inc.

Above all, we thank Ted Bones for his patience, commitment, enthusiasm, and support over many years.

Lesley Munro-Faure
Malcolm Munro-Faure

Introduction

Total Quality Management (TQM) is a proven, systematic approach to the planning and management of activities. It can be successfully applied to any type of organization.

The fundamental concepts behind TQM are simple:

1. A successful business relies on making profitable sales to its customers. A business will only retain the support of its existing customer base and attract new customers if it produces output (products or services) that conforms to its customers' requirements.
2. A business can satisfy its customers' requirements only if it:
   a. Identifies those requirements.
   b. Produces output that conforms to those requirements.
3. A business can maximize profits only if it produces its output efficiently. To do this, a business must direct all its activities towards producing the necessary output at minimum cost. This may be achieved by
   a. Ensuring that the design process results in output that conforms to customers' requirements and can be produced cost-effectively.
   b. Minimizing inefficiencies such as waste and rework when producing services or products.
   c. Reviewing all activities to ensure that they're directed at satisfying external customers' requirements. If they aren't, then consideration should be given to ceasing those activities.

Most managers are shocked by the cost of errors and waste that they've previously accepted as "normal." By focusing on eliminating this burden, an organization can significantly improve its performance.

Three companies that have made significant steps toward implementing TQM demonstrate the magnitude of the problem:

Company	Quality Costs
ICL	£160 million in 1987
Otis Elevator European Transcontinental Operations	29 percent of sales prior to 1987
National Westminster Bank PLC	25 percent of operating costs in 1988

This level of cost burden is typical of much of industry today. Similar results can be found in almost any organization.

We can develop a TQM environment only with the absolute commitment of management and all employees. But TQM can yield significant competitive advantage to any business that's prepared to invest the necessary time and effort to make it succeed.

The organization needs to be flexible and adaptable, continuously seeking to improve. This can only be achieved within a strong framework that responds to change while retaining effective control over operations. As a consequence there are a number of key elements that help management produce a TQM environment:

- A strong framework to retain order and control.
- The continuous striving for improvement.
- The adaptability to change to ensure that the organization responds to customer's requirements.

Figure i illustrates the components that help to produce a successful TQM environment.

Following a logical progression, this book's 10 chapters explain how management can introduce a TQM environment based on a wealth of practical experience.

Chapter 1: Total Quality Management—A Quality Revolution. TQM is a significant business management tool.

Chapter 2: Know Your Customers. The key to implementing TQM is to understand customers' needs and how the organization meets those needs.

Chapter 3: Quality Costs. The costs incurred through not meeting customers' real requirements the first time can be enormous. Only

FIGURE i
Components of Total Quality Management

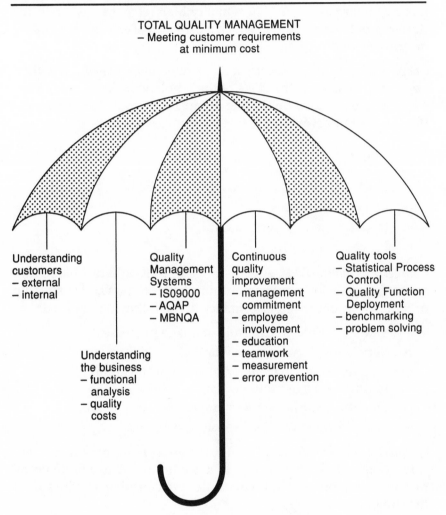

TOTAL QUALITY MANAGEMENT
– Meeting customer requirements
at minimum cost

Understanding
customers
– external
– internal

Understanding
the business
– functional
analysis
– quality
costs

Quality
Management
Systems
– ISO9000
– AQAP
– MBNQA

Continuous
quality
improvement
– management
commitment
– employee
involvement
– education
– teamwork
– measurement
– error prevention

Quality tools
– Statistical Process
Control
– Quality Function
Deployment
– benchmarking
– problem solving

by understanding how these costs are calculated can a business focus attention on the most significant areas for action.

Chapter 4: Functional Analysis. Tremendous opportunities for improving efficiency may be available from organizing the business so that it's really customer-oriented.

Chapter 5: Quality Management System Standards. The first step involves developing a strong management framework to ensure that customer requirements are fully defined, understood, and met by the organization. This Quality Management System forms the essential foundation on which a program of continuous quality improvement can be built.

Chapter 6: A Story of Continuous Quality Improvement. It's then necessary to harness the skills of the whole workforce to examine every activity carried out by the organization and identify opportunities for improvement. A six-step approach is followed:

a. Planning.
b. Understanding customers.
c. Understanding quality costs.
d. Quality awareness.
e. Measurement of performance.
f. Prevention of errors.

Chapter 7: Quality Tools. A wide range of tools and techniques are available to help management implement TQM. These help organizations improve performance in the following key areas:

a. Statistical Process Control—manage processes.
b. Benchmarking—achieve world class performance.
c. Quality Function Deployment—apply customer requirements to product design.
d. Quality Awards—understand current best practice.
e. Teamwork for quality—resolve problems.

Chapter 8: Problem Solving. A fundamental requirement for continuous quality improvement is a commitment to eliminate all problems that prevent individuals from performing activities right first time.

Chapter 9: Successful Implementation of TQM. By analyzing the application of TQM across a range of organizations, we can identify

a. The significant benefits from TQM.
b. Successful approaches and pitfalls.
c. How TQM can be applied to specific industries.

Chapter 10: What Can We Learn from the Quality Gurus? Much can be learned from studying the philosophies and methods of the "quality gurus," but it's important to adopt an approach that suits each individual organization, and to thoroughly research and plan the implementation to ensure that the organization "takes ownership" of the process.

Total Quality Management is fundamental to any organization's continued success. By following the approach outlined in this book, management can understand the concepts underlying TQM and the significant benefits it can bring. The comprehensive practical advice will enable management to implement the process of continuous quality improvement successfully in any organization that's determined to succeed.

Contents

Chapter One

Total Quality Management—A Quality Revolution

THE QUALITY CONCEPT

Quality is one of the most misunderstood issues in business today, yet it's central to the survival of even the largest organization. Quality is defined by customers. First of all, you agree on what the customer wants (the customer's requirements). Then you produce exactly what's wanted within the agreed time frame, at minimum cost. The perspective of the customer isn't always effectively addressed by Western companies. In many cases, Japanese competitors have gained an edge over their Western counterparts because they understand the need to satisfy their customers' requirements. Markets for home audio and video are cases in point; car and microchip manufacturing are examples where Western businesses are facing increasing competition.

There's only one key focal point for businesses in the world today: *the customer.*

Only businesses who focus on their customers' requirements will survive; this has been the driving force behind the leading elements in Japanese industry since World War II. Industries in the United States, Germany, and (as of late) the United Kingdom are rapidly recognizing the importance of this shift in focus and are responding. In some cases the response has been too little and too late. Adopting a strict customer focus may well emerge as the most successful strategy for remaining competitive in the face of the opening of the Single European Market and the implementation of ISO9000.

Quality is probably the best way of assuring customer loyalty, the best defense against foreign competition, and the only way to secure continuous growth and profits in difficult market conditions.

The quality concept isn't difficult to understand, but it does require a new focus of attention from everyone involved in business.

The Evolution of Quality

The concept of quality has grown a great deal since its early disciples defined quality as "producing output in conformance to customer requirements." The evolutionary path has passed through two generations already, and leading edge industries are pioneering third and fourth generations.

This evolution demonstrates how businesses are increasingly understanding and responding to their customers' requirements. The building blocks of a Total Quality Environment are illustrated in Figure 1–1.

- The first generation is to ensure that every customer's requirements are understood and are met. This marks the realization that customers will only accept output (whether it is a product or service) that meets their requirements. Any output that doesn't conform will be rejected. This leads to dissatisfied customers and additional costs for the organization. This stage is reached by ensuring that a management system exists to identify customer requirements and to ensure that those requirements are consistently met. Ensuring conformance to requirements may initially be achieved by checking and reworking/replacing any nonconforming output before releasing it to a customer.

  To reach this level, many organizations implement a Quality Management System (QMS) based on the guidelines in ISO9000 or the Malcolm Baldrige National Quality Award. Having initially been of particular interest to manufacturing organizations, this standard is now being adopted in such service industries as accounting and law.

FIGURE 1–1
The Quality Building Blocks

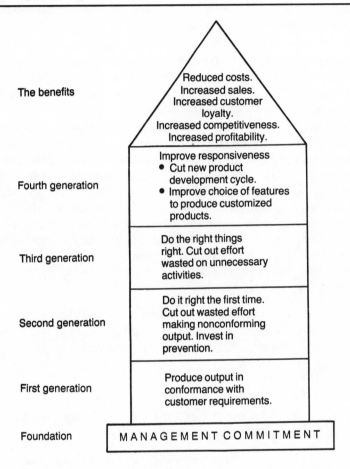

The benefits — Reduced costs. Increased sales. Increased customer loyalty. Increased competitiveness. Increased profitability.

Fourth generation — Improve responsiveness
- Cut new product development cycle.
- Improve choice of features to produce customized products.

Third generation — Do the right things right. Cut out effort wasted on unnecessary activities.

Second generation — Do it right the first time. Cut out wasted effort making nonconforming output. Invest in prevention.

First generation — Produce output in conformance with customer requirements.

Foundation — MANAGEMENT COMMITMENT

- The next generation aims to "do it right the first time, every time." Producing defective output is immensely wasteful in terms of time and money. By implementing preventive measures, companies can monitor processes and prevent errors from arising in the first place.
- The third generation recognizes that some activities are unnecessary. By analyzing the functions undertaken by an

organization (functional analysis), we can identify these operations. Internal meetings and many of the internal reports that are produced may be discontinued, freeing up valuable time and money in the process.

- The second and third generations of quality awareness have focused on producing conforming output more efficiently. The fourth generation focuses on the twin objectives of improving product responsiveness and improving the efficiency of the product development process.

- The fourth generation's objective is to shorten the time taken and to decrease costs incurred in bringing new products to the market. Being the first in the market with a new product frequently yields a significant competitive advantage. An example of the techniques being developed to achieve this objective is Quality Function Deployment (QFD). This methodology was originally developed at the Mitsubishi Kobe shipyard. QFD brings marketing, design, and manufacturing personnel together to determine customer needs and translate them into design specifications and manufacturing processes efficiently and effectively.

Each of these evolutionary steps marks a closer link between the producer and the customer. By developing this link the producer can strengthen its foundations. Ignoring the link's importance can lead to extinction.

Does Management Recognize Quality as One of the Key Competitive Issues of the 1990s?

The 1990 International Manufacturing Futures Survey conducted jointly by Boston University, the European Institute for Business Administration (INSEAD), and Waseda University in Japan produced an intriguing insight into current management thinking. This survey of manufacturing executives from over 500 large manufacturing businesses drawn from Europe, the United States, and Japan sheds light on how factories may develop in the future.

Earlier reports by the same institutes have described the quality revolution's spread from Japan (in the 1970s) to the United States in the 1980s and more recently to Europe. Improving product quality remains a key priority for management, but is increasingly becoming a qualification for entry into a market rather than a means to separate competitors.

When asked to rank five key competitive priorities over the next five years, respondents in three regions most often identified the following:

United States	Europe	Japan
Conformance quality	Conformance quality	Reliable products
Dependable delivery	Dependable delivery	Dependable delivery
Reliable products	Reliable products	Rapid design changes
High performance	High performance	Conformance quality
Price competition	Fast delivery	Product customization

Although each region is trying to develop more integrated factories producing improved-quality goods, they differ in their focus. US manufacturers are focusing on producing high-quality output at a reasonable price; Japanese manufacturers are developing systems allowing a continuing stream of new customized designs; and European manufacturers are streamlining operations to take advantage of the single European market and other markets. The same respondents were asked to identify the five activities that provided the highest payoff in the past two years (Table 1–1).

To develop a quality strategy and to ensure that it's a key part of the overall business strategy, you must understand what quality means, how it developed, and its possible future developments.

WHAT IS QUALITY?

The term *quality* has suffered over the years by being used to describe attributes such as beauty, goodness, expensiveness, freshness, and, above all, luxury. A car might be described as a "quality car" when in reality it's an expensive or luxurious car. Cloth might be described as a "quality cloth" when it's really an "all wool" cloth or a cloth with high density of threads.

TABLE 1–1
Effectiveness of Activities: The Five Activities Yielding the Highest Payoff

United States	Europe	Japan
Interfunctional work teams	Training of supervisors, management, and workers	Developing new processes for old products
Manufacturing reorganization	Manufacturing reorganization	Developing new processes for new products
Statistical Process Control	Linking manufacturing to business strategy	Quality circles
Linking manufacturing to business strategy	Quality Function Deployment	Computer-aided design
Just-in-time production	Developing new processes for new products	Quality Function Deployment

Source: J G Miller, A de Meyer, J Nakane, J S Kim, S Kurosa, and K Ferdows, "Factories for the Future," in J G Miller, A de Meyer, and J Nakane, *Benchmarking Global Operations,* (Homewood, IL: Business One Irwin, 1992).

All this makes quality look like a difficult concept to understand and almost impossible to manage. How can you manage something that's so imprecise and means so many things?

Before quality can be planned and managed it must be defined more precisely and meaningfully.

Many companies now define quality as total conformance to requirements; these requirements are the total customer requirement, not just a product or service specification. This broad, far-reaching application of quality to every activity has taken many years to develop and is a long way from where quality first began.

THE DEVELOPMENT OF QUALITY—AN OBJECTIVE STANDARD

Following World War II, manufacturing industry began to develop a specific meaning for quality. Driven by the need to meet customer demands for products that did what manufacturers claimed, quality began to mean the design and manufacture of a product meeting customer specifications and expectations. This was driven in Japan by the need to rebuild its manufacturing industry and in Europe and the United States primarily by the armed forces with their need for conforming equipment that allowed them to fulfill their military role.

The manufacturing industries adopted the term *quality* to mean "conformance to product requirements," whether these requirements were a stated specification or a perceived customer need. Industry was moving toward a philosophy that a product should unfailingly do what the customer needed and wanted it to do.

By adopting this definition of quality, management could measure, assess, and improve its quality performance. Quality became an objective concept. It was something that the whole work force could understand and measure, and for which they could accept responsibility. To achieve this product conformance, companies introduced the concepts of quality assurance and quality control.

Quality Control and Quality Assurance

Quality control is a system of activities designed to assess the quality of product or service supplied to a customer. If a product doesn't conform to requirements, it's reworked, scrapped, or downgraded. Quality control typically employs test inspection and repair techniques. Quality control is designed to answer the question, Have we done the job in accordance with the requirements?

Quality assurance is a management system designed to control the activities at all stages (product design; production; delivery and service), to prevent quality problems, and to ensure that only conforming products reach the customer. Key features of an effective quality assurance system are

- An effective Quality Management System (QMS).
- Periodic audit of the operation to ensure that it's effective.
- Periodic review of the system to ensure that it continually meets the changing requirements imposed on it.

TOTAL QUALITY MANAGEMENT (TQM)—A QUALITY REVOLUTION

"Quality" isn't just concerned with whether a product or service meets the claims made for it. Today's quality is much more than this. The modern concept of quality embraces how the company meets all its customers' requirements including how they're greeted on the telephone, how fast sales staff respond to a request for a quotation, having new products and services when required, and even ensuring that the invoice is correct!

Every contact with the customer, on every occasion, at every level builds a picture of the sort of company with which the customer's doing business. Of course, any product or service supplied has to meet its requirements; but this is the beginning— not the end—of the quest for a Total Quality organization!

A Quality Management System (QMS) designed to conform to the quality system standards is the starting point for Total Quality Management (TQM). Quality system standards define the control measures required to help ensure that the finished product or service conforms to the customer's requirements. However the standards aren't primarily concerned with achieving conformance to requirements in the most efficient or cost-effective manner. Nor do they focus on nonproduct–related activities.

The realization that applying quality disciplines to all activities would result in a more efficient and competitive company led to the evolution of TQM. TQM's aim is to ensure that each activity contributes to achieving the business's key objectives and is carried out efficiently. The basic philosophy of total quality is "do the right things right first time."

To succeed in today's competitive marketplace a company must supply products and services in accordance with the customer's requirements at minimum cost. To achieve this, the company must understand its role in the marketplace, organize itself to fulfill that role, and ensure that all employees understand and are committed to fulfilling the customer's requirements the first time every time, whatever task is being performed.

TQM generally requires a change in how a company operates. It requires quality to be the first priority of every employee and for their efforts to be focused on prevention of errors. It's no longer sufficient to rely on detecting and correcting errors—a costly, wasteful approach to assuring quality that's now largely redundant. Every department, every activity, every person at every level, starting at the top of the organization, must be wholly committed to the TQM philosophy.

Why Does Everyone Need to Be Involved?

TQM requires a change in the basic philosophy of everyone in the company, especially management. In the past we have generally followed the principles of management proposed by Taylor. Under this regime, the manager's role is to plan, organize, direct and solve problems. The worker's role is to carry out tasks as directed by the managers.

TQM requires us to recognize the contributions every employee can make and to harness the skills and enthusiasm of everyone in the business. To achieve this individuals must be provided with the skills, tools, and authority to investigate problems and introduce improvements. Managers must demonstrate that they believe their employees can make an important contribution to managing the business and must create an open atmosphere to allow this to happen. Teamwork is the key to the successful businesses of the 1990s and beyond. This radical change will only happen if it's actively and passionately led from the top and involves everyone. But it can't happen overnight, and it's unlikely to be painless unless it's carefully managed.

Meeting customer requirements. Customers' perceptions of their supplier are formed partly on the basis of the product or service they receive and partly on the basis of their day-to-day contact with the company. The receptionist who answers telephone calls, the security people who control access to the site, and the accounts person who sends out the invoice can all have a direct and important influence on customers. All these people must be involved in total quality in meeting the customer requirements, and in creating a world-class company.

The ability to meet these external customer requirements relies on a series of often complex internal supplier–customer links. The sales office sending out a quotation is the customer of the salesperson who provides the input for the quote. The person who packs the goods is the customer of the person who provides the goods, the person who provides the delivery note, and the person who provides the packaging material. A breakdown in any one of these internal chains may result in an error affecting the service the external customer receives.

TQM must therefore involve all the internal customer–supplier chains to ensure that external customers only receive conforming goods or services. No one is exempt from total quality.

Eliminating errors. We've already stated that TQM's role is to satisfy the internal and external customers and, through prevention, to eliminate causes of error. It's estimated that the costs of not getting the right things right the first time (non-conformance costs) can amount to 25 percent of turnover. By eliminating this unnecessary burden, companies can improve profitability in the short term and enhance competitiveness in the longer term.

Nonconformance costs may arise in any department. All departments spend time doing unnecessary activities, correcting their own mistakes, or rectifying other people's errors. Consequently all departments are open to Quality Improvement; no one is exempt.

The objective of TQM is to improve quality continuously by eliminating nonconformance in every activity throughout the company. Everyone, starting with management, is encouraged to refuse to accept the inevitability of error and to concentrate on preventing errors in the first place. Total quality leads the company toward new attitudes. Starting with senior management and working down through every layer of the organization and across every function, total quality involves everyone and influences the performance of the whole business.

The benefits of successfully implementing TQM are enormous: improved customer satisfaction; elimination of errors and waste; reduced operating costs; increased motivation and commitment of employees; improved customer satisfaction; increased profitability and competitiveness. Indeed, the company's very survival may be at stake.

In its initial stages, total quality often focuses on doing all activities right the first time. As TQM progresses, the company then begins to recognize that not all its activities are necessary; and that customer satisfaction could be increased (or the cost of non-conformance could be reduced) by carrying out different activities. Companies then look critically at their activities to identify those that are either unnecessary, inadequately focused, or inadequately performed. These are then subjected to an improvement program or discontinued.

QUALITY COSTS—A DRIVING FORCE

Costs are inevitably incurred in ensuring that products or services meet customers' requirements. These are the quality-related costs. An understanding of quality costs is essential for any business. Costs associated with the mismanagement of quality (costs of nonconformance) are often large, are nonproductive, and are avoidable through the implementation of TQM. Quality costs can amount to 25 percent of company turnover.

In most companies, the majority of quality-related costs are incurred putting things right after they've gone wrong. These are the costs associated with failure to achieve conformance to requirements and are generally known as the costs of non-conformance (CONC). Many companies are already aware of the product-related CONC (such as warranty, scrap, and rework), but ignore the CONC associated with, for example, administration, activities, or excessive debtor days. The calculation of CONC across the company often acts as a catalyst to convince management to implement a company-wide total quality program.

Companies suffering a high CONC generally also support extensive appraisal activities. Output from processes is checked at many stages in production. This appraisal activity and its associated cost are only necessary because the system produces so many errors. These must be found and corrected. Once the CONC is identified and the causes of failure are eliminated by introducing prevention activities; then extensive appraisal is no longer required.

Most companies find that a relatively small investment in prevention activities (such as training, calibration, equipment maintenance and planning) cuts both failure and appraisal costs.

Eliminating the CONC can increase profitability and improve the service provided to customers. These are important driving forces behind TQM.

SUMMARY—AND THE FUTURE

In today's market companies need to continually provide their customers with what they want. They must be innovative and quick to the market with new products, and do all this at minimum cost. Quality is vital in achieving these objectives. Only through understanding external customer requirements, organizing the company and harnessing every employee's skills to satisfy these requirements can companies succeed.

Industry has generally come to recognize quality's importance and is starting to implement TQM initiatives by meeting customers' requirements the first time every time. Japanese industry is moving toward another generation of satisfying customer requirements. They see the way forward as

1. Reducing the time it takes to bring new products to the market.

2. Improving manufacturing flexibility to encompass short-run production. This will enable them to provide a rapid response to customer orders.

Both these developments will improve responsiveness to their customers' requirements. Once again they may be able to pull ahead of their Western competitors unless the West responds to this threat. The competitive advantage available to companies that shorten product development cycles is immense. Independent consultant Donald Reinerstein reported in his book (*Developing Products in Half the Time*, published by Chapman and Hall) that in high-growth markets with product life cycles of some five years, a mere six-month delay in launching a product cuts its expected lifetime profits by a third. This is a substantial CONC and seems certain to be the next phase of the Total Quality revolution.

Table 1–2 shows the fundamental requirements of a total quality culture together with methods to help achieve these objectives. This table outlines the action plan necessary for companies that want to achieve a total quality culture.

TABLE 1–2
Fundamental Requirements of Total Quality Management

Fundamental Requirement	*Possible Actions*
1. Know your customers. • Know who they are. • Know their current needs. • Know their future requirements. • Respond to changing customer needs.	1. Customer surveys 2. Functional analysis 3. Quality cost analysis 4. Quality function deployment
2. Know your competitors.	1. Customer surveys 2. Competitor analysis 3. Benchmarking
3. Know your cost of nonconformance.	1. Quality cost analysis 2. Functional analysis
4. Measure your performance against key customer-driven parameters.	1. Customer surveys 2. Competitor analysis 3. Benchmarking
5. Make sure that all employees understand and commit themselves to the quality objectives of the business.	1. Functional analysis 2. Education and training 3. Communication
6. Achieve management commitment to continuous improvement of quality within the business.	1. Quality cost analysis 2. Functional analysis 3. Education and training 4. Communication
7. Define the purpose of each department and activity in terms of satisfying external or internal customer requirements.	1. Functional analysis
8. Enable employees to fulfill their commitment to quality by influencing the program of continuous improvement.	1. Education and training 2. Communication 3. Corrective action task force, Corrective action groups 4. Error Cause Removal system 5. Problem solving 6. Statistical Process Control 7. Recognition of performance
9. Replace inspection and correction techniques to control the quality of output with preventive actions.	1. Quality cost analysis 2. Functional analysis 3. Quality management system 4. Corrective action systems
10. Never accept nonconforming output in the form of product or services for external or internal customers.	1. Quality cost analysis 2. Functional analysis 3. Education and training 4. Communication
11. Plan effectively before undertaking actions.	1. Quality Improvement Team

How Can Businesses Develop a Leading Edge Total Quality Culture?

Every organization should determine whether it operates TQM. In most cases, companies operate some of the elements that make up TQM, but most companies have room for improvement. By instituting a process of continuous quality improvement, businesses may

- Improve competitiveness and profitability.
- Increase customer satisfaction.
- Reduce the costs of nonconformance.
- Increase employee motivation.

Chapter Two

Know Your Customers

WHO ARE YOUR CUSTOMERS?

A supplier–customer relationship is forged whenever a business purchases goods or services from another and each time a person asks another to undertake an activity. These examples illustrate the two principal categories of customer:

1. *External customers.* These are the ones who pay your bills! Businesses only survive if they meet their external customers' requirements.
2. *Internal customers.* Each transaction in a large business is the result of a number of internal supplier–customer relationships. The sales team concludes the sale; it specifies the characteristics required to the production team; the delivery team arranges for it to be delivered; and the finance team renders the invoice for the transaction. Each of these teams relies on inputs from their colleagues to enable them to complete their process right first time. Only by satisfying the (internal) requirements for each of these processes can the external customer's requirements be met.

This chapter describes how external customer requirements can be identified accurately, and how the operation of internal processes can be improved so that external customer requirements are met at the first attempt every time.

WHO ARE YOUR EXTERNAL CUSTOMERS?

All companies should know the names of their principal customers. Their purchasing departments are likely to be the focal points for component, material, and product purchases. But do you know who else within these businesses might assess your performance against their requirements for you as a supplier?

If the business is quality-driven, then its quality team might be monitoring the quality of the goods you supply, or the response times for service call-outs. If it's dissatisfied with your performance, it's likely to look for another supplier. Its goods receiving department may have requirements about when and how goods should be delivered. Its finance department will have requirements concerning the address and content of your invoice. Liaison with its marketing team might even yield an opportunity for the joint development of products to your mutual advantage.

Each of these customers may influence the decision to purchase goods or services from you. You must understand the requirements of all the groups within your customer's organization that influence their purchasing decision. Only then can you try to satisfy their requirements.

WHAT DO YOUR EXTERNAL CUSTOMERS REALLY WANT FROM YOUR BUSINESS?

External customers' requirements may be significantly different from what you expect. For example, a professional firm of lawyers or accountants, when asked to advise a client about appropriate locations for a new headquarters, might believe that the client only requires a one-off report, provided it's comprehensive, well written, and technically competent. But the client might really want a continuous flow of advice responding to the changing demands that surface as its business requirements become fully recognized. The report may be only one element in the service the customer really wants; but he will settle for that unless he can find a more responsive service elsewhere.

Meeting the external customer's requirements requires two major steps:

1. Identify the external customer's requirements.
2. Ensure that internal processes result in meeting external customer requirements at minimum cost.

TABLE 2–1

The Two-Step Approach to Meeting External Customer Requirements

Objective	Activity
Identify your external customers' requirements.	1. Identify the existing products and services you agree to provide to customers. • What services do you provide to your customers? • Do you enter into an agreement with all your customers specifying the services you'll provide, using standard terms of trade, an engagement letter, or contract? • If not, how do you know what your customers expect from you?
	2. How do your customers perceive the value of your products and services compared to those available from your competitors? Information to answer this can be obtained from a number of sources: • Customer surveys. • Competitor analysis. • Complaints log. • Trade surveys.
	3. Can you improve the products or services you provide to customers? Consider using the following techniques: • Customer surveys. • Competitor analysis. • Benchmarking. • Quality Function Deployment. • Marketing activities.
Ensure that internal processes result in meeting external customer requirements at minimum cost.	The key means for achieving this are • Functional analysis. • Continuous quality improvement. • Quality cost analysis.

There are a number of means to obtain the necessary information to enable you to complete these steps. Table 2–1 outlines an effective, practical approach.

"Hard" and "Soft" Customer Requirements

Customer requirements may be divided into two key categories: "hard" requirements and "soft" requirements.

1. *Hard requirements* must be met by the deliverable product or service. They're often specified in the contract and may include some, or all, of the following:

- Size, weight, color, texture, and taste.
- Functions, reliability, and facilities required.
- Packaging, labeling, and delivery times and methods.
- Cost and payment arrangements.
- Customer support required.
- Response times to failures.

These are the basic requirements for each product or service. They're the minimum customer requirements that must be met if a product is to be considered satisfactory.

2. *Soft requirements* relate to the impression given to the customer by the company they're doing business with. These factors convey a message to customers about whether they're welcome or just a nuisance. Are they kept waiting? This indicates to a customer that you believe your time is more valuable than theirs. Such little things show you really care for your customers. Your effort will generally be well received. Factors that may influence this impression include the following:

- *Telephone answering.* How easy is it to get through to the person you want to speak to? Are calls answered courteously and promptly? Do receptionists know where people are? Are messages taken reliably? If the contact isn't available, will someone else take ownership of the problem? Is the switchboard manned at all reasonable times, including lunchtimes and after office hours?

- *Security and parking.* What impression is given when people arrive at the site? Are security people courteous? Are they warned to expect all visitors? Is there a convenient, safe place to park? Do all visitors receive a map showing how to get to the location?

- *Reception and elevator area.* Does the reception and elevator area give the impression you want to give? Are these areas attractive and comfortable? Remember that for many operations, customers don't have many opportunities to assess the quality of your service. If they receive a bad impression during a visit to your premises, that could seriously impact future business. Are customers made to feel welcome? Are they offered coffee and a reasonable selection of reading?

• *Maintenance*. Are buildings and facilities clean and well maintained?

• *Correspondence*. Does all correspondence create a professional image? Is there a standard layout? Are letters well written and free from errors and corrections? Are all letters acknowledged and replied to promptly? Are customers kept informed of reasons for and likely duration of any delay?

• *Cars*. Are company cars kept clean and tidy?

• *Hospitality*. Are visitors kept waiting for extended periods on arrival while their contact arrives? Are they offered refreshments? Are the refreshments served in china or plastic cups?

• *Meetings*. Do your employees turn up for meetings on time? Are they adequately prepared for the meeting? Do they have all the equipment and information required? If your people are chairing the meeting, is there an agenda? Do meetings run on schedule?

These often-overlooked customer requirements can make a lasting impression. Every individual within the organization who makes any contacts with people outside the organization creates an impression of the company. A professional impression must be given at every level in every activity. The business must demonstrate that it's committed to quality and to customer satisfaction. Everyone is a potential future customer and should be treated as such.

The quality of output depends on the quality of internal processes and the internal supply chain. Understanding the underlying customer requirements is an essential first step toward improving your ability to meet those requirements. But how does a business meet the requirements of its external customers? External customer requirements can only be met by the correct functioning of internal processes.

FIGURE 2–1
Process Model

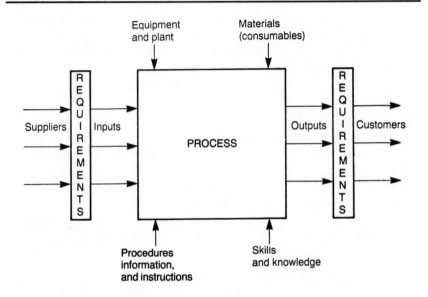

WHAT IS A PROCESS?

A *process* is any activity that takes an input and transforms it into an output. Figure 2–1 illustrates basic characteristics of a typical process. Any process can be described in this way.

A supplier is anyone who supplies the input; a customer is anyone who receives the output from a process. All activities within a business are made up of a series of often complex supplier–customer chains. Each person is a customer of the previous process in the chain and a supplier to the next process. If activities are to be carried out right the first time, it's essential that customer requirements for each process within the chain are identified and met.

Consider the supplier–customer relationships that arise in a meeting between a salesman and customer to discuss the services a business can provide. Here the customer requires a formal proposal within 48 hours so that she can award the contract. Figure 2–2

FIGURE 2–2
Illustration of Supplier–Customer Relationships

Activity	Comments	Common Failures
1. The salesperson meets with the customer.	1. *The customer supplies the salesperson with a briefing.* Here the salesperson relies on the information supplied by the external customer.	Not all requirements are identified.
2. The salesperson prepares a draft proposal in manuscript or by dictation. 3. The secretary types the draft proposal.	2/3. *The salesperson gives a draft proposal to a secretary.* At this point the salesperson is the supplier to a secretary. The secretary should insist on the salesperson providing enough information to enable the process to be completed right the first time.	The salesperson might have illegible writing, or an indistinct voice. The salesperson might not specify a time scale for completing the typing. The secretary might be overloaded and unable to meet the deadline. The salesperson might not deliver the draft to the secretary in time for it to be typed.
4. The secretary passes the draft proposal to the salesperson for review. 5. The salesperson reviews the proposal and signs it.	4/5. *The secretary returns the proposal to the salesperson.* Now the secretary is the supplier and the salesperson is the customer. Any deficiencies in the information given to the secretary will show up at this point. The action of reviewing a draft proposal is an appraisal activity. If the salesperson got it right when drafting the proposal, and the secretary typed it correctly, it could be run off in final in the first instance.	Typing might be delayed by interruptions. The wrong format may be used for the proposal. No spelling checks might be operated. Typing may be inaccurate. For important documents it might be acceptable to run off a draft at this stage. Routine documents should be run off in final.
6. The salesperson sends the proposals to the customer.	6. *The salesperson supplies the proposal to the customer.* The customer requires the proposal within 48 hours of the meeting.	Beware the U.S. postal service.

FIGURE 2–3
Customer–Supplier Chain

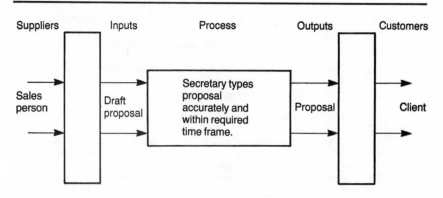

shows the activities associated with producing the output (in this case the proposal document).

Even apparently simple processes can require a number of inputs to enable it to produce the correct output. Consider the case of typing the proposal document. Figure 2–3 diagrams the process. Here, the key process requirements are

1. The proposal dictated by the salesperson. (These are the direct inputs.)
2. Equipment (here a typewriter/word processor and photocopier).
3. Raw materials (paper).
4. Knowledge of how the equipment works.
5. Procedures or instructions on how the proposal should be set out.
6. A dictionary or spell-check facility to eliminate spelling errors.
7. Experience or training to be able to type.

A number of requirements must be satisfied even for a simple process if the process is to be carried out right the first time. Establishing the external customer's requirements is an essential first step. This then establishes the process requirements. For example, if the customer didn't require the proposal until a week after the meeting, then the secretary wouldn't need the dictated draft proposal within 24 hours of the meeting.

FIGURE 2–4

Process Definition: Output to Customers

Who are my customers?	What do I deliver to them?	What are their requirements?	What is my current performance?	What actions can I take to improve?

FIGURE 2–5

Process Definition: Input from Suppliers

Who are my suppliers?	What do they deliver to me?	What are my requirements?	What is their current performance?	What improvement can be made?

FIGURE 2–6
Process Definition: Process Requirements

	What is required?	Does this exist now, reliably?	What improvements can be made	Who can make this happen?
Skills and knowledge				
Equipment and plant				
Materials				
Procedures, instructions, and information				

Understanding processes, how they're linked together in a customer–supplier chain, and the requirements for each process in the chain is essential if processes are to be carried out right the first time. This enables an organization to focus on increasing customer satisfaction and reducing the cost of nonconformance.

Figures 2–4 through 2–6 illustrate a useful series of questions that must be answered for each process to identify the requirements for that process. Only by knowing the answers to these questions can a business effect improvements.

Chapter Three

Quality Costs

The objective of a Quality Improvement Program (QIP) is to develop an approach which ensures that goods and services are produced that meet customer requirements for the minimum cost.

This objective may only be achieved by eliminating the costs associated with not getting things right the first time; these are the nonconformance costs of the company. We can only eliminate the costs of nonconformance (CONC) if they can be identified and evaluated. This chapter helps identify the CONC and other quality-related costs.

WHAT ARE QUALITY COSTS?

Quality costs are all the costs incurred by a business to ensure that the total service it provides to customers conforms to customers' requirements. These costs include the following:

- Costs directly associated with providing the end product or service that the customer purchases.
- Costs associated with support activities.
- Hidden costs such as missed opportunities and poor morale.

A secretary who spends 20 minutes trying to find her boss because he hasn't told her where he's going incurs a cost. She has wasted time that she could have spent more productively. This may also mean that she doesn't have time today to send out all the letters inviting potential customers to a company product seminar.

An incoming telephone call that isn't rerouted to a receptionist when a salesman is out of the office may persuade a customer to place her order elsewhere. Each of these failures may give rise to CONC.

THE IMPORTANCE OF IDENTIFYING THE CONC

Recognizing the amount of money wasted on finding and correcting nonconformance at the beginning of a QIP frequently underlines the strategic necessity of introducing the program. Findings from a number of businesses suggest that the CONC can amount to as much as 25 percent of turnover in both manufacturing and service industries! This is certainly a figure which grabs management attention.

Monitoring the CONC can provide a measure of the QIP's success. But it should be recognized that when a QIP is introduced, the CONC frequently appears to rise initially. This is because people become more aware of nonconformance and its associated costs as they become able to identify them. Consequently costs become included that wouldn't initially have been thought of as nonconformance costs.

Knowing the CONC associated with individual activities can help us prioritize corrective actions, focusing attention on the highest-priority areas. Being aware of the costs associated with errors will also help every department and individual in their commitment to perform every task right the first time.

THE IMPORTANCE OF QUALITY COSTS

Quality costs are important for a number of reasons.

1. They're often large. A government survey in 1985 recorded that quality costs in the UK may amount to 10 to 20 percent of turnover. These figures are also typically seen worldwide.

2. The size of these costs and where they occur are unknown for most businesses. Fewer than 40 percent of companies collect information on quality costs.

3. The great majority of costs (more than 80 percent for many companies) are associated with failure and appraisal activities.

4. Savings in quality costs have a significant, positive impact on bottom line results.

5. The large burden of failure and appraisal activities indicates that businesses tolerate a large number of defects, which they must then find and correct. Because appraisal methods

inevitably miss a proportion of failures, some nonconforming output will be received by customers. This results in dissatisfied, disloyal customers. Investment in prevention therefore results in more satisfied customers as well as reduced failure and appraisal costs.

What Does This Mean in Practice?

Consider the following summary of a company's profit and loss account:

Revenue	$10.0 million
Total costs	$ 9.2 million
Profit	$ 0.8 million

The company incurs a cost of quality amounting to some 25 percent of turnover ($2.5 million). Of this amount, 80 percent is incurred on failure and appraisal activities. Therefore the CONC is $2 million.

Consider the company's options to increase its profit to $1.6 million.

One satisfying way would be to increase sales volume, thus increasing its revenue. To achieve a profit of $1.6 million, however, it may need to double sales revenue. This is unlikely to be possible, especially in a competitive market or a recession.

Another way would be to cut costs. But to increase profit by $0.8 million, it would need to save almost 10 percent on all activities or make even larger cuts on selected activities.

A third way is to look at the costs of nonconformance and try to make savings here. To save $0.8 million it would need to reduce the CONC by 40 percent. Although not an easy task, it seems more achievable than doubling turnover. The advantage of implementing a quality improvement program that reduces the CONC is that it also reduces the failures seen by customers and improves the service they receive. So it should also increase sales revenue.

WHY MEASURE QUALITY COSTS?

Quality costs need to be measured because they're large (often ranging from 25 to 35 percent of operating costs) and unknown, and can have a significant impact on profitability and customer satisfaction. Measurements of these costs can also be used for the following purposes:

1. The size of quality costs can be used to attract management attention and shock it into making a commitment to implement a QIP.

2. Reporting quality-related activities in financial terms generally raises the importance of quality within the management team and ensures that it's given the same attention as any other activity with such a large potential impact on the company's performance.

3. Highlighting areas that incur a high cost provides ready targets for improvement. Once activities have been targeted for improvement, their results can be monitored to measure progress.

4. Knowledge of quality costs and where they occur enables decisions on quality to be made on a sound basis. The benefits, or otherwise, of any decision can be evaluated according to its effect on quality costs.

HOW TO CLASSIFY QUALITY-RELATED COSTS

One of the most useful ways of classifying quality-related costs is to distinguish between costs of conformance and costs of non-conformance.

Costs of Conformance

We can only reduce the CONC by investing in prevention activities. Investing in the prevention of errors enables failure and associated appraisal costs to be minimized. This is a fundamental driving force behind quality improvement! However, prevention activities inevitably result in some costs. These are *Prevention costs* (costs of conformance). This includes all the costs associated with any activity designed to ensure that the right activities are carried out right first time.

Prevention costs may include those associated with

1. Writing procedures defining how tasks are to be performed.

2. Process controls, such as Statistical Process Control (SPC).
3. Calibrating test equipment to ensure that product is produced within specification.
4. Training and educating employees so they understand how tasks should be performed.
5. Maintaining equipment.
6. Planning processes to ensure quality. Much of the Quality Improvement Team's work falls under this heading.
7. Working with suppliers to improve the quality of goods supplied.
8. Audit activities to ensure the continued effectiveness of the prevention system. (Any audit activities associated with the checking or correcting of errors are CONC costs.)

The key feature of a QIP environment is that failures aren't accepted as a normal occurrence. The root causes of any failures are identified and eliminated by the introduction of prevention activities. Failure is an exceptional occurrence. In this environment we don't need a vast appraisal activity. All we need is a small audit activity to ensure that the prevention system is working correctly.

So, after focusing on reducing failure costs, we can then look at reducing appraisal costs.

Costs of Nonconformance

Costs of nonconformance are all the costs incurred because failures occur. If there were no failures, there would be no requirement for appraisal and correcting activities. These are the costs incurred as a result of either

1. Not doing the right job (For example, costs incurred by an individual producing a regular report that no one reads is a CONC since it doesn't contribute to the success of the business) or
2. Not completing an activity right the first time. Obvious costs associated with not doing things right first time include scrap, warranty, and repair.

Nonconformance costs include the costs of failure and also many appraisal costs that are necessary only because of the high level of failures.

Costs associated with not doing things right first time. The most obvious quality-related costs are those associated with failure to achieve conformance to requirements. Termed *Failure costs*, they may arise either before delivery or after the product or service has reached the customer. Failure costs that are frequently quoted because they're easy to identify include the following:

In-warranty repairs	Correcting defects after the product has been delivered.
After-sales support	Solving problems the customer has when using a product or service.
Product recall	Repairing, handling, and investigating recalled products.
Scrap	Lost material, machine time, and labor.
Downgraded product	Product sold as seconds at reduced prices.
Rework	Labor, equipment, and materials used in repairing or reproducing defective work.
Lost efficiency	Reduction in the department's effective capacity because of effort diverted to allow corrective action. For example, part of the production line may be tied up with rework when it could be producing a new batch of product.
Customer complaints	Smoothing over problems in the field. This may include any incentives offered to pacify a customer (for example, extended warranty or reduced fees).
Liability insurance	Premium paid for product liability and claims insurance, and the cost of settling any claims.
Administration	All the administration, meetings, paperwork, and telephone calls associated with analyzing and resolving failures.

Other less visible failure costs that need to be considered relate to the following:

Excess inventory	Costs associated with holding excess inventory because of errors in forecasting (perhaps a marketing or purchasing error) or perhaps as a result of poor material control procedures.

Excessive debtor days	Costs associated with invoices not being paid on time. This might result from inadequate customer vetting, sending inaccurate invoices, or faulty or inappropriate goods.
Obsolete stock	Costs associated with stock no longer required. This includes storage, overhead, and scrap costs. This might result from a marketing, engineering, sales, or purchasing error.
Engineering changes	Costs associated with processing changes in specifications. Associated rework costs need to be added to this total.
Overtime	Excessive hours worked because of poor planning or controlling of activities.
Excess capacity	Extra capacity required to rework or replace failures.

There are also hidden costs associated with failure. These are generally more difficult to estimate, but include the following:

Lost opportunities	Income lost as a result of customers not placing orders. This may be due to a number of factors: Product late to market. Previous nonconforming deliveries. Poor routing of telephone calls when an office is empty or a line is busy or receptionists not passing messages to the salesforce. Salespeople not calling because they're sorting out problems elsewhere.
Poor employee morale	Costs associated with excessive staff turnover and reduced efficiency.

Failure costs occur in all areas of the company. However they're often accepted as part of the normal course of events and so are easily overlooked. We must adopt a rigorous approach to identifying failure costs. Table 3–1 shows typical quality costs associated with key departments.

Appraisal costs. The fact that errors occur is widely recognized in industry. To minimize the number of errors that reach their customers, many companies operate systems to find these errors. There are inevitably costs associated with finding these errors. These are the *appraisal costs*.

TABLE 3–1
Examples of Quality Costs by Department

Quality costs include:
Personnel costs.
Overhead costs (light, heat, and space).
Consumable materials.
Capital equipment depreciation.

Department	Prevention Costs	Appraisal Costs	Failure Costs	
			Internal	External
Design	1. Design procedures 2. Training 3. Functional analysis 4. Setting specifications for materials/products/services 5. Quality Function Deployment Understanding customer requirements before starting on designs 6. Reliability analysis 7. Design proving 8. Design reviews	1. Design specification for inspection equipment/procedures 2. Preproduction/prototype trials 3. Checking of drawings and specifications	1. Excess/obsolete inventory (unpopular designs) 2. Design changes 3. Project overspending	1. Product liability (for design failures) 2. Returned goods (for design flaws) 3. Rework/rectification (for design flaws) 4. Customer complaints (regarding design flaws) 5. Downgrading products (for design flaws) 6. Analysis of returned goods (for design flaws) 7. Orders lost because products weren't launched on time
Distribution	1. Distribution procedures 2. Training 3. Functional analysis	1. Inspection of finished products/services prior to dispatch	1. Rejects/rework due to incorrect packaging	1. Goods delivered to incorrect address
Finance	1. Finance department procedures 2. Training 3. Functional analysis	1. Internal audit 2. Checking invoices before sending	1. Issuing credit notes to correct invoices 2. Management reports not provided on time	1. Bad debts 2. Overdue accounts (beyond normal credit period)

Function	Prevention	Appraisal	Internal failure	External failure
Maintenance	1. Maintenance procedures 2. Training 3. Functional analysis 4. Scheduled maintenance	1. Inspection of plant	1. Production line stoppages 2. Investigation and repair following complaints, return of goods, warranty claims	1. Nonconforming product 2. Late delivery due to plant downtime
Marketing	1. Marketing procedures 2. Training 3. Functional analysis 4. Setting product or service specification 5. Market research, customer surveys	1. Checking letters and questionnaires before sending them out	1. Excess or obsolete stock because of poor forecasting 2. Lost customers 3. Fall in market share 4. Poor response time to queries 5. Lost sales because of poor forecasting	1. Product doesn't meet market requirements
Personnel	1. Personnel procedures 2. Training 3. Functional analysis 4. Staff appraisal 5. Staff surveys 6. Consultative committees	1. Checking appraisal returns 2. Checking candidate reports	1. Recruitment of unsuccessful recruits 2. Failure to fill post on time 3. Staff turnover 4. Employment disputes, strikes 5. Pursuing authorization to make employment offers	1. Poor customer relations due to inadequate training 2. Product not delivered due to plant stoppages
Production and materials control	1. Production procedures 2. Training 3. Functional analysis 4. Controls to ensure that processes remain in control 5. Specialist handling equipment and procedures 6. Preproduction and prototype trials 7. Evaluation of product/service specification (for production compatibility) 8. Production planning 9. Calibration of test equipment	1. Production/process inspection (on line and finished goods) 2. Inspection/measurement equipment	1. Scrap, waste, rework, rectification of faulty products 2. Replacement of defective product or repeating service 3. Downgrading of product or service 4. Excess or obsolete stock because of poor production 5. Reinspection 6. Analysis of failures 7. Excess capacity	1. Receiving, checking, repair, and/or replacement of returned goods/services 2. Handling customer complaints 3. Warranty claims 4. Product liability for production failures 5. Excess stocks of new materials, work in progress, and finished goods 6. Excessive delivery times

Continued

TABLE 3-1—Continued
Examples of Quality Costs by Department

Department	Prevention Costs	Appraisal Costs	Failure Costs — Internal	Failure Costs — External
Purchasing	1. Purchasing procedures 2. Training 3. Functional analysis 4. Supplier improvement program	1. Vendor auditing 2. Vendor approval/rating	1. Checking items before acceptance into stock 2. Excess stock of bought-in components from poor buying decisions 3. Cost of returns to supplier	1. Scrap material (not meeting specification/in excess of requirements) 2. Damages arising from product failure as a result of inadequate materials
Quality	1. Quality procedures 2. Training 3. Functional analysis 4. Quality Management System 5. Design of process controls 6. Auditing 7. Customer survey	1. Inspection of finished products/services at any stage	1. Quality system failure resulting in nonconforming product	1. Troubleshooting 2. Handling customer complaints arising from quality failures 3. Warranty claims arising from quality failures 4. Product liability arising from quality failures 5. Nonconformances raised by external auditing body 6. Audit deficiencies outstanding
Sales	1. Sales procedures 2. Training 3. Functional analysis	1. Checking quotes before sending out	1. Lost customers from inadequate service 2. Lost orders 3. Excess/obsolete stock from poor sales forecasting 4. Production overtime from poor sales forecasting	1. Handling goods returned as unsuitable 2. Dealing with customer complaints arising from goods returned as unsuitable
Service	1. Service procedures 2. Training	1. Inspection of repairs	1. Lost customers from inadequate service	1. Excessive turnaround time

3. Functional analysis
4. Evaluation of product/
   service specification for
   service compatibility
5. Preproduction and
   prototype trials
6. Calibration of test equipment

2. Lost orders
3. Excess/obsolete stock from
   poor service forecasting
4. Warranty after repair

Note: All costs associated with the quality department are quality costs. The department's objective is to reduce overall quality borne by the business by ensuring that

1. Procedures are in place that ensure that the right actions are taken; all actions are effected right first time; and all output is produced in accordance with pre-agreed–upon requirements.

2. The procedures operate effectively in practice.

It's sometimes thought that the full cost of the service department represents a cost of quality. If products were made properly in the first place, there would be no need to service them. However, service departments in a number of industries achieve a healthy income from maintaining equipment in good condition for customers. This chargeable activity isn't a true cost of quality. The cost of quality covers nonchargeable activities such as warranty work. The increasing drive toward long-term reliability of equipment, plus the increasing complexity of equipment are having a conflicting impact on many service operations activities.

Appraisal activities include the following:

- Checking a document for accuracy before approval.
- Inspecting goods received.
- Testing and inspecting a product between manufacturing and final checking.

We commonly expect errors to happen so we need appraisal activities to find them. If failures were eliminated, the vast majority of appraisal activities would also no longer be necessary.

Costs associated with doing the wrong things. The preceding sections illustrate costs associated with the failure to complete activities more efficiently (i.e., right first time). But what about activities that don't really further the business's objectives? In many cases, these activities can be discontinued. But few businesses address this important area adequately. A useful technique for understanding which activities perform a useful purpose is functional analysis, which is described in Chapter 4.

In many organizations, meetings are legion. Are they necessary? Are they all held for a predefined purpose? Are they managed properly? Is an agenda prepared to ensure that everyone is aware of the required preparation and proposed output of the meeting? Do meetings start and finish on time?

How many printouts do you receive? How many of these do you use? How much more valuable could the printouts be if you could specify the information you'd like and how you'd like to see it presented?

These are examples of activities that currently may not be contributing to the business's success. If they aren't contributing to its success, then the associated costs constitute nonconformance costs. They're the costs of failing to control the activities undertaken by the business.

What Costs Should Be Included as Quality Costs?

All costs associated with an activity should be included as part of the cost of quality calculation. The key costs are as follows:

1. Direct labor—standard and overtime rates for employees directly involved in the activity.

2. Indirect labor—costs associated with managing and supervising of direct labor.
3. Direct materials—cost of materials used in the activity (raw materials and consumables).
4. Occupancy—cost of space, light, heat, and power associated with the activities.
5. Administrative support services—costs associated with payroll, stores, and other support services associated with the activity in question.
6. Equipment—depreciation on equipment used in the activity.

We must capture the full cost of quality for each activity. Only then can we understand its full impact on the business. The necessary information generally should be available from the internal management accounts of the business.

HOW TO GATHER QUALITY COSTS

Each company must decide, for itself, the most appropriate method for collecting and categorizing quality costs. It must apply the chosen method consistently and use the information to improve its performance. Here are useful guidelines for gathering quality costs.

1. The starting point is to decide why you want to gather quality costs. Do you want to know the total for quality costs across the whole company as a target for overall improvements? Or do you want to identify the activities that are most important to the business, and then carry out a quality cost analysis only in these areas? The reason you want the costs will influence how you should go about collecting them.

2. Use existing cost management systems where possible. You may need to adapt the output from the existing system, but don't invent a separate new system. Table 3–2 illustrates the range of potential sources for quality cost data.

3. To ensure management attention, quality costs must be included in the regular management accounts. Therefore you should enlist the help and support of the finance department early on.

TABLE 3–2
Potential Sources of Data on Quality Costs

Salaries and wages analysis (include direct and indirect staff)
Department cost reports
Departmental budgets
Analysis of overheads (light, heat, power, etc.)
Product costing data
Space utilization reports
Scrap reports
Analysis of reworked product/services
Analysis of returned goods
Records of downgraded, scrapped product/services
Staff time reports
Staff travel/expense reports
Labor/equipment utilization reports
Material usage reports
Register of fixed assets used in departments
Inspection/test reports
Sales reports
Customer complaints log
Records/authorizations for repairs, replacements, refunds
Debtors' report
Analysis of credit notes
Cost of capital employed

4. Decide on the appropriate basis for analyzing quality costs to suit the business. Use the available guides but don't be restricted by them. Having established the ground rules, apply them consistently, or you won't be able to monitor progress.

5. The first estimate of overall costs doesn't need to be too detailed. Don't delay the QIP looking for pennies! Once the training and education program begins, people will be more enthusiastic and better qualified to identify quality costs. The information should then become more accurate.

6. Be prepared for quality costs to rise initially as people become better at identifying them.

7. Attribute costs according to where they occur (for example,

by department, supplier, or product). This will help guide subsequent investigation and cost reduction.

8. Target failure costs at the start.

9. Monitor overall quality costs periodically (perhaps annually). They don't need to be monitored too often as they usually change relatively slowly.

10. Quality costs should be gathered more accurately and monitored more frequently (perhaps weekly or monthly) for those areas targeted for improvement.

The Role of the Quality Improvement Team

The QIT's role is to devise a method for identifying total quality-related costs across the company. All quality-related costs must be included at this stage—not just the obvious costs associated with manufacturing. This analysis can then be used as a basis for measuring progress as the QIP is implemented. It can also be used to reinforce the need for implementing the Improvement Program when communicating with management and employees. The measurement of quality costs provides valuable management information and requires every manager and supervisor's active participation if it's to be a meaningful measure of current business performance.

QUALITY COST REDUCTION

Quality costs can be used as a basis to target areas for improvement. The first activities to target are those that (1) incur high failure costs and (2) have the greatest impact on customer satisfaction.

It's then appropriate to target other activities, such as the appraisal activities designed to identify failures.

Significant reductions in the CONC can, and regularly are, being made by companies. This reduction in wasted effort should be publicized and celebrated by organizations. It helps businesses satisfy their customers' requirements and usually makes their employees' work more interesting. By publicizing successes, an organization helps develop the momentum for the improvement program.

FIGURE 3–1
Typical Quality Cost Reduction

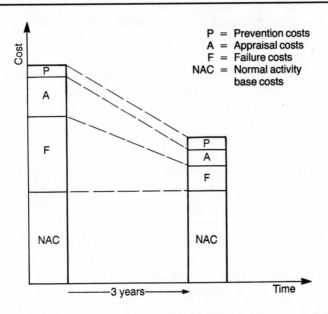

In the early stages of a QIP, it's useful to focus on reducing the CONC associated with individual activities because a reduction in overall quality costs can take a long time to flow through to the bottom line. A reduction in overall quality costs to one-third of their initial value may typically be made in three years. Figure 3–1 illustrates the impact of a typical QIP on quality costs over a three-year period. Here significant reductions have been made in failure and appraisal costs as a result of a small investment in prevention costs. This illustrates the objective of the QIP, which is to eliminate the CONC by investing in prevention.

Chapter Four

Functional Analysis

Quality is driven by customers' needs. Customer-oriented businesses are likely to be the only ones that will survive through the 1990s and into the 21st century. Technologically advanced companies and monopolies may keep going for a while, but they too must provide customers with the products that they require.

Functional analysis is the cornerstone of a successful program of continuous quality improvement. Businesses rely on their customers: functional analysis drives businesses to focus on satisfying those customers' needs. Put frankly, any activity that isn't directed toward this end may be superfluous, and the resources tied up should be considered for redeployment.

Functional analysis achieves its purpose by identifying

1. The purpose of the business as a whole in terms of satisfying external customer needs.
2. The purpose of each department in the business in terms of satisfying both internal and external customer needs.
3. Whether departments achieve their objectives in a cost-effective fashion.
4. The costs associated with any failure to work efficiently.
5. Areas for implementing corrective actions.

This radical approach requires each department to critically examine its role in achieving the business's overall objectives. This includes deciding why it exists and what it contributes to further the business's aims.

FUNCTIONAL ANALYSIS—THE METHOD

Figure 4–1's flowchart illustrates the steps within a typical functional analysis program, from establishing the requirements of the

FIGURE 4–1
Flowchart Illustrating the Functional Analysis Method

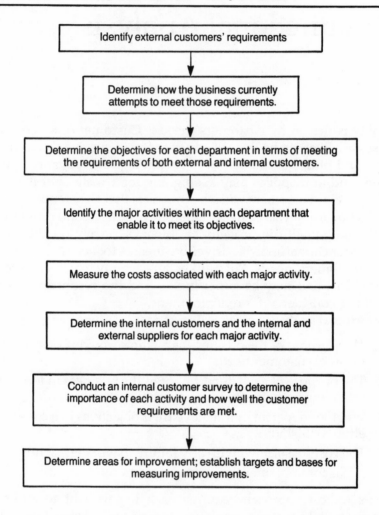

external customer, to setting detailed targets for improvement within each department.

Identify External Customers' Requirements

This step was detailed in Chapter 2.

Determine How the Business Currently Attempts to Meet Those Requirements

As a first step, senior management must determine why its business exists and what are its aims. Most businesses are set up to increase their shareholders' wealth. To achieve this end they must provide a product or service that satisfies their customers' needs. It's these commercial, customer-driven aims that interest us here.

A business might manufacture gasoline-driven engines. If so, is that the company's purpose? It's quite possible that management considers this to be the purpose of the company—and that it achieves its objective very effectively. But customers might very well look at the business differently. They might be looking for a power source to drive their vehicles. At the moment, gasoline engines may be the best form of power supply available, but customers wouldn't hesitate to use a different source in the future if circumstances change. If the company doesn't recognize that it's in the market to supply the customer need for power sources, it might well be left behind as technology or consumer tastes march on. One of the marketing department's functions is to ensure that this doesn't happen!

The whole management team should meet to determine why the business exists and its aims for the future. This vital step guides each function when determining its role within the business. It's useful to record the business's aims in a mission statement that can be published for the benefit of all employees.

All managers must demonstrate their commitment to the mission of the business every day and in every action they take. Employees quickly see through management initiatives that are all talk and no action.

Draft the Mission Statement

This is a definitive statement, made by the senior management team, of why the organization is in business. It should be short and clear, and should focus on the current and future customer requirements that the company must meet to survive.

Determine the Objectives for Each Department in Terms of Meeting the Requirements of Both Internal and External Customers

Having determined the aims of the business, it's necessary to determine why each department exists and what it actually contributes to meeting the overall business aims. Senior management should step back and review periodically (perhaps annually) each department's purpose and how departments should interact. The whole management team (not just individual department heads in isolation) must be involved in determining each department's role. Each function is both a customer and supplier to other departments and must meet those departments' requirements. Each function also has its own requirements that need to be met by the other departments. Thus all customers and their requirements must be identified before the role and purpose of each function is decided. This can only happen if all potential customers (i.e., all the other department heads) are present and contribute to this discussion.

To understand the purpose of each function, it's useful to take each function in turn and brainstorm four questions:

Why is this function required?

What does it contribute to achieving the business aims?

Who are its customers?

What are their requirements?

From the answers to these questions, each department's mission statement can be established in preparation for the next step of the analysis.

At the end of this phase the overall business aims and purpose will have been defined. The role of each function will also have been established in terms of what it does for whom, who its customers are (in many cases these will be internal customers) and how the satisfactory performance of these tasks can be measured. Once these key parameters have been established, each department can examine the activities it carries out. It can also devise means to measure how well it carries out its activities and the quality costs it incurs.

Identify the Major Activities within Each Department That Enable It to Meet Its Objectives

Modern businesses have become complex organizations. A typical business might include the following principal functions:

• The production department is the cutting edge of the business, producing the product or service actually required by customers. In a service business this might be the professional staff. In a manufacturing business this would be the production lines.

• *The marketing department* is responsible for interpreting customers' future needs in the light of the capabilities and aims of the business. It should ensure that the business produces the right product or service at the right time and the right price.

• *The finance department* ensures that customers are creditworthy and are invoiced promptly for all supplies at the correct price; that purchases are properly authorized and paid for; that all transactions are properly recorded; that management and financial accounts contain appropriate information and are produced promptly; and that tax, payroll, audit, and other compliance issues are handled effectively.

• *The personnel department* ensures an adequate supply of appropriate recruits; training needs are considered and effectively carried out; staff are properly treated, appraised of their performance, and counseled about their future; and reasons for poor staff retention are investigated.

• *The design (research and development) department* collaborates with the marketing and production departments to develop designs for new products that will satisfy anticipated customer requirements.

• *The service department* continues to meet customer needs once the product has left the factory. This may include installation, customer training, maintenance, and resolving customer problems and complaints.

• *The quality assurance department* ensures that the practices and methods adopted throughout the company result in products and services that meet customer requirements first time every time.

• *The sales department* obtains orders from customers, establishing requirements for product specification, price, and delivery schedules. It's then responsible for the accurate and prompt transmission of this information to production (to make the product) and finance (to invoice the customer for the sale).

• *The purchasing department* procures the necessary materials and services according to specification at minimum installed cost.

• *Warehouse and distribution operations* check goods received and dispatched; and ensure that goods are sent to the right customers on time.

Every department is assigned a range of specific responsibilities. Each department is also responsible for communicating with other departments on specific issues. Thus, for example, the personnel department will need to communicate with each department in relation to its employees. Every department is therefore a customer of the personnel department and it's up to each department to take part in specifying the objectives of the personnel department. This is true wherever departments interact.

Once the overall role of each function has been determined, department heads should work with their staffs to identify the major activities performed to meet their overall objectives. The major activities are either those on which the most time is spent, or those that the group feels are key to meeting departmental objectives. Investigating major activities can be time-consuming so care should be taken to avoid spreading resources too thinly.

At this stage, major activities may well be identified that aren't part of the department's role as defined by the management team. It may then be necessary to amend the department's role to incorporate this activity; or it may be decided to transfer the activity to another department; or the activity may not really be required by the business. The decision on what to do should be taken by the whole management team since it affects the primary role of a department.

Once the department has agreed on its major activities, these should be recorded so that each member of the department can see how they relate to the department's overall objectives (Figure 4-2). Table 4-1 illustrates the functional analysis approach as it's applied to a number of practical examples.

Measure the Costs Associated with Each Major Activity

When implementing a program of continuous quality improvement, one frequent difficulty is the collection of quality costs and

FIGURE 4–2
Functional Analysis: Major Activities

Department	Manager	No. in Dept.

The mission of this department is:

Major activities to fulfill this mission

No.	Activity	Percentage of time spent on this activity	Importance of this activity 1=Important 5=Not important
1			
2			
3			
4			
5			
6			

their use as a basis for introducing measurements of performance and improvement. It's relatively easy to determine the obvious quality costs associated with the product (such as rework, scrap,

TABLE 4-1
The Functional Analysis Approach (Data from Table 7-1)

Activity	Considerations	A Possible Way Forward
1. Raw materials and component stocks held by a manufacturing company	1. Stock costs money. Working capital is tied up; accommodation and staff are required to manage the stock; and it may deteriorate.	1. Consider just-in-time arrangements. 2. Benchmark best practice. *Consider this example:* Japanese car manufacturers maintained stock amounting to 0.2 days' requirements according to a survey in 1989. European car manufacturers maintained stock amounting to 2 days' production. This provides an obvious opportunity for savings.
2. Repair areas at production sites	1. If all products were made correctly the first time, there would be no need for any repair area or associated personnel.	1. Develop a strategy to reduce the number of repairs. You can then reduce the size of the repair area. 2. Benchmark best practice. *Consider this example:* Japanese car manufacturers employed an area equivalent to 4.1% of the assembly space for repairs in 1989. European car manufacturers employed an area equivalent to 14.4% of the assembly space for repairs. Repairing products a. Is more expensive than making them correctly the first time around. b. Ties up working capital in stock as the goods can't be sold. c. May mean that the goods can only be sold at a reduced price, as seconds. d. Is unlikely to capture all errors. Customers will be exposed to buying faulty product. e. Increases the likelihood that product will be scrapped as defective.
3. Employee training	1. Training employees is costly in terms of a. The cost of the training course. b. The opportunity cost of time spent training. 2. However training may be cost effective if `	1. Benchmark best practice. *Consider the following example:* A comparison of Japanese and European car plants in 1989 showed the following:

	Japanese Plant	European Plant
Productivity (hours per vehicle)	16.8	36.2
Assembly defects (per 100 vehicles)	60	97

| Absenteeism (%) | 5 | 12 |
| Training of new workers (hours) | 380 | 173 |

There may be a correlation between these statistics. Perhaps training does increase productivity, reduce absenteeism, and cut errors made in the production process.

a. Effective productivity increases. This may be a result of reduced scrap or increased throughput.

b. The value of output increases.

c. More sales can be made profitably.

4. Service activities

1. In-warranty service activity costs money and the business doesn't receive any additional income as a result.

2. The need for in-warranty service gives products a bad name. Customers will tend to avoid buying goods from manufacturers with a reputation for producing nonconforming product.

3. Out-of-warranty service activities are frequently a profitable line of business. Measures to enhance and develop this activity should be undertaken in such cases.

1. Identify the factors giving rise to in-warranty service work. These may include
   a. Poor production methods.
   b. Inadequate operator training.
   c. Poor user manual.
   d. Incorrect usage.

2. The factors giving rise to in-warranty service activities should then be eliminated by introducing preventive measures.

and customer returns), but significant costs are also incurred in less obvious administrative tasks.

The total quality-related cost should be determined for each activity. Quality costs may fall into four principal categories:

1. Employment costs associated with time spent on quality-related activities.

2. The cost of plant and equipment; materials and components used in processes.

3. The cost of the associated accommodation, power, communications, and other services.

4. Overhead costs associated with support functions.

Each major activity can be broken down into smaller sub-activities and the quality-related costs incurred can be analyzed as either prevention, inspection, or waste. Each department should define these for its own activities using the following guidelines.

Prevention costs relate to ensuring that errors aren't made when carrying out a task. This might include verifying that requirements haven't changed, checking that the materials and facilities required for a process are available; preparing and reading the procedure or instruction handbooks; and indeed doing anything else designed to ensure tasks run smoothly.

Inspection costs relate to checking for errors in either the inputs received from suppliers, your own work, or anyone else's work output before releasing the work from the department.

Waste costs relate to repeating an activity because of an error or simply not working at all, perhaps because a meeting was canceled at the last minute or was late starting.

In many cases, the largest single cost for these activities is the payroll cost. A reasonable estimate may frequently be obtained by analyzing the time spent on each activity. Employees should therefore be asked to record a daily time log for each activity for a period (perhaps a month) chosen because it represents the year as a whole. At the end of this period, time costs associated with these activities can be calculated by the department manager. (See Figures 4–3 and 4–4).

Using time records, the department manager can extrapolate to determine the approximate annual quality costs for her department. This is done by multiplying the times for the period under

FIGURE 4-3
Daily Time Log

Department		Major activity		Date

Time →											Quality = related time (hours)				
	Time spent on each subtask Each block = 30 mins														
Subtasks ↓	08	09	10	11	12	13	14	15	16	17	Sum	Prevention	Inspection	Waste	Sum
Totals															

FIGURE 4-4
Monthly Sum of Time Spent on Major Activities

Department		Period Covered

Time (hours)	Week 1					Week 2					Week 3					Week 4					Period total				
	NAT*	Quality time				NAT	Quality time				NAT	Quality time				NAT	Quality time				NAT	Quality time			
Major activity	Sum	Prev	Insp	Waste	Sum	Sum	Prev	Insp	Waste	Sum	Sum	Prev	Insp	Waste	Sum	Sum	Prev	Insp	Waste	Sum	Sum	Prev	Insp	Waste	Sum
No. 1																									
No. 2																									
No. 3																									
No. 4																									
No. 5																									
No. 6																									
Totals																									

*NAT = Normal activity time

FIGURE 4–5
Annual Quality Costs

Department	
Department head	
No. in department	

Major tasks:
1.
2.
3.
4.
5.
6.

For the period _____ to _____, the following time was spent on these
major activities and their associated quality-related activities:

Total time recorded against all major activities for the period (from Figure 4–4)		hours
Total hours worked by the department (number of people in department × hours in the period)		hours
Time spent on quality related activities during the period (from Figure 4–4)		
a. Prevention		hours
b. Inspection		hours
c. Waste		hours
d. Total		hours
Estimated annual quality costs $\dfrac{\text{Hours worked}}{\text{Time recorded}} \times \dfrac{\text{Total Quality}}{\text{time}} \times \dfrac{\text{Hourly}}{\text{rate}} \times \dfrac{\text{No. periods}}{\text{per year}}$	$	
Add on any other quality costs such as waste material → estimated quality costs for this department	$	

review by the hourly rate (including overheads) and grossing up to
represent a year. Figure 4–5 shows this calculation from the information recorded in Figure 4–4.

The other quality costs (such as costs of materials, plant, equipment, power and accommodation) should then be added to arrive at the total annual quality-related costs. This figure provides the group with an idea of the target for improvement.

Before beginning to implement this exercise, management must determine the purpose of collecting these costs. Any potential saving in time by employees might be seen as a threat by the work force. If management plans to retain the existing work force and redeploy personnel to more productive roles, then it must explain this message clearly to avoid misunderstandings.

Determine the Customers and Suppliers for Each Major Activity

A process model (see Figure 2–1) should be drawn for each major activity to identify the process, its customers and its suppliers.

For each major activity the group should identify who needs what it produces (its customers) as well as why and how they need it. It should also decide what it needs to enable it to carry out the activity (its inputs) and who supplies these inputs (its suppliers).

Conduct an Internal Customer Survey

Once the outputs and customers have been identified for each major activity, the group should then talk to each of its customers to determine how important the activity is to them and how well the output from the process satisfies their needs. Each customer and its requirements can be identified using the table in Figure 4–6 as a model. Table 4–2 forms a useful basis for recording results of a customer survey. At this stage the answer to the question, how well are we satisfying your needs?, is often a subjective judgment by the customer. In assessing performance, it's useful to identify with customers an objective means of measuring how well the group meets their needs. This measure can then be targeted as a basis for future improvement.

For each major activity a customer satisfaction index can be calculated based on the number of customers, how important the activity is to each customer, and how well each customer's requirements are being met. This information can later be

FIGURE 4-6
Customer Survey

	Department	Activity Ref. No.	Activity

No.	Customer	Customer requirements	What measurements are applied, or could be applied, objectively to measure quality of output?
1			
2			
3			

TABLE 4-2
Customer Survey 2

Activity number	Customer												Disatisfaction index:
	1			**2**			**3**			**4**			Sum of subtotals / No. of customers
	Importance 1=Strong 5=Weak	How well met 1=Well 5=Badly	Subtotal	Importance 1=Strong 5=Weak	How well met 1=Well 5=Badly	Subtotal	Importance 1=Strong 5=Weak	How well met 1=Well 5=Badly	Subtotal	Importance 1=Strong 5=Weak	How well met 1=Well 5=Badly	Subtotal	
1 Example	$5/1$	× 2	= 10	$5/5$	× 4	= 4	$5/2$	× 2	= 5	$5/4$	× 4	= 5	$\frac{24}{6} = 6$
2	$5/$	X	=	$5/$	X	=	$5/$	X	=	$5/$	X	=	
3	$5/$	X	=	$5/$	X	=	$5/$	X	=	$5/$	X	=	
4	$5/$	X	=	$5/$	X	=	$5/$	X	=	$5/$	X	=	
5	$5/$	X	=	$5/$	X	=	$5/$	X	=	$5/$	X	=	
6	$5/$	X	=	$5/$	X	=	$5/$	X	=	$5/$	X	=	

↑ The higher this index, the greater the need for improvement.

used as part of the decision making process to target areas for improvement.

Later, once the group fully understands its customers and how to meet their requirements, it can talk to its suppliers about what the group requires from them.

Determine Areas for Improvement; Establish Targets and Bases for Measuring Improvements

Having completed the customer survey and gathered data on the time spent on each activity, each department can target the areas that require improvement. This may be a complex decision based on a number of factors (such as costs associated with an activity, the activity's importance to its customers, how well the activity is currently being performed, and the scope for improvement). The group may then nominate areas for improvement. Each group will then decide who'll form and lead improvement groups. These groups will develop a proposed course of action to eliminate unnecessary activities and improve performance in important activities. The group will also recommend how improvements should be measured.

THE BENEFITS OF FUNCTIONAL ANALYSIS

In summary, functional analysis achieves the following major benefits for all businesses:

- It identifies external customers' requirements and focuses all activities toward meeting those requirements.
- The overall aims and purpose of the business are established.
- Each department's role in meeting those aims is established.
- The major activities each department carries out to fulfill its role are determined.
- Internal and external customers and their requirements are identified for each major activity.
- The performance of each activity is measured.
- Quality costs for the major activities within each department are collected. These may be aggregated with the

product-related quality costs to determine the quality costs for the business as a whole.

- Areas requiring improvement can be targeted and improvements can be measured.

- The whole process starts with top management and gradually involves everyone. This demonstrates management involvement and commitment to quality improvement, and at the same time ensures that everyone is involved.

- Individuals better understand the business, its aims, and how their daily activities help to advance those aims.

- Individuals understand how their output is used by their customers. This improves understanding of the customer–supplier chains within a company and the interdependency of functions.

THE APPLICATION OF FUNCTIONAL ANALYSIS TO KEY DEPARTMENTS

Functional analysis describes a method for analyzing each department's role within an organization to ensure that it's focused on meeting external customers' requirements.

This section records the results of functional analysis as it might be applied to a number of key departments in a business. Each organization is unique and has its own way of working. This section illustrates the functional analysis approach to stimulate ideas about what can be achieved in practice.

Each example follows the same basic format:

1. The mission of each department is described.
2. Principal roles of each department are defined.
3. Customers for each major activity are identified.
4. Key customer requirements are described.
5. Key measurements are identified that may be used as a basis for comparing performance against customer requirements.
6. Useful tools are identified that could help improve the department's ability to meet its customers' requirements the first time, every time.

TABLE 4-3
The Sales Department

The mission of the sales department is to
1. Maximize the value of profitable sales made by the company.
2. Accurately forecast order rates for production scheduling and financial forecasting purposes.
3. Ensure that orders are placed within an appropriate time scale.

Role	*Customer*	*Customer Requirements*	*Objective Measurements*	*Useful Tools*
1. Maximize the value of profitable sales made by the company	1. Sales manager 2. Shareholders	1. Maximize the value of profitable sales taking account of production and distribution constraints 2. For the purpose of monitoring performance, it's usually appropriate to consider the value of sales orders secured, the value converted into sales, and the amount of cash received. A sale is of no value until the cash is received.	1. Value of sales orders 2. Amount of cash received from sales made 3. Accuracy of quotes, measured as a. Profit achieved compared to budget b. Cost overruns	1. Sales order procedures. These should cover the making of sales, and describe the communication necessary between the sales team and, for example, the credit control department prior to effecting a sale.
2. Ensure that orders received are transmitted for production quickly and accurately	1. Production 2. External customer	1. The accurate and timely transmission of orders to the factory	1. Time taken to transmit orders to factory 2. Number of (or some measure of the cost of correcting) errors in orders received by the factory	1. Standard order procedures 2. Electronic transmission of orders 3. Accurate product database
3. Manage customer accounts	1. External customer	1. The professional management of the customer interface:	1. Time taken to acknowledge orders from customers 2. Number of errors in quotations	1. Secretary should know whereabouts at all times. 2. Standard quotation

continued

TABLE 4–3—Continued
The Sales Department

Role	Customer	Customer Requirements	Objective Measurements	Useful Tools
		a. Salesperson is contactable whenever necessary. b. Salesperson ensures that the customer is supplied with product that meets its real requirements. c. The company should ensure delivery of product conforming to the agreed-upon requirements at the right time, at the right place, for the agreed-upon price.	received by customers 3. Time taken to send quote to customer from the date of receiving the invitation 4. Percentage of quotes sent to customers within the agreed-upon deadline	procedure, incorporating standard terms of trade 3. Accurate product database
4. Minimize the cost of securing each order	1. Sales manager	1. Minimize the cost of securing each order	1. Number of successful (or unsuccessful) quotes 2. Value of successful (or unsuccessful) quotes 3. Percentage of successful (or unsuccessful) quotes 4. Cost of each quote or the cost of getting each order	1. Sales procedures

| 5. Forecast sales order volume for each product | 1. Production 2. Finance | 1. Accurate and timely forecast of anticipated orders for the next period | 1. Accuracy of order forecasts used for production scheduling or financial budgeting purposes (orders received as a percentage of orders forecast) 2. Timeliness of order forecasts, measured as percentage received on time, or as number or percentage received late | 1. Sales procedures |

TABLE 4-4
The Finance Department

The mission of the finance department is to ensure that
1. All customers are creditworthy.
2. All sales are invoiced promptly and accurately.
3. All transactions are accurately recorded in the accounting records.
4. All purchases are properly authorized, paid, and accounted for.
5. Audit and other compliance issues are handled correctly, efficiently, and promptly.
6. Appropriate management information is produced accurately and in a timely manner.

Role	Customer	Customer Requirements	Objective Measurements	Useful Tools
1. All customers are creditworthy.	1. Management team 2. Shareholders	1. Customers are good credit risks. 2. Customers settle outstanding accounts promptly.	1. Excessive debtor days 2. Value of debts outstanding over one, two, or three months 3. Cost of bad debts 4. Debt collection costs 5. Cost of the credit control department 6. Number (value) of customer accounts in solicitor's hands	1. Credit assessment procedures 2. Debt collection procedures
2. All documents (confirmation of order, delivery notes, invoices, statements of account, and credit notes) are accurate.	1. External customer	1. All documents are issued promptly and accurately.	1. Number of errors on invoices, etc. received by customer 2. Number/value of credit notes or other documents issued to correct errors in invoicing, etc. 3. Number of errors on invoices corrected prior to sending	1. Standard invoice format 2. Documented invoicing procedures
3. Time is minimized between sending goods/service to	1. Accounts receivable	1. Invoices are issued promptly and accurately so customers have no excuse for late payment.	1. Number of days between the delivery of goods/service and the dispatch of the invoice 2. The cost of capital tied up in overdue	1. Standard invoice format 2. Documented invoicing procedures 3. Routine, enforced billing

customers and the receipt of the full amount of cash outstanding.		2. Minimum delay between shipping goods and the receipt of cash	accounts 3. The number of days between completion of order and dispatch of goods 4. Number of days between the delivery of goods/services and the receipt of cash 5. The cost of chasing overdue debts 6. Value of outstanding invoices (broken down into "less than one month," "one month," "two months," etc.)	schedule
4. All purchases are properly authorized	1. Purchasing	1. No unauthorized purchases are made	1. Number of unauthorized purchases	1. Documented, enforced procedures relating to purchases of goods and services, governing a. Authorization of purchases b. Expenditure limits c. Documentation (e.g. purchase orders)
5. All transactions are accurately recorded in the accounting records.	1. Shareholders	1. All transactions are properly recorded in the accounting records.	1. Number of errors in the accounting records	1. Internal audit procedures 2. External audit
6. Appropriate management information is produced accurately and in a timely manner.	1. Senior management team	1. Timely delivery of accurate reports containing agreed-upon management information	1. Late delivery of reports (number of days) 2. The number (value) of errors in reports 3. Time wasted producing/reviewing unnecessary/inappropriate reports 4. Time wasted looking for important information	1. Agreed-upon timetable for preparation and delivery of reports to management 2. Agreed-upon list of key information for each report

continued

TABLE 4–4—Continued
The Finance Department

Role	Customer	Customer Requirements	Objective Measurements	Useful Tools
7. Tax, payroll, audit, and other compliance issues are handled correctly, efficiently and promptly.	1. All employees 2. Regulatory bodies	1. Accurate and timely handling of tax, payroll, and other procedures	1. Delays in receiving salary 2. Errors in salary/tax returns 3. Time taken to correct errors 4. Time taken corresponding to tax agency 5. Value of professional fees on these issues	1. Documented procedures

TABLE 4–5
The Personnel Department

The mission of the personnel department is to ensure that
1. There's an adequate supply of appropriately qualified recruits.
2. Training needs are identified and effectively implemented.
3. Staff are properly treated, appraised of their performance, and counseled about their future.
4. The terms of engagement (salary, hours, job description, and conditions of employment) for all staff are agreed upon with all staff members.

Role	Customer	Customer Requirements	Objective Measurements	Useful Tools

1. Recruit suitably qualified staff by the time required	1. All departments	1. Replacements are identified promptly after requirements have been specified.	1. Number of days in each department at less than full headcount
			2. Excessive overtime costs resulting from staff shortages
			3. Number of days/cost of training for new staff members in excess of standard requirements
			4. Time spent interviewing inadequately qualified candidates by
			  a. Personnel department
			  b. Each operating department
			5. Time taken to recruit for each vacancy
			6. Performance rating of recruits after six months' employment
				1. Formal record of agreed-upon target headcount for each department
				2. Budgeted overtime levels
				3. Training budget for new staff grades
				4. Recruitment procedures:
				  a. Preselection
				  b. Interviewing

2. Ensure that training needs are identified and effectively implemented	1. All departments	1. Staff receive adequate, relevant training.	1. Number of days training per department 2. Expenditure on training for each department 3. Number (or value) of operator errors resulting from inadequate training	1. Training budget for each department 2. Training schedule for each member of staff 3. Training policy and documented procedures

continued

TABLE 4–5—Concluded
The Personnel Department

Role	Customer	Customer Requirements	Objective Measurements	Useful Tools
			4. Time taken to effect agreed-upon training requirements 5. Rating by participants of training received	4. Consideration of training requirements at staff counseling
3. Treat staff properly, appraise them of their performance, and counsel them about their future	1. All employees 2. All departments	1. Staff are properly treated, appraised of their performance and counseled about their future. 2. Reasons for poor staff retention are investigated and overcome. 3. Staff are informed of and involved in company decisions.	1. Number of staff complaints (by department) 2. Number of staff who aren't appraised (by department) 3. Time devoted to appraisal and counseling of staff 4. Staff turnover (numbers and as a percentage of headcount) (by department) 5. Recruitment costs 6. Number of instances in which postresignation counseling isn't performed 7. Number/length/cost of strikes or other disputes 8. Percentage of negative comments from employee surveys	1. Staff handbook explaining procedures and standard terms of employment 2. Job specifications for all staff 3. Formal appraisal and counseling procedures (covering existing employees and resignations) 4. Records kept of agreed-upon follow-up action from counseling session 5. Staff consultative meetings 6. Employee surveys of (dis)satisfaction with the company's procedures

TABLE 4-6
The Warehouse/Stores Department

The mission of the warehouse/stores is to ensure that raw materials, components, and products are
1. Subject to appropriate procedures on receipt from internal and external suppliers (completion of receipt paperwork, inspected, recorded, and stored).
2. Stored safely and securely in good condition under appropriate conditions until required.
3. Accurately identified and made ready for collection by customers (whether internal or external) when required.

Role	Customer	Customer Requirements	Objective Measurements	Useful Tools
1. Receipt of goods from internal and external suppliers	1. Production	1. Goods should be received in good condition.	1. Number/value of damaged goods received into stock	1. Procedures for checking items before acceptance into stock 2. Ship to stock status for approved suppliers
2. Storage of goods	1. External customer 2. Production	1. Goods should be properly identified. 2. Goods should be stored in the correct location. 3. Goods should be stored securely. 4. Goods should be protected from damage and deterioration.	1. Number/value of items stolen, damaged, or subject to deterioration in storage 2. Time taken to pick stock items	1. Packaging and handling procedures 2. Stock management procedures
3. Checking and dispatch of goods a. Raw materials and components b. Finished goods c. Replacement goods	1. External customer	1. The correct items are received undamaged and at the right time.	1. Time to dispatch goods after receipt of request 2. Number of errors in goods dispatched	1. Packaging and handling procedures

Continued

TABLE 4-6—Concluded
The Warehouse/Stores Department

Role	Customer	Customer Requirements	Objective Measurements	Useful Tools
4. Receiving, checking, and sorting returned goods for replacement or repair	1. External customer 2. Production 3. Service 4. Design/ engineering	1. All goods returned are to be identified; replacements are to be sent out and the investigating department informed.	1. Time taken to send out replacement goods 2. Time taken to inform investigating department	1. Documentation procedures governing receipt of returned goods

TABLE 4-7
The Quality Department

The mission of the quality department is to help ensure that all departments in the business manage and exercise their responsibilities for quality effectively. Each department is responsible for the quality of its output and the quality of its internal workings. The quality department is responsible for advising and supporting other departments to achieve their quality objectives. It's also responsible for auditing their quality management systems to confirm compliance with procedures.

Role	Customer	Customer Requirements	Objective Measurements	Useful Tools

1. Managing of the quality management system	1. All departments
	2. External assessment body
	3. External customers
		1. Quality procedures established and followed for all departments	1. Number of audits carried out to schedule
			2. Average time to implement corrective actions
			3. Number of instances of noncompliance with procedures
				1. Quality manual setting out
				  a. The business's quality policy
				  b. Each department's responsibilities
				  c. Quality procedures to cover all operations
				2. Approved quality management system
				3. Quality audit timetable
				4. Quality audit checklist
				5. Documented quality audit procedures
				6. Audit training

2. Training personnel	1. All departments	1. Adequate, interesting, relevant training carried out to ensure that all employees understand their quality role	1. Participant rating of education program 2. Number of personnel trained (in each period/cumulatively)	1. Set formal objectives for each training course. These should be agreedupon with the head of the departments from which participants will be drawn. 2. Attendance rating for courses

continued

TABLE 4-7—Continued
The Quality Department

Role	Customer	Customer Requirements	Objective Measurements	Useful Tools
3. Establishing appropriate means of communication to keep all staff informed of the progress made by the quality program	1. All employees	1. Interesting and accurate information about the quality program to enable them to a. Understand how they fit into the wider picture b. See the benefits accruing to the business and hence to them (as employees) from their efforts c. Motivate them to continue to strive to improve performance	1. Employee awareness of quality 2. Rate of turnover of information on notices	1. Quality bulletinboard 2. Quality publication (newspaper/magazine/newsletter) 3. Quality section at key meetings
4. Facilitating the reduction in the cost of quality in each department	1. All departments	1. Accurate information on how the cost of quality is broken down by constituent activities 2. Accurate and timely calculation of the cost of quality in each department and for the business as a whole	1. Reduction in the cost of quality each period (by department and by the business as a whole) 2. Cumulative reduction in the cost of quality (by department and by the business as a whole)	1. Quality cost analysis
5. Advising each department on quality issues	1. Each department	1. Prompt, commercial advice on quality issues as they affect	1. Number of times that advice is sought from the quality department 2. Positive comments from customer	1. Log of advice sought maintained by the quality department

| | a. The external customer
b. Internal operations | departments on the promptness and value of the quality department's advice
3. Average time to respond | | 2. All other departments' periodic (say semiannual) evaluation, of the value and promptness of advice from the quality department |
| 6. Analyzing and interpreting customer feedback on the whole service provided by the business | 1. All departments | 1. Prompt, accurate feedback on customer perception of quality | 1. Number of customer reports obtained
2. Customer rating of overall service | 1. Source data for analysis:
a. Customer questionnaire
b. Customer complaints log
c. Warranty claims
d. Product liability cases |

Chapter Five

Quality Management System Standards

An effective Quality Management System (QMS) is a key building block for total quality. It is, however, only one element in a Total Quality Management organization. It describes a controlled, documented system of procedures designed to ensure that only conforming products or services are released to customers.

This can be achieved either by preventing errors from occurring in the first place or by checking the product or service to ensure that nonconforming product isn't released to the customer. A typical traditional QMS often relies heavily on a series of checking activities to identify instances of nonconformance. The errors are then corrected.

A traditional QMS doesn't generally cover other service and administration activities such as finance or personnel. To picture the key differences between a typical QMS and a Total Quality environment, it's helpful to compare their key features as illustrated in Table 5–1.

A number of quality system standards have been developed to describe the requirements for an effective QMS; perhaps the most important standard today is the International Standard ISO9000.

ISO9000—THE APPROVAL PROCESS

Conformance to one of the quality system standards may be specified between two parties as a contractual requirement. In this case conformance to the standard may be assessed by the customer placing the contract (second-party assessment). Alternatively, and more commonly, an independent assessment of a company's QMS can be carried out by an approved body (third-party assessment).

TABLE 5–1
Comparison of the Key Features of a Traditional Quality Management System and a Total Quality Management Culture

	Traditional Quality Management System	Total Quality Management Culture
Areas covered	Typically only product-related activities.	All activities within a company, including service and administration activities.
Focus on errors	Typically checking to ensure that errors don't reach customers.	Preventing errors from occurring in the first place.
Responsibility and involvement	Typically the responsibility of a quality department is to audit the system and recommend necessary changes.	Everyone is responsible for quality and striving for continuous improvement in all activities.
Benefits	Establishes basic controls over performance of activities. Reduces errors to customers and begins to reduce internal waste.	Builds on QMS. Focuses on eliminating errors and waste in every activity.
Customer focus	Focus directed at reducing errors in products or services received by the external customer.	Strives to ensure conforming outputs for all processes, whether for internal or external customers.

Any company may apply to an accredited body for approval. The company should ensure that the scope of the accredited body's approval covers the business activity concerned. It should then supply a copy of the documentation for its QMS to the approval body for review. Next the approval body notifies the company of any deficiencies in the documentation and seeks agreement on measures to rectify them. The approval body then undertakes an intensive audit of the operations of the company and either awards a certificate or notifies the company of the deficiencies found and seeks agreement on measures to rectify them. Following approval, the company is subject to periodic compliance audits by the approval body. Costs of the initial approval and subsequent compliance audits are met by the applying company.

BENEFITS OF AN APPROVED QUALITY MANAGEMENT SYSTEM

An approved QMS provides assurance to customers that the company is committed to quality and can supply products and services in accordance with their requirements. The standards only define what must be controlled, and not how individual processes must be controlled. Accordingly, a company that understands why it's introducing a QMS can implement a flexible system that suits itself and realize the benefits an effective QMS can bring.

An effective QMS should ensure that the business's activities are controlled and documented. This enables everyone to know what they're doing and how to do it. As a result, inefficiencies and waste may be targeted and eliminated. The benefits of an effective QMS are many but they can only be realized by a company that recognizes them, that's committed to the QMS, and that takes the time and trouble to implement a well–thought-out system that suits the company and advances its business objectives.

Here are some typical benefits of a well–thought-out, effective QMS:

1. Customers who are satisfied and loyal because goods and services are always produced according to their requirements.
2. Reduced operating costs as waste is eliminated and efficiency is increased as a result of eliminating nonconformance.
3. Improved competitiveness and profitability as operating costs are reduced.
4. Improved employee morale as staff work more efficiently.

An ineffective QMS is usually seen by everyone concerned as time-wasting and inefficient with no real benefit to the company except keeping the customer happy. This position may arise if management decides to implement a QMS without paying adequate attention to the business's requirements. This might happen if, for example, the company implements a QMS because of pressure from customers to seek ISO approval. This assures the customer that only conforming products or services will be delivered by the supplier.

However, unless the QMS is adequately planned, it may well be implemented without realizing the many benefits that an effective QMS would bring. In the worst case, a company might finish up with a system that's difficult to manage and doesn't advance its commercial objectives. Unfortunately this type of QMS won't advance the business's aims and won't even keep the customer happy for long because people will always try to find a way around it so nonconforming goods or services may well be released at some time.

An effective QMS can be implemented without being registered as complying with a quality system standard. However, in addition to providing information and guidance on how an effective QMS should operate, registration against a recognized standard has significant commercial benefits:

- It shows customers that the QMS has been independently assessed as effective. This is increasingly important as a marketing edge over competitors.
- It avoids duplication of customer assessments. Most customers accept and recognize the ISO9000 approval. Independent approval saves time and money for both customer and supplier. The companies can then concentrate on specific requirements for particular contracts or orders.
- It provides evidence of a responsible attitude to quality and product liability requirements.

REQUIREMENTS OF THE ISO9000 STANDARDS

There are three levels of approval within the ISO series:

1. ISO9001—quality systems specification for design/ development, production, installation and servicing.
2. ISO9002—quality systems specification for production and installation.
3. ISO9003—quality systems specification for final inspection and test.

The appropriate approval standard depends on the company's activities. Guidance is given in the introduction to each standard and in the guidance document, ISO9000, to help select the correct standard.

Each standard defines the activities for which a company must define appropriate controls. These range from ensuring that the company's quality policy is stated and that there are sufficient qualified personnel to carry out this policy; to ensuring that whenever defects occur, they're reported and actions are introduced to prevent their recurrence. Most well-run companies already carry out a number of the required procedures to control their business.

Once a company has determined the appropriate standard, it must ensure that its QMS conforms to it. One of the major activities when seeking approval for a QMS in a well-organized company is preparing documentation to describe all the quality-related procedures, and then controlling and amending the documents as the business evolves. It's important, as far as possible, to make the QMS reflect existing procedures, rather than change what's done to conform to a predetermined system. For this reason it's important to involve the whole company in documenting and implementing the QMS. A consultant can play an important role in training and interpreting the standards for the company. But beware the "off-the-shelf" QMS, whether produced internally or by a consultant! These may act as a straitjacket and will generally fail in the longer term.

The key requirements for an effective QMS are commitment from the top; a manager responsible for quality with sufficient resources to support her; documented procedures and records; and periodic, rigorous review of the system. These issues should be clearly addressed in the company's quality manual.

DETAILED REQUIREMENTS OF ISO9001

ISO9001 is the most comprehensive of the ISO9000 series. It contains the requirements for an organization involved in the original design, development, production, installation and servicing of products. A brief description of the principal features of ISO9001 is given in the remainder of this chapter. The other two standards contain appropriate elements from ISO9001. The clauses of each standard are detailed in Table 5–2.

TABLE 5–2
Clauses of the ISO9000 Series of Standards

	Number of Clause		
Title of clause	*ISO 9001 Design and Manufacture*	*ISO 9002 Manufacture*	*ISO 9003 Final Inspection and Test*
Management responsibility	4.1	4.1	4.1
Quality system	4.2	4.2	4.2
Contract review	4.3	4.3	—
Design control	4.4	—	—
Document control	4.5	4.4	4.3
Purchasing	4.6	4.5	—
Purchaser-supplied product	4.7	4.6	—
Product identification and traceability	4.8	4.7	4.4
Process control	4.9	4.8	—
Inspection and testing	4.10	4.9	4.5
Inspection, measuring, and test equipment	4.11	4.10	4.6
Inspection and test status	4.12	4.11	4.7
Control of nonconforming product	4.13	4.12	4.8
Corrective action	4.14	4.13	—
Handling, storage, packaging, and delivery	4.15	4.14	4.9
Quality records	4.16	4.15	4.10
Internal quality audits	4.17	4.16	—
Training	4.18	4.17	4.11
Servicing	4.19	—	—
Statistical techniques	4.20	4.18	4.12

MANAGEMENT RESPONSIBILITY

Quality Policy

To ensure that quality is taken seriously by all members of an organization, senior management should define and publish the company's quality policy. This defines the quality objectives for all employees and helps to demonstrate senior management's commitment to quality. Senior managers are then responsible for ensuring that this policy is understood and implemented throughout the company.

Organization

To ensure that an effective QMS is implemented, the role and responsibilities of all functions that affect quality must be defined. This is usually achieved by an organization chart and job specifications. When considering the organization required to assure quality, the company should identify the test, inspection and other monitoring activities required (including audit and design review) and ensure that sufficient trained personnel are available to carry them out.

It's also important to nominate one manager with the necessary authority, resources, and responsibility to ensure that the QMS is implemented and maintained. Managers should have sufficient freedom to carry out this task without conflicting with their other responsibilities.

To ensure that the QMS is properly implemented and continues to meet ISO9001 requirements, a system of quality audit and management review procedures should be implemented.

QUALITY SYSTEM

Having nominated a manager and decided on the organizational structure to assure quality, the company should consider the Quality Management System it will introduce. This system should be fully documented. The activities that the system should control are detailed in the remainder of the standard.

QMS Documentation

To ensure that a system of standard procedures is applied to control the quality of product or service, a comprehensive set of documentation is required to describe appropriate procedures.

The quality manual describes how a company ensures conformance to ISO9001. It usually starts with a statement of the quality policy and a definition of how this is put into practice by addressing each of the requirements of ISO9001. Detailed control procedures and other documents are referred to as is appropriate. The manual is a formal declaration by the company of how it ensures quality and forms a documented set of managerial instructions on quality matters.

Control procedures define in detail the methods and controls adopted throughout the organization to assure quality, and might include quality procedures, design procedures and standards, manufacturing procedures, sales procedures, and data processing procedures. These procedures generally affect a number of people or departments, and frequently cover interfaces between functions. Individual work instructions are referred to where appropriate.

Work instructions define procedures for specific tasks or processes. They generally apply only to one task or to a small group of people. Examples include specific inspection instructions, test specifications, drawings, planning instructions, and calibration methods.

For example, consider the procedures required to define how in-process testing is controlled. The quality manual may discuss the overall policy on testing and may refer to a routing procedure to detail how the process is controlled. The routing procedure may define who makes a decision on what testing is required for a given item and how the system ensures that the item follows this routing. The routing procedure may state that all testing is carried out in accordance with the appropriate test specification. The test specification then describes what tests a particular item is subject to at a given stage during its manufacture.

Quality documentation is one of the keys to running an effective QMS. As a result, you must define how each level of documentation is controlled. It's also important to understand the relationship between documents to ensure that any changes take account of all the interrelated effects that might occur.

CONTRACT REVIEW

Once it's documented and implemented, the QMS defines how an organization assures the quality of the product or service it expects to provide. When accepting an order or contract to supply a product or service, it should ensure that it's capable of meeting the specific requirements. Accordingly, all orders or contracts should be reviewed before acceptance to ensure that the requirements are capable of being met. Orders or contracts shouldn't be accepted unless the company can meet the requirements. The following issues must be addressed at this stage:

1. Are the processes and equipment used capable of meeting the requirement?
2. Does the company have sufficient skilled personnel?
3. Are the methods currently used for testing, inspecting, and monitoring output adequate to meet the requirements?
4. Are the equipment and methods currently used for taking measurements and testing capable of the required accuracy?
5. Does the company fully understand the acceptance criteria? All those items that determine whether the item meets the customer's requirements should be written down and fully understood. This includes a proper definition of any subjective judgments such as "smooth finish," "scratch-free," or "blue."
6. Are all the necessary processes (including design, production, inspection, and test) compatible and capable of producing the product/service in accordance with requirements?
7. Do procedures exist to produce appropriate records?

A documented system should exist to ensure that this review is undertaken before an order is accepted. The system should ensure that the following points are checked:

1. The requirements are clearly stated in writing.

2. Any differences between the order and the original quotation/tender are resolved.

3. The company is capable of meeting the requirements.

It's usually possible to implement a fairly simple procedure to check points (1) and (2) when standard or repeat orders are received. It may then be possible to restrict checks to identifying unusual features and ensuring that the version required is fully documented before accepting the order. A more rigorous procedure should be implemented whenever new orders, non-standard orders, or special contracts are received. This will require a more detailed check against the preceding criteria. A documentary record should be kept to demonstrate that this review has taken place. For companies that don't usually produce standard items but work to specific contracts, the preceding points are often documented as part of a quality plan prepared specifically for individual contracts.

DESIGN CONTROL

The standard contains detailed requirements on how the design process should be controlled, and specifies that procedures to cover planning, design input, design output, design verification, and design changes should be fully documented:

Planning

It's essential that all staff understand their role and responsibilities in the design process and how they interface with other groups. The standard specifies that

1. The organization for each design activity should be documented so responsibility for each activity and interfaces between activities are defined.

2. The person responsible for each activity should have the necessary qualifications and sufficient resources to carry out the activity.

The standard requires procedures to specify how and when information is transmitted between groups. Timely flow of controlled and accurate information is essential to ensure that the design process is carried out effectively and without errors in cases where a number of groups work on specific elements of complex designs.

Design Input

Design requirements may be received directly from external customers or from internal sources such as the marketing department. Before accepting a design requirement, the design department should review it to ensure that it's sufficiently detailed to enable them to know what's expected from the design process.

Design Output

Output from the design process may consist of drawings and specifications supported by calculations, analyses, tests, and reviews to demonstrate that the design conforms to the input requirements. Design procedures should ensure that the design output

1. Meets the input requirements. It's only possible to do this if input requirements are adequately specified.
2. Contains instructions to define how conformance of the product or service can be verified during production.
3. Meets all the necessary regulatory requirements. The design process should ensure that all regulatory requirements are considered, not only those specified as part of the input requirements.
4. Meets necessary safety standards. The design department should identify all parts of the design that are critical to safety so they can be carefully monitored during the production process.

Design Verification

Procedures should exist to ensure that the design output conforms in all regards to the input requirements. Design verification should be planned and performed, and the results should be fully documented as part of the design process. A number of methods may be acceptable depending on the circumstances. Typical methods include holding design reviews, undertaking tests, carrying out checking calculations, and comparing the new design with similar, proven designs.

Typically a combination of these methods might be adopted. The company should consider carefully which methods are most appropriate for any given design project. Unless a design is proven before it's released for production, significant rectification costs and wasted time will likely arise during the production process.

Design Changes

Whenever a change is made to a released design (for example, a new material is introduced), the change should be proven, approved, and communicated to everyone concerned in a controlled way. The procedures necessary to control design changes usually form part of the system for document control.

DOCUMENT CONTROL

An effective QMS ensures that all activities are carried out in a controlled way, so that everyone knows what they're supposed to do. This requires documentation of how tasks should be performed. Because many processes are related and interdependent, it's important to ensure that any change is implemented by everyone at the same time. This requires a system to ensure that documents are controlled so that (1) everyone who needs to use a document has easy access to it and (2) only the current version of a document is available at any time. This avoids confusion and mistakes.

Procedures should cover the origination and amendment of documents, detailing who holds the document, who may authorize changes, how documents are reissued, how obsolete documents are withdrawn, and a system for verifying the current version (perhaps using a master list). Key documents that must be controlled include (1) the quality manual and procedures, (2) department manuals and procedures, (3) work instructions, including test, inspection, and planning documents, and (4) drawings and specifications.

PURCHASING

To ensure the quality of the end product or service, you must ensure the quality of bought-in services and materials purchased. This applies equally to component suppliers and subcontractors. The buying company is responsible for ensuring that its supplier's quality system is effective, and should ensure that

1. The supplier is capable of meeting the customer's requirements. This may be established by supplier assessment, verification of third party approvals, and review of past performance.
2. The supplier is provided with sufficient written data to enable a complete understanding of the requirements.
3. Products and services can only be purchased from approved suppliers.
4. A supplier's performance is regularly monitored and corrective actions are introduced where appropriate.

PRODUCT SUPPLIED BY THE CUSTOMER

Items may sometimes be supplied by a customer to be built into the end product. The company should introduce a procedure to ensure that these items are checked, identified, securely stored, and used as specified in the contract.

PRODUCT IDENTIFICATION AND TRACEABILITY

All companies should implement procedures to enable them to identify each product, subproduct, component, and raw material at each stage in the manufacturing process, from goods inward to final dispatch. This helps avoid the possibility of products or components being mixed up and perhaps fitted in the wrong place. Unique part numbers and revision numbers are a common means of achieving this objective.

In some industries more rigorous procedures may be needed. For example, in the defense and aerospace industries it may be necessary to be able to trace every component back to its original manufacturing batch to enable component failures to be investigated or to trace all other critical users so replacements can be fitted before further failures arise. A system to ensure full traceability can be very costly and time-consuming to implement. As a result, it's not a mandatory part of the standard. Traceability should generally be specified in individual contracts unless it's required as part of the industry standards or by law.

PROCESS CONTROL

A system should be implemented prior to commencing production to ensure that process controls are adequate to ensure that products and services conform to specification. The system should ensure that

1. The activities and equipment required to produce the output are identified.
2. Instructions are prepared describing how activities are to be performed. These instructions should detail
   a. Training and skills required.
   b. Set-up/start-up procedures.
   c. The order in which activities should be carried out.
   d. Material and equipment requirements.
   e. How the process is to be monitored.
   f. Maintenance requirements.
3. Instructions describe how the output from a process is assessed to ensure that it conforms to requirements. This can include tests, inspection methods and workmanship standards.

Process control may be applied equally to the administrative activities carried out in the organization. Special processes such as heat treatment, nondestructive testing, and welding are employed in some industries. The output from these processes can't be fully assessed by subsequent inspection or testing. Deficiencies may only show up after the product is in use. These processes may well be critical in the manufacture of products such as, for example, pressure vessels. To ensure product quality in these circumstances, it's necessary to apply additional special control procedures during manufacturing. Detailed standards exist for a number of processes governing the qualification of operators, appropriate procedures, and the records required to demonstrate conformance to procedures. These standards only apply to certain industries.

INSPECTION AND TESTING

Inspection and testing are means of assessing whether processes have been carried out correctly and whether the product conforms to specification. The standard requires that inspection and testing should be considered at all stages in the production process, and be carried out where necessary. Records should be kept as evidence of the tests performed.

The standard focuses on three principal areas in relation to test and inspection: receiving inspection, in-process inspection and testing, and final inspection and testing.

Receiving Inspection

Incoming goods should be checked to ensure that they conform to requirements. The type and level of inspection depends on the controls exercised by the supplier and on the supplier's previous performance.

In-Process Inspection and Testing

In-process test and inspection procedures should identify all nonconforming product. Activities that monitor process parameters and indicate a likelihood of nonconforming product are generally more cost-effective than inspection or test activities that only detect nonconforming product after production. In service activities, the term *nonconforming product* applies to instances where the required service levels haven't been met (for example, if 72-hour delivery is promised but not achieved).

Final Inspection and Testing

The appropriate level of final test and inspection may vary in the light of the overall control environment and should include a check to ensure that all the specified operations have been carried out.

Inspection is generally carried out after an activity has been completed. As a result, it does little other than sort good product from bad. Companies should therefore consider carefully the level, nature, and quantity of testing/inspection introduced. Where possible, effort should be directed at preventing errors from occurring in the first place. Merely finding errors once they've occurred is expensive (in terms of time and material wasted) and does nothing to prevent errors from recurring in the future.

The standard is concerned to ensure that adequate controls exist to make sure that products and services conform to specification. It's permitted to modify the control environment to take account of changed circumstances. Individual inspection and testing activities to ensure product conformance may be removed provided it can be demonstrated that prevention activities ensure that the errors concerned no longer occur. To operate a cost-effective QMS, procedures should be subject to periodic review to identify appropriate prevention activities that may replace test/inspection procedures.

INSPECTION, MEASURING, AND TEST EQUIPMENT

The performance of measuring and test equipment is vital to product integrity for all companies that rely on test and inspection procedures to verify product conformance.

Equipment used to verify that a product conforms to requirements must be reliable and capable. The standard requires that a system is introduced to ensure that the right equipment (regularly calibrated to ensure that readings are reliable and accurate) is used in the right way. The system should address the following issues:

1. Appropriate equipment should be selected for the measurement required.

2. Equipment used to assure product quality should be regularly calibrated, and the calibration status should be obvious to the user.

3. The calibration methods should be documented to ensure traceability of the calibration to national standards. Recalibration should be performed frequently enough so that it occurs before equipment goes out of calibration.

4. A system should be in place to assess the validity of any measurement taken using an instrument that's subsequently found to be out of calibration.

5. Calibration records should be kept for each item of measuring equipment.

INSPECTION AND TEST STATUS

Product must be labeled clearly and unambiguously to ensure that anyone who may need to use it knows the inspection/test status of the item. This ensures that only proven, conforming product passes to the next stage in the process. Methods such as tags, stamps, labels, route cards, color coding, and location may be used to indicate the three test states: awaiting inspection/test, passed inspection/test, and failed inspection/test.

CONTROL OF NONCONFORMING PRODUCTS

Nonconforming product should be clearly identified to ensure that it's not used. A procedure should describe who's authorized to decide the means of disposal for nonconforming material (rework, repair, use in another application, or scrap), how the decision is communicated, and how subsequent operations are controlled. This information should then be used to drive the corrective action activity. For service activities, "nonconforming product" applies to areas where service levels haven't been met (for example, a client report issued late or containing errors).

CORRECTIVE ACTION

A key element of any QMS is the continuous improvement of quality. The system should ensure that actions are introduced to prevent problems from recurring, that the effectiveness of the prevention activities are verified, and that any change in procedures is properly documented and implemented. A procedure should define the responsibility for initiating and implementing corrective actions. Where possible, the system should allow anyone who discovers a problem or error to highlight the need for corrective action. Specific areas where procedures are required include

1. Investigating the causes of nonconforming product and introducing actions to prevent recurrence. For service activities this applies to recording any instances where service levels haven't been met, and implementing corrective action.
2. Analyzing processes, concessions, quality records, service records, and customer complaints to detect trends and introduce actions to prevent nonconforming products or services.

HANDLING, STORAGE, PACKAGING, AND DELIVERY

A procedure is required to ensure that the product is adequately packed, handled, and stored to prevent damage or deterioration at all stages from the receipt of goods to safe delivery to the customer. Protection measures might include site security to prevent vandalism or theft; packing or handling procedures to protect the finish on a product; or special handling techniques to prevent, for example, damage to electronic components through electrostatic discharge.

QUALITY RECORDS

Records may represent the only evidence that designated quality procedures have been applied to any given product or service. As a result, it's important to decide (1) the nature (including duration) of the records required to demonstrate this compliance and (2) the procedures to ensure that they're properly maintained, stored, and retrieved.

INTERNAL QUALITY AUDITS

To ensure that the QMS is properly implemented and continues to meet ISO9001 requirements, procedures should be defined covering two key activities:

1. Management review to ensure that the QMS continues to meet the standard's requirements. It's pointless to ensure that everyone is working to the QMS if the QMS itself isn't adequate to fulfill the requirements laid down by the standard. Senior management should regularly review the current system and implement corrective actions. This may include a review of audits, quality costs, outgoing/in-process quality measurements, and customer complaints. A record should be kept of the review, together with resulting actions.

2. Quality audits to ensure that everyone is working in accordance with the QMS. The quality audit procedure should define the following points:

   a. Audit methods.
   b. Responsibility for scheduling and carrying out audits.
   c. How the audit schedule will be determined.
   d. How audit results will be recorded.
   e. Corrective action and follow-up procedures.

Auditing is a key requirement of the standard. Only through auditing can a company determine whether the QMS is properly implemented. A skilled process, it should be carried out by trained personnel if it's to yield positive results.

TRAINING

Individuals should have access to the correct procedures, tools, and skills to carry out tasks in accordance with requirements. The appropriate skills may be acquired through a combination of qualification, training, and experience. A system should be designed to identify training needs for any activity affecting product or service quality. Detailed records should be maintained of an individual's capability to carry out specific assignments.

SERVICING

Where servicing is an important part of customer requirements (for example, the regular servicing of heating equipment or the installation of computer networks), the preceding procedures should be applied to the service activity to ensure that it conforms to requirements.

STATISTICAL TECHNIQUES

Statistical techniques may sometimes be applied to verify a product or process's acceptability. Where these techniques are used they should be thoroughly understood and documented. Statistical techniques may include

1. Inspection sampling plans where the acceptability of a batch of product is determined by the inspection of a sample.
2. Statistical Process Control where control of a process is achieved by monitoring the control parameters.

Chapter Six

A Story of Continuous Quality Improvement

For many companies, the costs of not getting things right first time (nonconformance costs) can amount to 25 percent of turnover. Eliminating this unnecessary burden enables a company to improve profitability in the short term and enhance competitiveness in the longer term.

Nonconformance costs may arise in any department. All departments spend some time doing things over again or rectifying other department's errors. Consequently all departments are involved in Quality Improvement; no one is exempt. Each and every individual is involved in ensuring that the right things are done right the first time.

The objective of Quality Improvement is to continuously improve quality by eliminating nonconformance in every activity throughout the company. The benefits from implementing a successful Quality Improvement Program are enormous: improved customer satisfaction; elimination of error and waste; reduction in operating costs; higher motivation and commitment of employees; increased profitability and competitiveness. Indeed the very survival of the company may be at stake.

Implementing a Quality Improvement Program is, however, not a step to be undertaken lightly. It demands absolute commitment from everyone, starting with senior management, if it's to succeed. It frequently requires a change in company culture and a radical rethink of every activity performed in the company. Senior management's commitment is the most important factor in ensuring the program's success; it's also the most difficult to achieve. There's no easy method for gaining this commitment. It requires constant attention, persuasion, and powerful evidence of the benefits that can accrue from Quality Improvement.

The effort required to implement a successful Quality Improvement Program is considerable, but the cost of not implementing one can be catastrophic. Inadequate attention to consistently meeting customers' requirements frequently results in business failure. Total Quality is only for survivors!

This following case follows the steps Alpha Systems took to implement a Quality Improvement Program. Although the company is fictitious, the story reflects the experiences of a number of real companies. The basic approach adopted by Alpha, and the problems it encounters, are common to many businesses, whether manufacturing or service, large or small, high tech or traditional.

But the story only represents one possible way of implementing Quality Improvement. Every company is unique. Consequently every improvement program will be unique. The aim of this chapter is to provide insight into what's possible. Whatever methodology is used, there are a number of key steps that any program must include:

1. *Planning for Quality Improvement:* This phase is key to any Quality Improvement Program's success. The objectives of this phase are to:
   a. Secure the active commitment of senior management to the continuous improvement of quality.
   b. Determine the most appropriate means of implementing Quality Improvement within the organization.
   c. Develop a detailed plan to guide the implementation of the Quality Improvement Program.

2. *Understanding customers:* Companies only exist because they serve their customers' needs. Quality Improvement is about improving a business's ability to meet customer requirements. To improve quality, it's essential to
   a. Understand the external customers, their requirements, and how well those requirements are being met.
   b. Identify how internal processes work to meet external customers' needs. Only by improving the performance of these processes can a business better meet its external customers' needs, at minimum cost.

3. *Understanding quality costs:* Non-conformance costs arise because things go wrong. Activities that generate high quality costs are either not satisfying customer needs or not working efficiently. So it's essential that the Improvement Program

identifies the magnitude of quality costs and where they occur. This information can be used as a focus to drive the program.

4. *Quality awareness:* A Quality Improvement Program relies on the complete commitment of all employees. All individuals must be educated to ensure that they understand their role and how they can contribute to Quality Improvement. Employees also need to be kept informed of progress

5. *Measurement of performance:* It's only possible to focus on improving performance if the current performance of processes is measured. Improvement goals can then be targeted and improvements monitored.

6. *Prevention:* Businesses have traditionally relied on checking output for errors and then correcting them—a very inefficient way to run a business. The cornerstone of Quality Improvement is recognizing that errors aren't inevitable—they can be prevented. Action is necessary to ensure that any problems preventing quality improvement are identified and corrective actions are implemented to eliminate them. A system is required to achieve this on an ongoing basis.

The following story illustrates how a business might implement a Quality Improvement Program incorporating these key requirements.

Case Study

Part 1: Background of Alpha Systems

Alpha Systems designs, manufactures, and services electronic instruments. It has been reasonably successful over the years. The case study begins a couple of weeks after the annual strategic planning program. The personnel involved are:

Michael Wright	general manager
Richard Harrison	manufacturing manager
Jane Reed	purchasing manager
David Bergman	engineering manager

Maria D'Angelo	service manager
Tom Webster	sales manager
Julie Ford	quality manager
Alan Peters	human resources manager
Adrian Claussen	financial controller
Marcia Wu	program administrator

Michael Wright has been the general manager of Alpha Systems for three years. He had been promoted from sales manager in another division of the Alpha group. Michael had set himself the objective of revitalizing the company and significantly improving profitability. He hoped to achieve this within five years.

Since his arrival, Michael had systematically examined every activity in the business. He had restructured, modernized, introduced new systems and methods, and carried out training at all levels in the company. The products seemed to be what the market required and everyone was working hard, but still there was no significant improvement in profits.

Michael wondered what he could do next. Running out of ideas, began to wonder if he really had what it takes to turn the business around. Whenever things seemed to be going well, a new problem emerged. Things just never seemed to run smoothly.

The previous year Alpha had lost a major order because the tender didn't arrive on time. It had been asked to bid late. The sales and marketing people had done a great job putting together a detailed presentation at short notice and the customer seemed very impressed with the product. As long as the price was right, it looked like the order was in the bag. The salesman put the order in for typing and marked it urgent—he also spoke to the sales office in advance so they could rush it through when it arrived. Unfortunately he included only the customer's name on the order and not its address. The sales office looked up the address on the database and sent the quote off. The quote went to a division of the company with whom Alpha had previously done business, not the division that had requested the quotation. By the time the mistake had been discovered, the tender closing date had passed and the order was lost.

Then, six months ago, the manufacturing line came to a complete halt. The display panels used on all the instruments had cloudy windows instead of clear ones. This made the display very difficult to read. The quality manager reacted swiftly. She withdrew the whole stock of windows and had them individually checked. This yielded enough clear panels to start the line again. She took the remaining panels to do battle with the supplier. But the supplier had never been told how clear the panels had to be and had no means of checking them for clarity. Alpha relied on checking them when fitting them to the instrument. This problem batch of panels had particularly thick windows that made them appear cloudy. As soon as he knew of the problem, the supplier's inspector visited Alpha and determined visually how clear the window needed to be to ensure a clear display. He then assured the quality manager that no more cloudy windows would get past him. The problem was resolved and the line has now been running for six months with no further problems. However the line had lost two days' production.

Michael called a management meeting to discuss the continuing lackluster results. He didn't see why the rest of the team shouldn't share the responsibility. The team agreed they'd done all the right things in restructuring and modernizing Alpha. They'd simply run into bad luck recently with a series of "one time only" problems. Now these had been resolved (the quality manager gave details of the actions taken), so profits should soon rise. Michael was somewhat reassured and closed the meeting in a more positive mood.

Returning to his office, he found Adrian Claussen, his financial controller and longest-serving team member, waiting for him. Adrian was worried. He had been with the company for 10 years and had seen these "one time only" problems throughout that time. He did't see why they were miraculously going to disappear this time. Sure, there was a lot of activity, and a lot of problems had been resolved. But as soon as one lot of problems was resolved, another crop would appear. They were all becoming experts at resolving problems. He often wondered why they never saw the problems coming so they could prevent them from arising in the first place.

Michael felt his spirits drop again. After Adrian left he toured the company to talk to some old timers and see how they felt. If Adrian was right, then something radical had to be done. They couldn't spend every day staggering from one crisis to the next, never moving forward. Alpha was in business to produce electronic instruments, not to become expert troubleshooters. Perhaps that was where his profit was going. He was running a "ghost factory" whose mission was to solve problems. There had to be a better way.

A few days later Michael called the quality manager into his office.

"Julie," he began, "since the management meeting I've been thinking a lot about quality and the problems we've been having. I think we may be talking ourselves into believing that things are getting better. I was talking to Fred, the buyer, last night about the great work your team has done to resolve the panel display problem. He said a similar problem arose about five years ago and he'd expect it to happen again another five years from now! It really made me think about the value of all our effort solving problems. We seem to spend a great deal of effort finding and fixing problems rather than preventing them from occurring in the first place. If all we do is keep fixing problems, there will always be new problems to take their place. What ideas do you have about what we could do?"

Julie thought for a while before replying. "I've been meaning to talk to you for a while, Michael, about the possibility of implementing a Quality Improvement Program. I think we spend all our time fixing problems because that's the way we've always worked. We haven't got any systematic means of preventing errors from occurring. So we wait for them to occur and then go around fixing them. A Quality Improvement Program would completely change our way of working so that we invest effort in getting things right up front. That way we prevent errors from occurring, rather than fixing them afterwards."

"Have any other companies that you know implemented this type of program? And what have they achieved?"

"A couple of recent seminars have given me some useful details about companies that implemented this type of program. They seem to have gained significant benefits. Would you like to read the information and see what it's all about?"

"Yes, that would be interesting. If we did decide to go down this route, how long would it take you to get it all underway? We could certainly do with some quick results on this."

Julie drew in a breath. "It's not quite as simple as that, Michael. We only get one chance at this. So we need to make sure we understand what we're doing before we rush into it. The one thing that comes through loud and clear from my reading is that this isn't a quick-fix motivation campaign. It's about changing the culture of the company and everyone in it. We need to make everyone believe that preventing defects is possible and is what we, the management, want them to do. It will need the full commitment of everyone in the company, starting with you, if we're going to succeed. It certainly isn't something that I can implement alone. There's no formula or management technique to make it happen. We need to make those changes one step at a time, taking everyone in the company with us at each stage. A number of different approaches have been developed for implementing Quality Improvement. Read the material I've pulled together and then we can decide how to proceed."

"OK, Julie. You've convinced me that I need to slow down and take things one step at a time. I'll read that material over the weekend. Perhaps we could meet first thing on Monday to discuss where we go from here. There's just one thing before you leave; why doesn't our Quality Management System achieve it all for us? It's approved to ISO9000; I thought that was all about preventing defects and ensuring conformance."

Julie thought before replying. "Quality Standards like ISO9000 are designed to prevent customers from receiving nonconforming products or services. They don't really focus so much on achieving those requirements without errors or rework on the way. Also they don't cover all the other activities where we generate errors and waste, such as accounts, personnel, and administration. Although we involved the work force when we implemented the Quality System, we never really sold them the idea that they're personally involved in improving their own activities. To some extent they feel that the Quality System will do it all for them. Provided they work within the system, conforming products and services will result. I think the Quality System is essential because it establishes a baseline and framework, but now we want to involve the work force in making improvements in the way we all work. This builds on the Quality System and takes it to the next level."

"Oh, I see. Or at least I think I do. The Quality System has resulted in a controlled way of working in those areas associated with the products and services we sell to our customers. What we want to do now is to release the creativity in our people to improve the way we work in every activity we carry out. Then we can continue to meet our customers' requirements—but without all the errors and waste on the way. I've certainly got a lot to think about. I'll see you on Monday morning."

PLANNING FOR QUALITY IMPROVEMENT

Before a Quality Improvement Program (QIP) can be successfully implemented, senior management must recognize the need for Quality Improvement and must understand the total commitment required from them if it's to succeed.

Having committed themselves to implement Quality Improvement, management must then put together a detailed plan to guide the implementation.

Management Commitment and Involvement

Having recognized the need for Quality Improvement, the first objective is to secure management commitment to the new company culture, focusing on preventing errors, rather than on merely fixing them once they've arisen.

It's then necessary to gain the support and commitment of the entire work force. The attitudes and actions of employees are generally determined by what they believe management wants of them. It's therefore essential that management defines clearly and unambiguously its requirements in relation to quality. This is recorded formally in the company's Quality Policy.

The Quality Policy is an important statement of management's intention as regards quality. But it's every manager's demonstration in their day-to-day work that they're never prepared to compromise their commitment to the Quality Policy that will make a Quality Improvement Program succeed.

Gaining senior management's support and commitment isn't easy and is one of the major reasons for the failure of a Quality Improvement Program. The go-ahead to implement a program may be relatively easy to attain. It's the personal commitment and involvement from every manager that's difficult. Gaining this commitment requires persuasion, practical examples, reports on the benefits of a QIP, and continuous effort! Any and every means possible should be used, including

- Estimate of the cost of nonconformance. This demonstrates the cost of not committing to Continuous Improvement.
- Obtain customer input on current performance and how well their requirements are being met.
- Describe other companies' experiences and the benefits they've realized.
- Consider using videos, articles, and press clippings on Quality Improvement to reinforce the message.
- Conduct training and seminars.
- Hold a pilot run in a department committed to Quality Improvement to demonstrate the benefits.

Although management commitment may be difficult to attain, it generally gets easier as the program develops and the benefits of success begin to be realized. Publicizing and celebrating early successes is an essential part of increasing the momentum of a Quality Improvement Program.

Quality Improvement Structure

In most companies, significant changes are required when implementing a Quality Improvement Program. To plan and pilot this implementation, most companies form a Quality Improvement Team (QIT). The team should be composed of a chairperson, an administrator, and a representative of each department.

Selection of the chairperson and administrator is important since they'll become deeply involved in the program and will direct the running of the QIT. Chapter 7 details the QIT's role.

Case Study

Part 2: In Michael's Office

Julie turned up at Michael's office on Monday morning and was pleased to find Michael obviously expecting her. Too often in the past she had turned up for appointments with Michael to discuss quality matters only to find something more important had come up and Michael wasn't available. Perhaps this was a sign that things were really changing!

"Morning Julie," said Michael, "I spent quite some time over the weekend reading about improvement programs. They certainly seem to have produced impressive results elsewhere. I've decided that we'll launch a program here and it seems that the first thing we need to do is to determine our Quality Policy and then get the rest of the management team to understand and sign up to it. Once that's achieved we can form the team and really get underway. I've had a go at writing a policy. In fact, I all but copied it from one of the examples in the information you provided, and I'd like your opinion."

Michael passed over the following statement for Julie's comment:

> The Alpha Quality Policy is to understand our customers' requirements and ensure that we meet those requirements first time every time.

Julie read the policy several times and then smiled. "It seems absolutely fine to me, Michael. We could include a lot more on customer satisfaction, reducing costs, and the like, but I think that will just confuse the issue. This way it's short and to the point and no one can misunderstand what we want them to do. It looks good, although we'll need to make sure everyone understands that they may have internal and external customers."

"Excellent," replied Michael. "I suggest we arrange a meeting of the management team next Tuesday to convince them of the need for an Improvement Program and get them to sign up to the Quality Policy. I also like to agree on who'll be chairperson and administrator of the QIT since they seem to be important roles. I suggest we spend some time discussing that now. I know from our discussions on Friday that you can't implement the program alone, but shouldn't you at least chair the team?"

"I'd certainly like to be, but I don't think it is appropriate, Michael. If we really want to get the message across that quality is the responsibility of everyone and not just the quality department, then we should elect someone else as chairperson. I do agree that it should be a senior member of management. Perhaps you should do it?"

"That might be a good idea. Certainly, I have to make sure it succeeds. If it doesn't, then I may not have a business to run in a few years. But, if I do it, people might agree just because I suggest things rather than because they're really committed and involved. I think, if possible, we should think of someone else."

Julie thought before replying. "What about Tom Webster, the sales manager? He's obviously very close to our customers and could provide valuable feedback on how they view us as a company. He often has to pick up the pieces when things go wrong, and pacify the customers. Somehow, I don't think he'd agree to do it, though."

"Tom would do an excellent job," Michael replied. "The only problem with having Tom is that it might make people believe the program is solely about the external customer, in effect a Customer Care Program. We also need to get the message across that to eliminate errors and waste, we must satisfy internal customers at every stage; the person next in line who receives the output from our activity. I think Tom would bring valuable expertise to the team but I don't think he should be chairman."

"Just a minute. I've had an idea," Michael exclaimed. "What about Adrian? He was the one who put the idea into my head in the first place by suggesting that we ought to be able to see problems coming and so prevent them. He's a long-standing and well-respected member of the management team. He has high personal standards and would be invaluable in putting a cost to the current levels of waste and errors we're suffering. He's genuinely concerned that we're becoming a company of trouble shooters and I think he'd welcome the opportunity to do something about it."

"If we can convince him that the Quality Improvement Program will be implemented everywhere, including his finance department, then I think he'd be an excellent choice. If we get him on board, it will convince a lot of the others that the program has a good chance of success. Adrian has a reputation for only backing those projects that are dead certs. What about one of my quality engineers as the administrator? Marcia Wu would be an excellent choice. She's bright, good with people, and a born organizer. I think she'd relish this sort of opportunity."

"OK," replied Michael. "I'll get Val to organize a meeting. If you bring Marcia along, we can introduce her to the management team. I suggest we save asking Adrian to be chairman until the end of the meeting."

Case Study

Part 3: The Initial Management Meeting

Julie introduced Marcia to the management team as they arrived but at this stage did not explain what she was doing at the meeting. Michael welcomed everyone and opened the meeting.

Michael   I'm pleased you could all make it this afternoon. I'd like to discuss the proposal that we implement a Quality Improvement Program within Alpha. Let me briefly outline our position. For the past three years our sales have been around $40 million despite the expanding market for our products. So we're losing market share to our competitors. Our profit for the year is forecast at $610,000, only 1.5 percent of sales. When I took over, I firmly believed that within five years we'd return at least 5 percent of sales. If we don't improve our profits, then not only will I be out of a job but the Alpha group will probably be looking for somewhere more attractive to invest its money. We need to improve our ability to satisfy our customers and also improve our profitability by reducing internal costs and increasing sales. Our recent problems with quality have really made me think about where we're going and seem to tie up with our poor profitability. Unless we deliver to our customers what they ordered when they require it, we'll never be able to increase sales. We also seem to spend a great deal of time and effort solving problems and virtually no time at all preventing problems from occurring in the first place. Julie and I have found some very positive information on companies who've recognized similar problems and have implemented a Quality Improvement Program with some impressive results. I'd like us to implement such a program here and this is what I'd like to discuss today.

Tom   I agree, Michael. We need to greatly improve the products that manufacturing delivers. I'll certainly support a Quality Improvement Program in manufacturing.

Michael   Thank you, Tom. But, you know, it's not just the manufacturing area that's involved in generating errors and rework. Although we do have problems with some of our products, we also have problems in the nonmanufacturing areas. Product quality isn't enough. Every task performed and decision taken has to be of a high quality. To survive today, we need to get the whole act right, not just the product. Remember last year when we lost that big order because the proposal didn't arrive on time? I know your people did a great job on the proposal and presentation. But we just failed to send the proposal to the correct address. That had nothing to do with the product at all. I'm sure we all know of other examples where silly errors have caused us real problems. In fact, Julie has estimated that, in common with many other companies, as much as 25 percent of our effort in all departments may be involved in doing jobs over again. We need to be able to harness all that effort productively.

David   I agree with you that every department generates errors and rework, but I really can't believe that a quarter of my people's effort is being spent on unproductive tasks.

Richard   Well, you're always moaning about your people spending time in production sorting out problems. Perhaps if the product was right in the first place, they wouldn't need to waste that time. Also my people wouldn't have to sit around waiting for your people to turn up!

Tom   I suppose if we even look at this meeting, there's been a lot of wasted time. Two people turned up 10 minutes late so the rest of us had to sit around and wait. Just think what that must have cost. I do agree, though, that 25 percent seems a bit farfetched.

Michael   Maybe 25 percent is too high, but perhaps we shouldn't get too bogged down with the exact percentage just yet. As part of the program we'll find out what it really is and I expect we'll all be quite surprised. I don't suppose we're that much better than other companies, so I expect our quality costs will be approaching 25 percent. Let's accept 25 percent for the moment. Then, given our current salary bill of $12 million, we're spending $3 million doing things over again. That doesn't include scrap material or costs associated with excess inventory and the like. And $3 million certainly seems a target worth working for. Even if we only eliminate a proportion of it, it'll do a lot to improve our profitability.

Adrian   I agree we won't be able to save the whole $3 million. We have to invest some money in running the program and training people. But if we really can eliminate errors and rework, then we should also see additional benefits. People get fed up doing rework and solving the same old problems over again. I think the program would boost people's morale and their loyalty to the company. I've read a bit about Quality Improvement Programs, and a lot of attention seems to be given to getting people to work together in teams and giving them the power to make changes.

Michael   At this point I'll ask Julie to tell us a bit about the program.

Julie   Before we start on the program, I'd like to spend a bit of time discussing what quality means. In normal conversation, we all seem to use the term quality in a vague way to denote some measure of goodness or worth. We also confuse quality with elegance, luxury and all sorts of subjective things. Everyone uses quality in a different way and none of us really understands what the other means. When I started looking at the Quality Improvement Program, I realized that defining quality in subjective terms doesn't really mean anything. Before we can have a Quality Improvement Program we must clearly define quality in objective terms. Quality to us must mean conformance to requirements. Then everyone can understand what it means. If we want something to be more elegant or more powerful, then we must change the requirement; but quality must always mean conformance to requirements. Using this definition also makes it easier to understand that quality applies to everything, not just the product.

David   It certainly makes sense to me to have a clear definition of quality. I know in the past I've always had difficulty describing what quality is. I usually finish up being rather vague and waving my hands around a lot.

Tom   It would certainly make for fewer complaints from our customers if we always made everything conform to their requirements. But isn't it going to cost a lot of money?

Julie   If we don't do it, then it's going to cost more than money—it's going to cost us our business. If we don't supply to our customers' requirements then someone else will; and eventually we won't have any customers left. But the second fundamental of the Improvement Program is that it's always cheaper to do things right the first time rather than correct them later. So we're going to have to change the way we work. We'll need to invest effort up front getting things right. We'll then save the money we currently spend fixing things.

Michael   Julie and I have spent some time drawing up a Quality Policy. I'd like you all to read it and decide if you can commit to it. If we can't all commit to it, then the program can't go any further.

Michael handed round the policy. They all silently read it.

David   It seems to summarize what you've just told us about the program. If we're to keep our customers and reduce costs, then it seems to me that we have no time to lose. You can certainly count me in.

Tom   If we do decide to go ahead, how long will it take to get this thing up and running?

Julie   This isn't something we can do overnight. It will take a lot of careful planning. The first thing to do is to set up a project team to plan how we'll implement the program. I think that if we start now, we can have the team formed within two weeks and begin training them straight away after that. The whole program may well take a year to really get going. This is just the start of a never-ending commitment to Quality Improvement. But before we can start, we need to select a chairperson for the QIT.

Michael   I think this is where I come in. Julie and I have discussed it and we would like you, Adrian, to head up the Improvement Team.

Adrian   But I don't know anything about Quality Improvement.

Michael   Neither does anyone else here, so we'll all be learning together. I think you've already shown that you believe we need to improve and that the program's aims are achievable. That's the main qualification you need. Also, Marcia here will act as administrator, so you'll get a lot of help from her.

Adrian   OK, I'll do it. But I've got a lot of questions. What do I do? Can I pick my own team? How much time will it take? And what's all this about training?

Julie   You'll be chairman of the Improvement Team, whose job is to plan and pilot the program. I expect it will take about 20 percent of your time. But we thought that probably wouldn't be too much of a problem as you've got your MBA student for the rest of the year. Yes, you can pick your own team in conjunction with the department heads. Every department should be represented on the team and the person chosen should have the authority to make commitments on behalf of the department. Once chosen, you and the rest of the team will spend four days learning what the program is all about.

Adrian   Well, that's a bit clearer. As far as the team goes, shouldn't it be the people here?

Julie   You don't have to have the people here on the team. We could involve other members of each department instead.

Adrian   I don't mind that. There are a few people I can think of that I'm sure would do well on the team. But I do need to know that they have the full support of each of the managers here. It can't just be used as a way of the manager opting out of the program.

Michael OK, Adrian, we'll leave it to you to talk to each of the departments and come up with a team, and then Julie will arrange the training. I suggest, though, that you keep Julie on the team. I think we could do with her help. And Tom could provide some useful input on our customers' perceptions of us.

Alan What about the union? If they don't cooperate, we'll be in real difficulties.

Michael I agree. It's vital that we involve them as soon as possible. Let's give Adrian a few days to think through the program and then Adrian, Alan, and I will talk to the union. I don't really anticipate any problems provided we explain what we're doing and why. They're generally a pretty sensible bunch.

David Just a minute. I think we're getting a bit ahead of ourselves here. I for one feel that I'm being steamrolled into something I don't really understand. We really need to think about this and discuss it a bit more before we go ahead.

Michael Do other people feel the same way as David?

There were a couple of nods and a few people looked away at this point.

Michael OK, I suggest we get someone to come in and talk to us in further detail about Quality Improvement, its benefits, and what's involved. I've just been reading about what other companies have achieved, so I'm all fired up and can't wait to get on with it. Julie, would you please arrange for someone to come in and talk to us early next week. Also I suggest you let everyone have a copy of those articles you lent to me so they can be prepared.

UNDERSTANDING CUSTOMERS

The Importance of Customers

This section focuses on customers, how their requirements are identified, and how these requirements are communicated throughout the business. Organizations only continue to exist because of their ability to meet their external customers' requirements. External customers' needs must drive all the internal processes within the organization. Continuously improving the effectiveness of the internal processes is no good if, at the end of the day, they aren't producing the outputs that the customer requires. Organizations must understand

1. Who are their external customers and what are their requirements.
2. What internal processes produce the service or product required by the external customer.
3. How their customers perceive their current performance.
4. How performance can be improved.

When implementing a Quality Improvement Program, it's easy to fall into the trap of becoming focused internally—concentrating resources on improving internal processes and reducing costs at the expense of external customers' needs. Understanding customer requirements is an essential part of any QIP.

Getting Information about Customers

A comprehensive picture of customer requirements must be determined. This isn't restricted to the product or service delivered to the customer, but covers the total service required from the organization as a supplier. There may be a number of different customers to consider, even within the same organization. The person who places the order has requirements; the receiving department where goods are delivered has requirements; the user has requirements; the person who pays the invoice has requirements. A company that wishes to succeed must be aware of all these requirements and constantly improve its ability to meet them.

There are a number of sources of information on customer requirements:

- Customer surveys and trials.
- Trade surveys and trials.
- Working with selected customers.
- Competitor analysis.
- Focus groups.
- Benchmarking.

- Customer complaints.
- Legal and guideline standards.
- Informal customer comments and potential customer comments received from sources such as the sales force after customer visits and feedback from other employees as well as comments heard at conferences, training courses, and trade exhibitions.

Every contact with an existing or potential customer at any level in the organization is an opportunity to learn more about their requirements. This information must be tapped and used to improve the business's ability to meet customer requirements.

INTERNAL PROCESSES

An external customer requirement can only be met if internal processes within an organization are set up effectively to deliver the requirement. A breakdown in the internal supply chain often results in failure to meet external customer requirements. An important part of Quality Improvement is the analysis of the whole organization to ensure that it is set up effectively to meet its customers' requirements. The following steps can help you achieve this.

1. Identify the basic purpose and objectives of the business. What customer requirements does it exist to fulfill?

2. Identify existing and potential customers of the business. Tap as many sources as possible to ensure that their requirements are understood. This includes understanding why potential customers aren't actual customers!

3. Identify each department's overall role in meeting customer requirements and business objectives. This may reveal that changes are required in the roles of departments within the organization.

4. Identify the internal processes that link together to meet external customer requirements. Ensure that external customer requirements flow back through the supply chain to determine the customer requirements for each internal process. Only by doing this at each stage in the supply chain can external customer requirements be met.

5. Measure performance overall and for each process.
6. Introduce improvements to each process to improve performance.

Case Study
_____

Part 4: The Management Meeting

Michael   Adrian, you've asked to discuss the concept of functional analysis at the meeting. Perhaps you could tell us all a bit about it—I certainly haven't used it before.

Adrian   Functional analysis seems to be an important element in the Quality Improvement Program. It helps ensure that we understand our customers' requirements and are set up to meet them. Basically, it requires that we identify the purpose of our business: the customer needs we exist to fulfill, and how we go about fulfilling them. Then we develop this to decide the objectives of each department within the business—their reasons for existing. We can then identify the specific tasks each department carries out to meet its objectives and decide whether these tasks are carried out in the most effective way. We can then target areas for improvement and introduce measurements to monitor the improvement.

Tom   I don't quite understand what you're driving at, Adrian. Surely Alpha's purpose is to produce products that customers want to buy. The marketing people should identify what people want to buy. The engineers should design the product; production should make it; and the sales team should sell it.

Adrian   You're probably right, Tom. That's broadly what we do today as a business and within each department. But, functional analysis requires us to put aside what we've always done and take a radical look at our business. What customer needs do we fulfill? We don't exist to supply electronic instruments; we exist to fulfill a customer need to make accurate fluid flow measurements. In a few years from now that need may not be fulfilled by electronic instruments at all—some other technique may have replaced it. If we take our eye off the ball of customer needs, we may continue to make bigger and better electronic instruments that no one wants any more.

We need to apply this way of thinking to each of our functions and decide what customer needs, whether internal or external, they exist to fulfill. We should forget what each of us have always done and start again from basics with our focus on customer needs and requirements.

Michael You certainly sound enthusiastic about this concept, Adrian. It requires each of us to look again at why Alpha exists and how we organize our business. It sounds exciting to me and seems to offer a great deal—if we can carry it out successfully. I suggest we have a go now at deciding why we exist as a business—perhaps a brainstorming session would be a good way to start. We may not come up with our definitive mission today, but at least we'll be underway.

Richard I agree that our business must always be focused on meeting customer needs, but I don't think that, at the moment, we know enough about our customers to do that. Our marketing people are involved with customers when drawing up the product specification, but there must be more to it than that.

Julie You're right, Richard. The customers have many more requirements than just those associated with the product. Last week I logged a complaint from a customer's controller. He was annoyed that many invoices he receives have an error on them. The product we're supplying may be excellent, but the impression we're giving to the finance guy is poor. All these people have an influence on whether the customer continues to do business with us. Although the product may be good, we're costing them (and us) a lot of money to sort out problems on our invoices! We need a method to ensure that we understand all the customer requirements.

Tom I've got an idea that might help get this off the ground. Why don't we organize a meeting or series of meetings with our customers and find out what they really need from our business? It won't give us all the answers, but it should at least point us at areas where we need to dig a little deeper.

Michael That's a good idea, Tom. It could help us get closer to our customers. I suggest that we consider having a series of breakfast meetings and invite perhaps a dozen people to each. We'll need to look at a cross section of companies, and a cross section of functions. Perhaps we could look at each function in turn at a separate meeting. Julie, will you and Tom get together and come up with a suggested list? Perhaps you could start by having a look at your complaints log and inviting some of those complaining companies.

IDENTIFYING QUALITY COSTS

The objective of the Quality Improvement Program is to develop an approach which ensures that goods and services are produced that meet customer requirements for the minimum cost.

One way to accomplish this is to eliminate the costs associated with not getting things right the first time—the costs of non-conformance (CONC).

The Importance of Identifying the CONC

Recognizing the amount of money devoted to the CONC at the beginning of a QIP frequently underlines the strategic necessity of introducing the program. Findings from a number of businesses suggest that the CONC can amount to as much as 25 percent of turnover in both manufacturing and service industries—a figure that grabs management attention.

Monitoring the CONC can provide a measure of the QIP's success. But we must recognize that when a QIP is introduced, the CONC frequently appears to rise initially. This is because people become more aware of nonconformance and its associated costs as they become able to identify them. Consequently costs become included that wouldn't initially have been thought of as non-conformance costs.

Knowing the CONC associated with individual activities can be used to help prioritize corrective actions, focusing attention on the highest-priority areas. Being aware of the costs associated with error helps every department and individual in their commitment to perform every task right the first time.

Distinguishing among the Quality-Related Costs

One of the most useful ways of classifying quality-related costs is to distinguish between the costs of conformance and the costs of nonconformance. Costs of nonconformance are all the costs incurred because failures occur. If there were no failures, there would be no requirement for the activity. Costs of conformance are all the costs associated with preventing nonconformances.

Cost of nonconformance. The most obvious element of CONC are the costs associated with failure to achieve conformance to requirements—the *failure costs*. Failure costs occur in all areas of a company. They're often accepted as part of the normal course of events and so are easily overlooked.

Failure costs' existence is generally well recognized in industry. To minimize failure costs, many companies operate systems to find failures. There are inevitably costs associated with finding these errors. These are the *appraisal costs*.

Today many of us expect failures to happen so we need appraisal activities to find them. If failures were eliminated, the vast majority of appraisal activities would also no longer be necessary.

Cost of conformance. To reduce the CONC, we need to invest in prevention activities. Prevention activities inevitably result in some costs. These are *prevention costs*. Investing in the prevention of failure enables failure and associated appraisal costs to be minimized. This is the fundamental principle underlying Quality Improvement.

The key feature of a QIP environment is that failures aren't accepted as a normal occurrence. The root causes of any failures are identified and eliminated by the introduction of prevention activities. Failure is an exceptional occurrence rather than the norm. In this environment we don't need a vast appraisal activity; we only need a small audit activity to ensure that our prevention system is working correctly. So after focusing on reducing failure costs, we can then look at reducing appraisal costs.

The Role of the Quality Improvement Team

The role of the QIT is to devise a method for identifying the total quality-related costs across the company. All quality-related costs must be included at this stage—not just the obvious costs associated with manufacturing. This analysis can then be used as a basis for measuring progress as the QIP is implemented. It can also be used to reinforce the need for implementing the Improvement Program when communicating with management and employees. The measurement of quality costs provides valuable management information and will require the active participation of every manager and supervisor if it's to be a meaningful gauge of current business performance.

The objective of the QIP is to eliminate the CONC by investing in prevention.

Case Study

Part 5: A QIT Meeting

Following their introductory training course, Adrian calls a QIT meeting to order.

Adrian   Well, after our training course, I for one was staggered at the number of activities that we've all accepted as being part of our normal business, but that actually are only necessary because we keep getting things wrong.

David   I agree. It's quite depressing to think that we've been managing the business so badly all these years.

Jane   At least we've now recognized it and are doing something about it. I'm sure there are a lot of people out there who haven't even gotten to that stage yet.

Adrian   Since the last meeting, I've been doing some work on our quality-related costs and reckon that, just looking at the obvious costs, they're about 10 percent of sales or $5 million. Of course, some of these costs will be prevention costs, but I think that's only a very small part of the total. I'm sure the amount we spend on inspection and rework far outweigh what we spend on prevention. Anyway, here's a copy of the figures.

	$000
Field service	850
QA dept	340
Inspection	600
Scrap	1,200
Warranty	1,500
Rework	300
	$4,790

They're far from the true total, but at least they provide a basis for discussion.

Julie   They're very interesting figures, Adrian, but I agree that they're too low. They're probably only about half of the true total since they involve mainly the production-related areas, and many errors occur in the other departments.

David   I can easily see how we can arrive at the CONC in manufacturing, but I don't see how it can apply to a creative area like design where you exist by developing original ideas.

Jane   What about designs that aren't implemented? And what about all the changes you carry out once the design has reached production. Those cost a fortune and always seem to delay the launch of our new products.

David   Those changes are almost always because manufacturing can't make the product. They have nothing to do with engineering. We only do the changes to make life easier for them.

Julie   What about introducing a prevention activity. By ensuring that the manufacturing department is included at the earliest stages of your designs, we'll know we can manufacture a product before you release the design from engineering and won't need all the changes. The costs of all the changes are certainly a nonconformance cost resulting from a failure to prevent errors at the design stage.

Richard   I agree, Julie. Surely there are similar examples in every department. Would you, Adrian, spend some time between now and the next meeting discussing nonconformance costs with each department head? That way we'll have a more realistic figure to discuss at the next meeting.

Maria   One thing that worries me is that the whole of my service department has been included as a CONC. Does that mean that they'll all be out of a job as the QIP progresses?

Julie   All my department is included as a CONC as well. We need to make sure we understand what will happen in these areas as the QIP progresses and CONC is eliminated.

Alan   Yes, we're certainly not going to get much support for the program if people feel their jobs are threatened—especially the union people.

Marcia   The position is obviously quite complicated. But in principle if we improve the quality of our products and services, we'll increase our sales and profitability because we'll give customers what they require all of the time. The money we save from reducing CONC can be invested in growth. The QIP will highlight activities and specific job functions that are no longer required; but as we grow we should be able to redeploy those people in more productive jobs. For example, as we improve our outgoing quality we'll no longer need so many field service engineers. But we may be able to use them for advising customers and salespeople of new applications for our products. Their role could change from customer repair to customer support. This is an area where we're very weak now. It should also help us win more orders.

Alan   Thanks, Marcia. That's helped set my mind at rest. I hadn't really thought of it that way before.

Julie   I agree that the QIP isn't a head count reduction program. We want to keep all our people and develop them in roles that are more productive for the whole company. But whatever happens, we need to succeed with the QIP. If we don't, we'll all be out of a job as another business folds. And no one wants that to happen.

Adrian   Thank you, everyone. If no one has anything further, I suggest we close. The next meeting is in three weeks. That will give me plenty of time to put together details of the quality-related costs in conjunction with each of you. I for one can't wait to see them. I think they'll be very interesting.

INCREASING INDIVIDUALS' COMMITMENT TO QUALITY

This section explains the importance of involving everyone in the Quality Improvement Program and describes effective means for achieving this objective. To be successful, a Quality Improvement Program often requires a complete change in how an organization is run.

1. All employees require a greater understanding of customer requirements and the internal processes needed to meet these requirements.

2. It will no longer be acceptable to rely on finding and fixing errors. The organization must become committed to investing resources in preventing errors from arising.

3. Individuals should be empowered to take actions to improve the quality of output from their own work areas.

To achieve these changes requires the commitment of every employee within the company. The required level of personal commitment is only likely to be achieved if every individual understands the aims and benefits of the program, the role they can play, and how they can implement improvements in a successful QIP. A number of activities can help achieve this personal commitment to Quality Improvement:

1. *Education.* Individuals need to understand the reasons for the change, what it will mean to them, and how they're equipped to contribute. The training must be relevant and interesting, and must enable people to understand and participate in Quality Improvement.
2. *Communication.* A constant flow of information is necessary. It should describe progress made by the QIP, how and when individuals will be involved, and the successes achieved.
3. *Recognition.* A system to recognize and publicly reward those who make an outstanding contribution to Quality Improvement can greatly encourage employee commitment.

Education

After the management team agrees on the need for Quality Improvement and accepts the program in principle, the QIT should attend an intensive training course. This course should explain their responsibilities for implementing the Quality Improvement Program and ensure that they thoroughly understand how it can be implemented. This course may be run internally or by an external trainer depending on the level of existing expertise within the company.

Having been trained, the QIT should plan the education program for the rest of the work force. The whole work force must be included in the training program. Everyone has their part to play in a company. A receptionist may help to gain or lose a customer as easily as a manager. If a message isn't passed on quickly, the customer may choose to look elsewhere for his needs. Production line staff are likely to know more about the things that are wrong where they work than their managers and supervisors. They've probably been living with the problems and fixing things for a number of years.

Experience has shown that the most effective approach to training within a company is to cascade the learning process from the manager to the supervisors and then to individual employees. The duration and content of the education program depends on the individuals being trained. But they should all understand why the program is required and their personal involvement in the drive for improvement. At each stage the supervisor should be actively involved in the training. This ensures that supervisors fully understand the program and how it affects their areas of the business. It also provides an important opportunity to demonstrate their commitment to the program to their teams. This approach has the added advantage of helping to develop a team approach in all areas of a company. This can result in a dramatic improvement in performance as people become personally committed to their team.

Once teams form and begin looking at areas requiring improvement, they'll need training in how to analyze and resolve problems. It's no good asking people to make improvements if they haven't been given the tools to enable them to do so. The training program should be designed to enable them to use the essential problem solving tools. The techniques taught will depend on the business, but may include functional analysis, data gathering, Pareto analysis, brainstorming, fishbone diagrams, and process control.

In view of the time and experience required to produce training material, many organizations use externally generated training material. If external material is used, it must be adapted to ensure that it's relevant to the organization and to the individuals being trained.

Case Study

Part 6: Following the QIT Training Course

Adrian is talking to Julie and Marcia following the QIT training course.

Adrian Now that we've been trained, I think I understand what's involved in the program but I'm a bit unsure of where we go from here on education. I know we're supposed to train our next line of management. But is the QIT really supposed to do that? If we are, then what are we going to do about material. I certainly haven't got time to generate all that along with everything else.

Marcia I understand why it's important to educate everyone, but why don't we just get the people who did our training to come and do the training for us. That would certainly save us an awful lot of time and effort.

Julie We could do that and, as you say, it would save a lot of effort, but I don't think it's the right thing to do. The cornerstone of the program is the commitment of every manager. Because we want to change attitudes and minds, it isn't something we can use outsiders for. What's really needed is to convince our people that we—the managers and supervisors—have really changed. We must demonstrate that we're working in a different way and want them to do the same. Sure, a consultant could come and tell them that we've changed, but I don't think they would believe it.

Marcia I suppose that if managers don't train their people themselves, then they could opt out of the program altogether. If they're responsible for training their people, they'll really have to understand the principles and believe in it.

Adrian OK, I agree. Each manager should do his or her own training. But what about material. We can't expect each manager to generate his or her own and I haven't got time. What about you, Julie?

Julie I suggest we ask the consultants to generate the training material—under our supervision, of course. Then each manager can add local examples to suit the group he or she is training.

Marcia That sounds good to me. Everyone gets the same basic message but with local examples. The managers don't have too much preparation to do and we don't delay the program for weeks while we generate our own material. Would you like me to talk to the consultants about it?

Julie Thanks, Marcia. That would be useful.

A few weeks later Richard arrived in Julie's office looking perplexed.

Richard Julie, I've just had a conversation with Marcia. She told me we'll be spending time this year training everyone in the department. I can understand that the supervisors need to know about the program but surely it's a bit over the top training my people on the line. I don't see that they'll be interested. I thought I'd just issue a memo to them all to let them know what's going on and leave it at that.

Julie   I know it's a big investment, Richard, but I think it's worth it. This Improvement Program is all about changing the culture of the company and we can only do that if we can change the attitude of everyone in the company. Your people are just as important in this as you and me. When it comes to improvement, I bet your people know far more about the things that are wrong in their work area than you or your supervisors. They are the ones who've been living with the problems and fixing them for years. If we want them to make improvements, we have to help them to believe they have the ability to do so. Education about the need for improvement and some techniques they can use to analyze and solve problems will give them confidence that they can do it. I think that once they've been trained and we show them we want their support, you'll be surprised at just how much they contribute! And to make things easier, we can schedule the training for less busy times in the month.

Communication

The objective of the communication step is to explain the need for improvement to all employees and prepare them for the commitment required to the Improvement Program.

At some point everyone will receive training on their involvement in the implementation of the program. But it's important to keep everyone involved right from the start. The most effective means of developing commitment is to ensure that people know what's going on. If people aren't kept informed from an early stage they may feel left out of the program. This could result in the belief that the program isn't for them. This could undermine the program and lead to resentment by some employees. Early involvement of everyone helps to generate the enthusiasm and commitment necessary to ensure the program's success.

In the early stages it's particularly important to communicate any successes achieved as a result of the program. This encourages all employees to become involved, and also encourages those who are currently struggling to introduce improvements.

An important part of the Improvement Program is to develop a team approach between employees and their supervisors. Ensuring that key messages are communicated to employees by their immediate supervisor helps this team building process. It also demonstrates the supervisor's involvement and commitment to the program.

Effective methods for communicating. The communication activity has two essential components, both of which need to be planned by the QIT:

1. General information about the Quality Improvement Program can be communicated through posters, competitions, a company magazine, or special events. This material must be interesting, varied, and up-to-date. A steady stream of information should be supplied to employees to keep them informed of progress and developments. If this stream dries up, it's likely to be seen as yet another management fad implemented without commitment. This will undermine its continued success.

2. Regular meetings between employees and their supervisor should be used to reinforce the general information produced by the company on the Improvement Program, focusing on the particular department in question. These meetings should also be used to discuss specific nonconformance problems affecting the department and the necessary corrective actions. As well as producing results, this primes employees for the education and operational steps of the process.

Case Study
___

Part 7: A QIT Meeting

Adrian is standing in front of the team at a regular Quality Improvement Team meeting.

Adrian   The most important thing about communication seems to be that everyone must receive sincere, easily understood messages. The most effective way to achieve this is through their supervisors and peers since these are the people with whom they work every day and who have the most influence over their opinions. If we get this step right, it will make our job much easier because people will become enthusiastic about the program and want to be actively involved.

David   What about organizing a meeting where Michael talks to everyone about what we're doing? The supervisors could all be there to signal their support for the program and everyone will hear the same message at the same time.

Marcia   I think individual meetings with the supervisor would be better although it will require more effort than just having one big meeting. We need such a change in how we work that it's essential that we explain the situation carefully to everyone and that each person hears it from his supervisor. Any other way, people might not feel involved or they might feel their supervisor isn't involved. If they don't feel involved, they can't become committed.

Jane   I think Marcia's right. At a big meeting people can just sit back and listen without really becoming involved. At a meeting with their supervisor, whom they know well, they're much more likely to challenge an idea and ask questions, which should result in their being more involved and committed at the end of the day.

Julie   We also want to ensure that the communication meetings are a regular event so people understand that this is an ongoing process and not just a nine-day wonder. That wouldn't happen if we just had a big meeting with Michael. I think Marcia's right; we should do it through the supervisor. If we encourage regular meetings between supervisors and their people, then we've started to build a means to enable groups to look at their activities and identify areas for improvement. If we can all agree that supervisors are the best people to give the message, we can then discuss the message we want them to get across.

David   OK, you've convinced me. The supervisor is the key to getting our message over so that the work force will really believe we're serious about this whole thing. I think the message needs to be simple and clear. We, the management team, have recognized that we've never clearly told the work force that we require every job to be done right the first time. That's what we're now asking them to do and we'll help them by fixing the problems they identify and by investing time and effort in preventing failures. If we all work on it together, we can eliminate errors. The program is just a means to ensure our achieving that goal.

Richard   That sounds like a clear basis for our message, David. I think the supervisors will believe in it and the work force will understand what it's all about and will respond positively.

Adrian   Having been briefed earlier by Marcia on the advantages of supervisors holding regular communication meetings with their people, I've already spoken to Michael on how we might handle this and we've come up with the following suggestion. Michael and the QIT will meet all the managers and supervisors next Thursday to explain the program and its importance to the future of our company; the steps we need to take to improve our operations; and the fundamental role played by managers and supervisors in ensuring the program's success. We'll then ask each of them to organize regular meetings with their teams to discuss the Improvement Program and begin identifying and introducing improvements. We'll provide information on the program, the measurements that have been introduced so far and the costs of nonconformance that we've identified to date.

Maria   That sounds like an excellent first step. But how do we know that the supervisors will actually hold regular meetings?

Julie   They'll only continue to hold the meetings if they believe we, their managers, are interested. We, therefore, must also hold regular meetings with our immediate subordinates to discuss the program, the measurements they're making, the problems they're finding, and the corrective actions introduced. I suggest we then report back to the QIT. That way we'll get a much better feedback on how the program is being received and the progress being made.

Tom   I think we all agree on involving the supervisors in regular communication meetings. If we take up Julie's suggestion and all hold regular meetings with our people, that should ensure that supervisors know we're committed. That should encourage them to continue to hold their meetings. What about organizing some general information on the program that we could display around the building. That way we'd keep the message in front of everyone all the time.

Maria   That sounds like a good idea, Tom. I think we need someone to be responsible for coordinating the information, making sure the material is always fresh and up-to-date. Perhaps Alan could do that if we all provide ideas and information.

Alan   That's fine by me, provided everyone comes up with information and keeps it up-to-date. Nothing signals to people more clearly that a program is running out of steam than a pile of out-of-date information.

Marcia   I've already ordered some posters. I also had an idea last night that perhaps we could organize a competition to design some more. It would help generate enthusiasm and would certainly be a lot cheaper than getting them done outside.

Alan   Good idea, Marcia. I'll see about arranging a competition. We could discuss it at the next meeting. Where do you suggest we display the posters you've ordered once they arrive?

Tom   Not on the existing notice boards, that's for sure. I think we should invest in some new notice boards just for QIP information. That way we won't get lost among the company baseball team scores!

Julie   I think the budget could stretch to a few notice boards; I'll get them organized. But I think we need a bit more than a few posters. We've now established measurements in all departments. I suggest that in addition to reviewing them at QIT meetings, we could also put up the charts showing progress on the notice boards.

Marcia   I'm not sure that just putting up all the measurements will be very meaningful. What about featuring one department each month? Each department could describe the measurements they've introduced, what they've achieved, and their experience with the QIP.

Maria   That sounds like a good idea. It should certainly generate interest. But perhaps, rather than making a decision now, we should use the time before the notice boards arrive to think about what we're going to put on them. Meanwhile what about getting Michael to do an article on the program for the company magazine?

Alan   I could ask Michael to do that for us. I could also arrange to set aside a regular slot each month for a feature on a different aspect of the Improvement Program.

Adrian   Excellent. I think we've made great progress today. Perhaps we should decide on the next few topics for the magazine, and who'll write them, at our next meeting. And now, if no one's got anything else to discuss, I suggest we go and tell our managers and supervisors about Thursday's meeting.

A couple of weeks later the assembly and production control supervisors are talking.

Carl   How did your production control people react to your communication meeting, Harold?

Harold   Well, to begin with they all had their "quality is nothing to do with me" look on their faces, so I knew I had some work to do. I told them all about the program, what's happened so far, what's planned from now on, and how it will involve them. Then I told them about your problem with missing components in the printed circuit board assembly area. We talked for a while about how this could be caused and eventually worked around to the point where they recognized that some of the problems could be caused by us. We're responsible for planning the flow of every item through that area and touch every component and piece part several times on its journey through to test. So we could be responsible for the wrong components being in the bins. Once we got to this point they became more interested and I even had some suggestions on how we could improve things to avoid the problem in the future. I think we'll make progress but it's going to take time. They need to know we are serious about it before they put any effort into it themselves.

Carl The supply of information seems to be the key to success. I told my assembly people about the problems the testers find with our boards and they were staggered. They've never had that sort of information before because things have always been put right by repair. Jack suggested that from now on they do their own rework so they know about the problems and can prevent them from happening again. It sounded like a good idea so I'm going to speak to Richard about it tomorrow. I must say I've been quite surprised by the response. I thought they'd be cynical about the whole thing but so far they've been very positive. There aren't too many ideas at the moment and I seem to do most of the talking but I think that will change once we've been meeting for a few weeks and they're more confident.

Harold My people were all keen to know when their training will take place. Do you know anything about that?

Carl No. We're meeting Richard tomorrow. Why don't you raise it then? I expect everyone will be interested in knowing.

Harold OK, I will. It should be an interesting meeting. I'm going to raise the training issue; you're going to talk about having rework done by assembly people themselves instead of going to repair; and I know Arthur from test is going to query those costs of nonconformance figures we were given at that meeting with Michael last week. I'm looking forward to it!

Recognition

The need for recognition. Most people want to get more out of a job than just their wages or salary. Job satisfaction and feelings of appreciation can be just as important.

A QIP increases all employees' involvement in their work and gives them a say in how their job can be done more effectively. Many organizations also adopt some form of recognition for significant contributions to Quality Improvement.

The monetary value of most awards isn't particularly important. The key feature of any award process is that it allows management to signal to all employees that they treat the award seriously.

Winners need to know that management appreciates their contribution and that their contemporaries know that they've made an exceptional contribution.

Fundamentals of recognition. When implementing a recognition system, the following features are important:

1. How much an individual values the award depends not on its monetary value but on how seriously management takes the award. Try to make the award something the employee can remember or keep. Something the employee can wear or use at work is a good idea. This will be noticed by her contemporaries and mark her out as an award winner.

2. Make a big thing of presenting the award and ensure that everyone knows about it. In addition to making the individual concerned feel good, this generates further enthusiasm for the program and keeps the momentum going.

3. Ensure that everyone knows how the award can be won, who makes the decision, the selection criteria, and how an individual or group is nominated.

4. Ensure that the selection system is fair and is capable of recognizing all significant contributions whether these are by a group or an individual.

Case Study

Part 8: A QIT Meeting

Adrian   The purpose of today's meeting is to discuss how we should reward those people who make an outstanding contribution to Quality Improvement. Hopefully it should be fairly straightforward. Any suggestions?

Jane   I think that if people are going to value the award, it needs to be something worth having—cash or a holiday. Also we need to make a big deal of it and let everyone know who's won.

Julie   I agree that we should make a big thing of it, but I don't think we should spend a lot of money on the award itself. I think what people really value is honest appreciation for their efforts and for everyone to know that their contribution has been recognized. The way to do that is for management to be involved and interested in what they've done, not just to throw money at them.

Richard I think Julie's right on this one, Jane. It's a bit like presents at Christmas. The one that you really appreciate and value isn't necessarily one that costs a lot of money; it's the one that someone's really thought about that counts. I think it will be the same here. We need to show appreciation for their efforts, not try to buy their involvement in the program!

Alan Yes. It's like the long-service awards that the departmental managers give out. If they just leave it on someone's desk or even send it through the mail, the guy wonders why he bothered staying all that time. If the manager organizes a presentation and perhaps lunch for a few friends, the person feels important, remembers the day, and wears the award with pride. That's what we want to achieve with the quality awards.

Adrian I also think we should concentrate on the dignity of the presentation rather than on the value of the award. Marcia, you've been looking at this. What have you found?

Marcia I think you're right, Adrian. What really counts is how the award is treated by senior managers and how the presentation is carried out. We certainly don't want them sent in the mail! The most important factor is that the individual feels management takes the award seriously and that everyone in the company knows about the award and the winners. The award doesn't have to be expensive, but it should be something the recipient can be proud of. I suggest we hold a lunch for the award winners where the presentation will be made. We should also make a big feature of these awards in the magazine. We've already introduced an award for the best error cause removal (ECR) idea adopted each month, and that's gone down well. Winners and their suggestions are featured in the company magazine and Michael gives them a bottle of champagne at a presentation in the department. Actually the department seems to appreciate the chance to meet and chat with Michael as much as the winner appreciates the champagne! I suggest for the other awards we have a quality cup on which winners' names will be engraved. This can be permanently displayed in the reception area with a feature on the current winners. We could also give each individual a small award to keep—perhaps a pen or a pin which they could wear. I propose we set up a formal recognition system to award exceptional performance in the following areas: groups that meet their improvement goals; individuals who make an outstanding contribution; and the best ECRs submitted. That way we have group and individual recognition. We encourage individuals to contribute, we keep progress groups going, and we stimulate the ECR activity. We could make the awards each quarter.

Jane   You've certainly done a lot of work on this, Marcia and have come up with some good ideas. One suggestion I'd like to make is if we're not going to give awards of greater value, why don't we ask one of the directors to present the awards. We rarely see them here and I think it would make the recipients feel special to meet them.

Adrian   I agree, Jane. I'll ask Michael to talk to the corporate people and see if one of them could come to the awards lunch to make the presentations and talk to the winners. Also, Marcia, I think it's important that the selection of award winners is seen to be fair. I'd like you to choose an awards committee whose members are drawn from across the company. This committee will then select the award winners. At our next meeting I'd like to review the committee's proposals on how they'll select the award winners and whether they agree with your proposals on the awards to be given. Perhaps they'll have some different ideas. It's important that we can publish the selection criteria so everyone can see they're fair. All workers then have an equal chance of winning and know how to nominate someone for an award.

PERFORMANCE MEASUREMENTS AND TARGETS FOR IMPROVEMENT

This section explains the importance of introducing objective measurements in all departments of the organization, and then setting targets for improving performance.

Accurate measurement of the quality of all processes is the cornerstone to improvement—until we know where we are today, we can't improve. Objective measurements enable management and employees to focus attention on areas of weakness and to monitor progress.

Since all departments are involved in meeting customer requirements and in generating and fixing errors, all departments should be involved in the Quality Improvement Program, and all departments need to introduce appropriate measures for performance to be monitored.

Measurements can be used to highlight opportunities for improvement and also to monitor the program's success. All measurements that are introduced must fulfill two primary objectives:

1. They should be meaningful to the business. Improvements in these areas should lead to improved business performance.
2. The measurements should be performed by individuals or work groups.

It's often difficult to define measurements that meet both objectives. As a result, introducing measurements is often best approached from two angles:

1. *From the top down.* These are the initial measurements introduced and performed by managers and their departments. They are key functional measures where improvements will result in direct, tangible benefits to the business. These measurements effectively define the big picture into which the other measurements will fit.

2. *From the bottom up.* These are measurements introduced directly by individuals and work groups as the program progresses and individuals become involved in the program. They're often measurements of smaller, more personal activities that are frequently more meaningful to the individuals than the "big-picture" measurements.

With any Improvement Program, it's important to have both types of measurement; one without the other reduces the benefits of the Improvement Program. Bottom-up measures on their own can trivialize the program as the benefits to the business may be relatively small. Top-down measurements on their own can limit the extent to which individuals become involved in Quality Improvement. This can prevent individuals from realizing the important role they play.

Fundamentals of Top-Down Measurements

Before introducing new measurements at the beginning of the QIP, it's essential to focus attention on those areas with a real impact on the business. This helps to set the scene for a forward-looking program that individuals can recognize is driven by business needs. Once the program has been running for a while, individuals and groups will begin to introduce measurements of their own.

The following sequence has been found, in practice, to provide an effective way to identify appropriate measures.

1. Identify the basic purpose of the business and its objectives. The whole management team must be involved at this point. Results of this analysis should then be interpreted for each department. Functional analysis is a key technique at this stage.

2. Identify key measures of performance for each department. For example, a key measure for the personnel department might be to ensure that each of the other departments has its full quota of staff. The appropriate measure in this case might be variances from target head count.

3. Each department then establishes a number of functional measures. Functional measures reflect each department's major activities to meet its key objectives. (For the personnel department one functional measure might be the time taken to agree on the job specification once the vacancy has been identified.) Improvement in these functional measures can then be monitored. Progress in the functional measures supports the department's overall business objectives.

4. As the program cascades through the organization, these measurements will be developed and added to until everyone has established performance indicators within his or her own work area.

5. These measurements should be reviewed as part of the annual business planning cycle to ensure that they continue to reflect the overall business objectives.

Each measurement should be agreed upon and performed by the department being measured. Only then is the department likely to take the measurement seriously.

Measurement is only effective if it produces information that people can easily understand and use. Data must, therefore, be accurate and the operating and reporting methods must be straightforward.

Once accepted by the departments concerned, all measurements should be prominently displayed for everyone to see. This ensures commitment to the measurements by the department being measured, and allows an opportunity for everyone interested to participate in the Improvement Program. Measurements aren't just for managers; they're for everyone involved in the process.

Measurements should be made regularly. The frequency depends on the specific measurement being made.

The measurement of quality in practice. Most companies operate systems to measure performance within manufacturing divisions but have difficulty in deciding on measures to use within other areas. Here are some examples of measures that may be appropriate within other areas:

Engineering	Number of engineering changes
	Software bugs reported in released software
	Number of weeks that projects are delayed
Sales	Time to respond to requests for quotations
	Percentage of orders incorrectly entered
	Comparison of actual orders against forecast
Service	Turnaround time for repairs
	Warranty claims after service
	Excessive spares inventory
Accounts	Incorrect invoices raised
	Debtor days outstanding
Personnel	Time to fill vacancies
	Staff turnover rates
Administration	Number of items returned due to typing errors
	Number of hours late producing the typed copy
	Time taken to pass messages to the recipient

One of the most useful ways to display measurements is via trend charts. These charts should be posted on a regular basis (daily, weekly, monthly) to record progress over time. But the charts only record status and progress. It's the action taken as a result of the information on the charts that results in improvement.

Case Study

Part 9: A QIT Meeting

Adrian   OK everyone, the purpose of today's meeting is to discuss how we'll implement the measurement step. I've asked Marcia to summarize the purpose of the measurement step and then we can discuss it.

Marcia   The measurement step is one of the most important in the program since it's through measurement that we can target and monitor improvement. Improvements in performance in each department are the visible evidence to everyone of how we're progressing with Quality Improvement. The first step is to ensure that each department proposes a number of measurements of their performance that they'll commit to improving. Once the measurements have been agreed to, we can then make sure they're prominently displayed for everyone to see.

Jane   I can't see the point in doing that. It's just asking for trouble. Surely measurements are for us, the managers, to use.

Richard   Maybe that's how it used to be. But from what I understand, we're now asking everyone to improve things. It will be difficult to get them interested in improving things if we don't give them any information on how they're doing. Besides, no one will want their measurement to be getting worse, will they? I think that if they're displayed, people will be more committed to improving them.

Jane   Within the purchasing area all we can measure is how well our suppliers are doing. I can't see any supplier being happy at having its reject rate displayed for all to see—especially its competitors!

Alan   Surely there are some measurements of how well your department does its job. What about measuring how long it takes to process a purchase requisition or the number of times a part is ordered from a nonapproved supplier? As far as suppliers are concerned, I suggest we tell them what we're doing and agree with them on how the measurements will be made and then help them with improvements. After that if they don't like it, or don't improve, I suggest we start looking for another supplier.

Adrian   So what we're asking for is a proposal from each department of the measurements it will make and display for all to see?

Julie   That's right, Adrian. Measurements that the departments themselves agree with and own.

David   What concerns me, Julie, is that departments may choose things that are fairly easy to improve so they'll look good, but that are so trivial that people think the whole program is a bit of a joke. We could be sunk before we've even begun.

Richard   Does it really matter how trivial they are as long as they improve?

Adrian   I think that once the program is more established, you may be right Richard. But at the moment all people can see is how much we're going to spend on training this year. They'll want to see us getting our money back by making improvements in significant areas. David's right. We need to make sure the measurements are significant. What do you suggest, Julie?

Julie   I've got a couple of suggestions. One is that we need to involve Michael and the rest of the management team who aren't part of the QIT on this issue. We need the management team to define the overall business objectives and each department's role in ensuring that those objectives are met. Then we can devise the significant measures in each department that actually advance those objectives. My other suggestion is that we get Tom's people to devise and carry out a customer survey asking them what they think of our total performance as a supplier. This will need to include questions that aren't related to the product itself—things like what they think of the time it takes us to return calls. We could use this information to determine areas where we need to introduce measurements and improve performance.

Adrian   That sounds like an excellent idea. What do you think, Tom?

Tom   It's something we've never done before. It will need careful planning for us to ensure we get the information we need. If it works it could provide vital information on the areas where we need to take action to improve our customers' perception of us. I'll get my people to have a look at it and report back at the next meeting. I think they'll be excited at the prospect, but we'll need some help when it comes to actually carrying out the survey.

Adrian   Good. If you can let me have the relevant information, Julie, I'll tackle Michael about organizing a management meeting to discuss it. I suggest we all read the material carefully so that when we come to the meeting, we'll have some ideas!

Fundamentals of Bottom-Up Measurement

Once the QIP is underway, the training has begun, and measurements are introduced, individuals will begin to see evidence of the value of the program in their work. This will generate enthusiasm for the program. It's important to turn this enthusiasm into action. Only then can the Improvement Program develop fully throughout the company.

At the program's outset, the department heads will each have identified a number of top-down measures to be used as a basis for improvement. Their staffs will have been given the objective of improving their performance against these measures. But the initial measures may seem remote to the work force, and so not seem fully owned by them.

To maintain employees' enthusiasm they must be fully involved in the program as soon as possible. Perhaps the best way to achieve this is to let them identify a set of objectives that they take ownership for. Each group will then be responsible for introducing corrective actions and measuring improvement.

Each group's supervisor should sit down with their team and agree on improvement goals. Wherever possible these goals should come from the group itself although the supervisor may need to set the ball rolling by suggesting possible goals. Goals may be for the group as a whole or for individuals within the group. The goals should be specific and measurable.

Once selected, goals should be posted in a conspicuous place and progress should be monitored. Managers must monitor and encourage improvements, which should be widely publicized.

Case Study
_____

Part 10: A Sales Department Meeting

The sales department was holding its regular quality meeting. It spent some time discussing improvements against existing departmental measures. Sally was the sales team leader.

Sally   So far, we've all been trained and have been meeting for a few months to discuss how we might improve our performance against the measurements Tom suggested. Now we have the opportunity to introduce our own measurements and set our own targets for improvement. This is the time that we try to identify for ourselves any other areas in which we can make improvements. It will then be up to us to decide what activities we want to improve and introduce measurements to monitor progress.

Jack   It's all very well for us to decide on new areas to improve, but what about the measurements we've been taking to date? Do we just drop those?

Shirley   Oh no, I don't think we should drop those. They seem to be important and we're already starting to make improvements. For example, we've seen a great improvement in the accuracy of our sales forecasting. We're now at the stage where we can give manufacturing a firm idea of the number of items we expect to ship in the next month. In the past I know they've been pulling their hair out because they couldn't plan their production schedules on the figures we were giving them. I used to see differences of ±30 percent between confirmed sales orders and our forecasts. Now, although we're down to ±15 percent, we can't rest on our laurels. I think it's essential that we keep trying to improve on this. The drive on the shop floor to turn orders around within a month depends on accurate forecasts.

Sally   OK, if everyone else agrees, then we'll continue to measure and improve our sales forecast accuracy. I agree that it's a vital area. But what other measures should we introduce. One idea I had, after a complaint from a customer the other day, was to measure the time it takes us to send out a quotation. If a customer doesn't receive the quote promptly, we might not even be considered for the order.

Jeremy   What about keeping a measure of the total number of minutes people turn up late for meetings? We spend ages hanging around for people before we can start, especially at the monthly sales meeting. I expect that if we just start measuring it we'll see an improvement without taking any other action at all!

Shirley   Maybe people turn up late because the meetings aren't very productive. Maybe we could devise some means of assessing each meeting for its effectiveness. We could give each meeting a score and monitor that.

Jeremy   You mean we could give points for things like whether a meeting was necessary? Was an agenda circulated before the meeting? Were people properly prepared? Had the actions from the previous meeting been completed? Did the meeting run to time? It sounds like a good idea to me considering how long we all spend at meetings. We'd need to make sure the scoring method was sensible and simple.

Liz   One thing that would really improve life for us secretaries is if we didn't have to keep retyping things because the salesperson has made changes. It's really annoying to get a piece of work back for changes when you think you've seen the last of it.

Marian   Yes, I'd agree with that, especially for long proposals. Maybe we should concentrate on those and measure the number of changes that are made once a proposal has been typed.

Liz   Another thing that causes difficulties for us in the office is when we can't get hold of salespeople because we don't know where they are. We usually need to get hold of them because a customer has a query so it's annoying for customers too.

Jeremy   As far as the salespeople are concerned, we're often criticized by customers for not getting back to them quickly enough. It's usually caused by our not receiving messages from the message desk promptly.

Liz   Maybe we should measure both the delays in messages reaching salespeople and the number of times the salespeople are uncontactable—because I expect they could be linked.

Shirley   I'm usually on the receiving end of complaints, from the shop floor because there are errors on sales orders. They're always coming up here to say that a certain part number doesn't exist or we haven't included the version that the customer needs. It would certainly make my life easier, and theirs too no doubt, if we could resolve this.

Sally looked around to see if there were any more ideas before she joined in.

Sally   Well, I didn't know there were so many problems! There are bound to be some areas where improvement could make a real impact on the business. But if we try to do too many things at once, we're almost bound to fail. I think we should select two or three measures in addition to the sales forecast measure and really concentrate on making significant improvements in those areas. I've made a note of all the suggestions. I'll ask Susan to type them up, with no changes of course, and get her to circulate them to you all. I'd like you to think about them and then, at next week's meeting, we can decide on the ones we'll implement.

PREVENTION

This section focuses on the need to adopt prevention as the system for Quality Improvement throughout the organization. It explains the Zero Defects concept and the importance of introducing effective corrective action systems to eliminate the causes of nonconformance and prevent their recurrence.

The Zero Defects Concept

To implement a successful Quality Improvement Program, a company must adopt prevention as the system for managing quality. Prevention requires everyone within the company to believe that (1) errors aren't an inevitable part of working life and (2) correct systems, training, equipment, materials, and, above all, personal attitudes can prevent errors from occurring. This belief is summarized in the Zero Defects concept. There's some question as to who first propounded the Zero Defects concept, but it's most closely associated with Philip Crosby and has been extensively used by him and his consulting organization in implementing Quality Improvements in many organizations worldwide.

The fundamental principal underlying Zero Defects is that all operations can be done right the first time. Zero Defects doesn't mean that everything has to be gold-plated or that the place has to be crawling with inspectors. It simply means that each and every one of us has to believe that it's possible to carry out activities without error. Errors aren't inevitable. We shouldn't anticipate errors and then build up massive systems to find and correct them. If we expect errors to occur and build systems to deal with them, they'll happen. We're then effectively saying that errors don't matter. We will find and fix them. This is a very costly path to tread.

If errors aren't expected to occur, and preventive actions are introduced to eliminate problems, then errors won't happen. The new attitude is that errors aren't tolerated. A big fix-it outfit shouldn't be available just waiting for errors to happen. Everyone will be more careful and will work to eliminate the causes of errors so that eventually they'll no longer occur.

In our personal life we don't expect to put on odd shoes in the morning on a given number of days in a year. If we did expect this to happen, we could ask our partner to check our shoes every morning before going out and then rectify any errors found! This would prove very costly in terms of our partner's time and patience. We don't, however, expect this to happen because we implement a preventive action such as putting our shoes in pairs when we take them off.

The Zero Defects philosophy requires us to apply our personal standards to our work and asks everyone else in the company to do the same. By adopting the Zero Defects concept, employees underline their commitment to the attitude and belief that errors aren't inevitable. Errors can be avoided by applying prevention techniques.

The Fundamental Importance of Effective Corrective Action Systems

The fundamental objective of corrective action is to ensure that, having identified a problem, the action taken ensures that it doesn't recur. The corrective action should be designed to prevent the same type of error from happening again, not just today but forever. Although at the start of a Quality Improvement Program it's important to focus attention on major problems, in the long run no error is too small to require corrective action.

We've already discussed the need to introduce measurements of performance in all areas of the company. These provide raw data so we can identify and evaluate a problem's impact. The correct use of effective measurements enables us to monitor the progress resulting from corrective actions taken to eliminate problems.

But it must be stressed that measurements only provide information. It's the actions taken as a result of this information that produce the necessary improvements. We therefore must make sure that an adequate system is in place to ensure that effective corrective actions are taken when a problem is identified.

The Failure of Typical Existing Corrective Action Systems

Most companies already operate corrective action systems. The resolution of audit deficiencies, and meetings with suppliers to review the reasons for rejected components and to improve performance are examples. But existing systems in many companies fail to succeed for three main reasons:

1. The actions taken as a result of problems often aren't really preventive actions. They may fix today's problem but generally don't introduce the long-term improvements necessary to prevent the problem's recurring in the future.

2. Many companies don't operate a mechanism for collecting details of employees' day-to-day problems. This can be countered by introducing an Error Cause Removal (ECR) system.

3. Many companies' typical approach to resolving problems is to form a team of managers and supervisors. These teams are formed on an ad hoc basis and meet to try and resolve significant

problems as they're identified. By only using managers and supervisors in these teams, we restrict the number of problems that can be tackled, and frequently don't get the benefit of the practical experience of the people actually doing the job on a day-to-day basis.

Features of an Effective Corrective Action System

To be effective, corrective actions must be carefully designed to eliminate the problem concerned once and for all. Six features typically need to be present for a corrective action system to be effective:

1. An effective mechanism must exist to identify the problems to be solved. It's important to analyze systematically the features of a business and examine whether processes could be carried out more effectively. It's also important to establish a mechanism (an ECR system) to identify practical problems facing the work force.

2. Once a problem has been identified, all the people concerned with the problem must be involved in developing corrective actions via a corrective action group.

3. Someone within each group, frequently the supervisor, needs some knowledge of problem solving methods.

4. Progress should be reported to team members regularly.

5. Corrective actions should be carefully assessed to ensure that they're the most effective means to eliminate the problem once and for all. Once the actions are introduced, their results must be monitored to ensure that they achieve their objectives.

6. Management must support the activity and demonstrate its commitment by taking an interest in the progress made.

Corrective Action Groups

Besides improving existing corrective action systems, it's generally necessary to consider introducing formal problem solving groups. The two most important types of group are

1. *Progress groups* (also known as *process action teams* and *quality circles*. A progress group is generally a small group of individuals from within one department who carry out similar work. The group meets regularly to identify, implement, and monitor the

progress of corrective actions for problems arising within its work area.

2. *Corrective action task force*. Complex problems frequently arise during the course of a Quality Improvement Program. A corrective action task force is an interdepartmental group with a member from each department affected by the problem.

The Error Cause Removal (ECR) System

An important feature of a successful Quality Improvement Program is the introduction of a simple method that allows any individual to bring out into the open problems preventing his or her performing error-free work. Management can then target these problems to find a solution. This is the Error Cause Removal system. This type of system differs from a suggestion scheme because, in this case, the employee need only identify the problem. (In a suggestion scheme individuals are only asked to contribute if they can propose a solution. Thus a whole host of problems go unidentified and unresolved). Many companies operate ECR systems. In some cases they fall into disrepute because there's no real management commitment to solving problems identified. As a result, individuals have to wait a long time for what's often an unsatisfactory answer. Eventually the system is no longer used. Like quality circles, an ECR system is only likely to be successful as part of a Quality Improvement Program. In this case management actively wants to know about problems and is committed to effecting solutions.

The following features should be present for an ECR system to work effectively:

1. The system should be introduced early in the Quality Improvement Program so it's available for individuals to use as they become involved in the program.

2. The forms should be short, simple to complete, and readily available.

3. ECR reports should initially be submitted to the individual's supervisor. An ECR report should be acknowledged within two days of receipt.

4. If the problem can't be resolved by the supervisor, then the form should be sent to the department responsible for the

problem. The individual should receive a reply from the department within two weeks. This reply should give details of the decision or a report on the actions taken so far together with an estimated completion date.

5. If it's decided to do nothing about an ECR report, this should be cleared with at least the next level of management. The individual must be given a clear explanation of why no action is being taken.

6. Every ECR should be taken seriously. No one should be criticized for raising an ECR.

7. All corrective actions introduced must resolve the problem permanently through preventive action. They should not just fix the problem in the short term.

8. The system should ensure that each ECR is resolved at the lowest possible level of supervision. Of all ECRs raised, experience has shown that 85 percent can frequently be resolved by the first level of supervision and 13 percent at the next level; only 2 percent might need to be referred to the department head or the QIT.

9. The system's efficiency should be monitored by the QIT. It should look particularly at the response time and the actions taken. If either is unsatisfactory, individuals will cease to use the system and the Improvement Program will lose credibility.

Case Study

Part 11: A QIT Meeting

Adrian   I've been asked by the magazine editor what we'd like to say in the next issue of the company magazine. Does anyone have any suggestions?

Alan   What about featuring the progress made by the task force we set up three months ago to look at why it takes so long for new product designs to reach the customer? Remember we had a heated discussion with just about everyone being blamed from manufacturing to engineering, purchasing, marketing, and back again. In retrospect it was a tough task to set for our first problem. But they've made excellent progress so far and are proposing some radical changes in how we approach this whole activity.

David   I understand they'll have finished their report next week and I suggest we wait to hear what they've got to say before we publish a report. If we wait, we could run a far better story in the next issue. They've apparently had a lot of difficulty estimating the CONC. It was particularly difficult to estimate the cost associated with lost customers through our not having a new product available when we said we would. But I believe they've now come up with a rough figure that they're happy with, though they wouldn't tell me it. They want to save that until they do their formal presentation to us so I guess it must be quite interesting! Anyway they feel they're now ready to present their proposals to us for our approval to implement. I'd like to have a special meeting of the QIT next Tuesday for this if everyone can make it.

Maria   What about the Progress Groups then? Have we got any information on how they're going?

Adrian   Marcia, have you any information?

Marcia   I haven't yet completed a review of the current status in all departments, but I can give you my general impressions. Most areas are continuing to hold regular communication meetings with their supervisor. But in some areas these are becoming a bit stale and no real progress is being made with identifying performance measurements or implementing corrective actions.

Jane   From the experience I've had with my people, the process gets a real boost once people have been educated about the program. Maybe part of the problem is that our education timetable has been slipping.

Marcia   I think you're right, Jane. We certainly haven't trained everyone yet.

Adrian   Right, I've been monitoring progress on the education step and frankly we could do a great deal better. I think this is something we should tackle straight away. I'd like each of us here to commit to completing the training of all our people within the next three months. This means we need to draw up a timetable and tell each individual the date their training will take place. That way we're likely to stick to it! Perhaps for the next issue of the magazine we could do an article on education. Jane, you seem to be the furthest ahead in this area, so would you draft an article on your department's experience?

Jane   That's fine by me. I should be able to finish it in time for the copy deadline next Wednesday. I'll let you look at it before then.

Julie   I'd also like to suggest that once a month at the QIT meeting each member summarizes the progress made on each of the improvement steps within his or her area.

Adrian That sounds like an excellent idea to me, Julie. It would have been a good idea to do that from the beginning but I didn't think of it. It's another example of how we need to plan carefully every step we take and implement preventive actions! Before we go I'd like to ask Marcia to bring us all up to date on the ECR system we've introduced. What's happened so far, Marcia?

Marcia Well, as you know, we introduced the ECR system a month ago. In the first month we've received 110 ECRs.

Richard That seems a lot. How on earth will we be able to keep up, especially if they keep coming in at the same rate?

Marcia Fortunately we set up the ECR system so that most problems could be dealt with by the first level of supervision. That has spread the load. Supervisors can either solve the problem directly if it's within their control, or they can refer it to their counterpart in the department who's responsible for the problem. Many of the ECRs raised in this first lot have been dealt with by the individual's own progress group. Although they're outside the individual's direct control, they're within the control of the progress group. Supervisors have picked these up and referred them directly to the progress group. In the future I hope, individuals will refer these sorts of problems directly to the group instead of raising an ECR.

David Are there many that can't be dealt with by the supervisors?

Marcia A few. At the end of the first month 10 had been passed up to a manager. What I've done this month is just circulate a brief description of the ECRs raised so you can all see the sorts of problems being highlighted.

Alan It's amazing that there are so many problems out there making life difficult for people when most of them can be resolved relatively easily once someone knows about them.

Adrian Unfortunately that was a fact of life under our old system of working. We used to just live with the problems. Now we've committed to ensure that problems preventing error-free work are resolved. Is there any way to monitor the ECR system to ensure that problems are resolved speedily? That way we can establish our commitment to the program. If ECRs aren't acted on promptly, then the system will fall into disrepute. Can you have a look at a way of doing that, Marcia?

Marcia Yes. It'll take me a little while to set up. By the end of next month I'll start reporting the ECR status.

Here's a sample of the initial ECRs received at Alpha.

- Why is the soldering machine so far away from assembly? By the time the boards reach me, half the components are loose. I have to push them all back in place before they can be soldered.

- The orders we receive from sales have only the customer's name but not the address. Some customers have more than one address so we have to contact the salesperson to find out the correct address.

- The person who unloads at Receiving can't recognize components. The paperwork is never with the right stuff and we spend a lot of time sorting this out.

- There's always a line to use the fax machine. I spend a lot of time waiting there. Why can't we buy another one?

- Front panels come packed in lots of 10. We issue them in lots of 5, which means unpacking them and then packing them up again. Why can't the supplier send them in batches of 5?

- We leave the lights on when we go home because the bank of switches isn't marked to show which switch turns off which lights. Why can't they be marked so we can turn the lights out and save electricity?

- My PC and printer are different from other secretaries'. Why don't we all have the same models so that if one breaks down we could use someone else's?

- The customer database only has the company name and not the buyer's name. Whenever I want to call a customer that I don't know, I have to scout around to see if anyone knows the buyer's name before I call her.

Chapter Seven

Quality Tools

STATISTICAL PROCESS CONTROL (SPC)

Statistical Process Control (SPC) enables an operator to determine whether a process is producing and is likely to continue to produce conforming output. It does this by measuring key parameters for a small sample of the output produced at intervals while the process is operating.

This information can be used as a basis for making adjustments to the inputs or, if necessary, to the process to prevent non-conforming output from being produced.

SPC also enables a business to reduce the variations in the output from a process, although relatively few organizations use SPC in this way.

Producing products that are just within the specification may be acceptable today, but any variation from the target nominal value may result in rejects and rework further along the chain. Variations from the nominal value can also cause significant problems in view of the interdependence of components in complex products. SPC enables businesses to constantly improve the performance of the process to reduce variation in output. This ability to reduce variation from the nominal value may provide a distinct competitive advantage and may enable premium prices to be charged for products.

Features of an SPC Environment

In a traditional quality control environment, the quality of output is assessed at the end of each process by answering the question, Has the output been produced according to the specification?

This question leads to appraisal and correction activities. The business has to check the output from each process to see whether it conforms to requirements. If it doesn't conform, then it must be reworked or replaced. These activities are an admission of the failure to define and control processes to ensure that they produce conforming output.

SPC represents a preventive approach to the manufacturing process. In an SPC environment, output quality is assured by concentrating on the design and operation of the process itself rather than waiting until the output has been produced and then inspecting and sorting it.

Three key questions are asked when using SPC methods:

1. Is the process capable of producing conforming output?
2. Is the process actually producing conforming output (checked by examining in-process samples)?
3. Can the process be improved to reduce variability?

To benefit from SPC, management must invest the necessary time and money in equipment as well as in training and educating employees so they understand both the philosophy of prevention and how to operate the SPC equipment. An effective SPC environment is one that constantly strives for (1) continuous improvement in the operation of processes and (2) reduction in variation in output.

To operate an SPC environment, the following conditions need to be satisfied:

- The requirements of the process must be defined.
- The process should be set up so that it can produce conforming output.
- Operators should be provided with equipment to enable them to monitor critical attributes of the process while output is being produced. This information enables them to assess whether the process continues to produce output meeting the requirements.
- The operator should be trained to make the necessary adjustments to the process or its inputs if the process moves away from producing output at the nominal specification.
- The process should be constantly monitored. This enables the operator to fully understand it, so that opportunities for improving its performance (by reducing variation in the

output and increasing conformance to the required nominal specification) may be identified and implemented.

Achieving the required level of commitment and cultural change is a long-term activity. A number of years may pass before a complete change is achieved.

Benefits of SPC

The implementation of SPC offers three significant advantages for many types of business. First, it reduces the quantity of non-conforming output. Concentrating on the process itself rather than on postprocess inspection also reduces the amounts of wasted time and materials expended on rework and repeating processes; it cuts the inspection effort required; and it improves the quality of the working environment. This can have an important positive impact on employee morale if managed correctly. No one likes reworking or repeating processes that weren't adequately controlled in the first place.

Second, most inspection processes miss some nonconforming output. Even where all output is inspected, some 15 percent of the errors are commonly missed. These nonconforming products are then sold to customers. If nonconforming output is prevented in the first place, customers are less likely to receive nonconforming products or services.

Third, continuous improvement of processes and reduction in the variation in output enable businesses to compete in terms of both performance and price.

PROCESSES

SPC requires the careful design and monitoring of processes. To understand SPC we must therefore understand the meaning of the term *process*. (Figure 2–1 illustrates principal characteristics of a process.)

Inputs are received from a supplier. (The requirements for these inputs need to be defined.) The process transforms these inputs into outputs for delivery to a customer. (Customer requirements also need to be defined.) The outputs may be a product (for example, a set of accounts, a typed letter, or an assembled printed circuit board) or a service (such as answering the telephone or delivering a training seminar).

To produce conforming output, the process may need to use

1. Direct inputs such as a draft letter, bare printed circuit board, components, or financial data.
2. Equipment and facilities (such as a manufacturing plant, typewriter, computer, calculator, or training room).
3. Skills and job knowledge.
4. Procedures describing how the process is to be performed.
5. A specification defining the performance standards required of the process.

Once a process has been defined, SPC can be used to ensure that output conforms to requirements. However SPC methods can only be used once a process is "in control" and capable of producing conforming product. For a process consistently to produce conforming product it must be capable of both producing conforming product and operating under control so only conforming product can be produced. Non-conforming output is produced because of variation in the inputs or the process itself.

When a process is first set up, it may not be "in control." In this case, we must investigate why the process can't produce conforming product so that the causes can be identified and eliminated. Chapter 8 describes a comprehensive practical problem solving methodology that may be useful in these circumstances. The principal methods it describes are

Process flowcharting

Brainstorming

Cause and effect diagrams (Ishikawa diagrams)

Voting and weighting

Bar graphs

Pareto analysis

Scatter diagrams

Force field analysis

The remainder of this chapter focuses on the use of control charts.

Causes of Variation in a Process

Variation can arise as a result of two principal factors:

1. *"Assignable"* or *"special"* causes. This form of variation is assignable to a specific cause such as differences between the performance of different machinery, operators, or materials. This type of variation isn't random and can lead to excessive process variation. If assignable causes of variation exist in a process, then the process is defined as "out of control."

Variation due to assignable causes is often excessive and SPC methods can't be used to predict these variations. Before control charts can be used, therefore, the process must be adjusted so that it becomes "in control." All assignable causes of variation must be eliminated.

2. *"random"* variations. These arise as a result of the interaction between a multitude of factors, such as temperature, atmospheric pressure, and the normal operating tolerance of the machinery. These variations are random, are generally small, and can't be assigned to any specific cause. A process is said to be stable or in control if process variability is the result of random variations alone. SPC monitors random variations and, by plotting the trend in this variation, predicts the point at which the process is about to produce nonconforming product. The operator can then make the necessary adjustments to ensure that the process continues to produce conforming output.

Attributes and variables. If the output of a process can be measured as a continuous variable (for example, the voltage of a power supply, diameter of a wire, or cycle time), then no two measurements will be identical and the variation will generally follow a normal distribution curve. The parameters of this curve are well understood. It's the characteristics of this curve that are used as the basis for control charts for variables.

Where the output of a process can't be measured as a continuous variable but only as a discrete value (for example, the number of typing errors in a report, number of customer complaints, or number of wrong components assembled), these are termed attributes. In this case the variation in the parameters follows a binomial distribution. This is used as the basis for control charts for attributes.

Characteristics of the normal distribution curve for variables. A normal distribution will result if variations in the parameter being measured are randomly distributed (that is if variations are just as likely to be upwards as downwards from the central value.) A normal distribution produces a symmetrical bell-shaped curve (Figure 7–1). This curve can be defined by two parameters:

1. The mean (μ) is the central value. It's calculated by dividing the sum of the individual values by the number of observations:

$$\mu = \frac{\overset{n}{\underset{1}{\sum}} x_n}{n}$$

2. The standard deviation (σ) measures the spread of values around the mean. It's calculated by summing the squares of the differences between each measured value and the mean, dividing this sum by the number of observations, and then taking the square root of the result:

$$\sigma = \sqrt{\frac{\overset{n}{\underset{1}{\sum}} (x_n - \mu)^2}{n}}$$

The standard deviation is a key parameter in setting control limits for SPC purposes because a known proportion of the population lie within a range specified by the standard deviation from the mean:

- About 68.3 percent of the items in the population lie within a range defined by "the mean ± one standard deviation."
- About 95.4 percent of values are in the range defined by "the mean ± two standard deviations."
- About 99.7 percent of values (i.e., virtually all the values) are in the range defined by "the mean ± three standard deviations." This range defines the so-called "natural process capability" of the process. The process produces output within ± three standard deviations of the mean virtually all the time.

These values are used to predict the point at which the process is about to produce nonconforming output so the operator can implement preventive actions and keep the process within limits.

Establishing the Capability of the Process

Before control charts can be constructed, we must ensure that the process is consistently capable of producing conforming product.

FIGURE 7–1
Normal Distribution Curve for a Continuous Variable

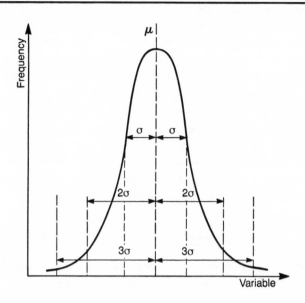

One way that the natural capability of a process can be compared to the output specification is by using a simple index. C_p compares the actual range achieved by the process with the acceptable range or tolerance. It is calculated as follows:

$$\text{Process capability } C_p = \frac{\text{Tolerance range}}{\text{Actual range } (6\sigma)}$$

If C_p is greater than 1, it means that at least 99.7 percent of the outputs from the process are contained in a range with the same breadth as the acceptable range.

But this measure doesn't take into account that the process mean may not conform to the required nominal value. So the process may produce output that doesn't conform to requirements. A second index, C_{pk}, takes into account both the range and the centering of the process:

$$C_{pk} = \frac{\text{Upper limit} - \text{Nominal}}{3\sigma} \quad \text{or} \quad \frac{\text{Nominal} - \text{Lower limit}}{3\sigma}$$

The difference between C_p and C_{pk} is analogous to the difference between precision and accuracy. A process is said to be accurate if the mean of its output conforms to the specified nominal value. But a process is said to be precise if there's little variation in its output; the lower the standard deviation, the higher the precision.

For a process to be capable, both C_p and C_{pk} must be greater than 1. If they're less than 1, then less than 99.7 percent of the output from the process will fall within the acceptable range (i.e., the process won't consistently produce conforming output). If C_p and C_{pk} equal 1 then just 99.7 percent of output from the process will fall within the acceptable range; but any slight variation in the process will produce nonconforming product. To operate with a margin of safety and ensure the production of output within the required limits, then C_p and C_{pk} should approach 2.

Using Process Control Charts for Variables

Having established that the process is capable of meeting the output requirements, the process control charts illustrated in Figure 7–2a may be used to plot actual output. Trends in the value of the output produced are monitored and actions taken if the process is seen to vary excessively as a result of assignable causes.

The charts show warning and action limits for the process. These are based on the 2σ and 3σ points from the normal distribution curve mentioned. At intervals during the process the operator takes a sample (of at least four items) from the output and takes measurements. Results are plotted on the control chart. Adjustments to the process are made based on results from the sample. Any variation in the process due to random causes should give a value within the action limits points (1 through 7). If the value plotted falls outside the warning limits (points 8 and 12) this may still be due to random variation (there's about a 1 in 40 chance of this happening), but it's grounds for suspicion that an assignable cause may be present. If this happens, then a further sample is taken immediately and the result is plotted. If this second result is within the warning limits, then the process is allowed to continue (points 9 and 13). If the second sample is again outside the warning limits, then action should be taken to adjust the process. If the value falls outside the action limits, this indicates the presence of an assignable cause that should be investigated and the process should be adjusted.

The charts should be easy to understand and interpret. An experienced operator will frequently be able to tell the most likely cause of an error based on the characteristics of the process control plot.

Any changes to the process and additional samples should be recorded on the control chart when they take place. In practice coded marks are commonly used to mark changes in operator or materials or in the setup of the equipment. This information helps us identify causes of variation in the mean or range of output.

What Types of Control Charts Are There?

The most commonly used charts for variables are mean and range charts. Examples of mean charts appear in Figures 7–2a and b.

For a mean chart, the mean of the measurements taken from each sample is plotted on the control chart.

For a range chart, the difference between the highest and lowest value in each sample is plotted on the chart.

Using Process Control Charts for Attributes

For attributes, the output follows a binomial distribution. In this case, number-defective or proportion-defective charts are commonly used to record variation. Warning and action limits may again be calculated, and the control charts are used in the same way as for variables. Other charts—such as moving average (or range) or cumulative sum (cusum) charts—may also be valuable. Cumulative sum charts are powerful tools for detecting trends or changes in attributes.

What Is the Role of the Operator?

SPC relies on the close control of the operating characteristics of processes. If a process starts to move out of control, it's necessary to implement prompt corrective action. To do this, operators should be given responsibility for ensuring that the process remains in control, producing output that conforms to

FIGURE 7–2a
Mean Chart—Stable Process

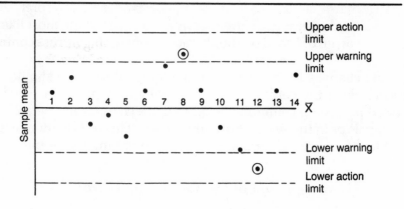

FIGURE 7–2b
Mean Chart—Drifting Process

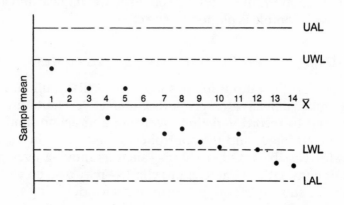

requirements. To enable them to take this responsibility, they must be given the necessary training, procedures, tools, authority, and information to do the job properly.

It's generally helpful to keep the information supplied to the operator to the minimum required to enable the process to be managed effectively. Providing too much information can create confusion.

Although control charts can be drawn manually, in organizations where they're routinely used to control a large number of processes, computer control of these charts is useful.

Modern computer-driven process control systems may be programmed to present only those charts that are going out of control, and may issue operator instructions about how to bring them back under control.

Summary of Steps to Set Up a Control Chart for Variables

1. Take a minimum of 20 samples of the output. Each sample should contain between 4 and 10 items.
2. Measure each item and record the results. Calculate the mean and range within each sample.
3. Calculate the average mean and range of all the samples.
4. Using standard tables draw the control charts, and the action and warning limits.
5. Having plotted the control charts, take at least 20 sample measurements over a period of time to determine whether the process is in control (i.e., whether the variation in the process is due solely to random causes).
6. If the process is out of control, then actions must be taken to eliminate the assignable causes.
7. If the process is in control, then determine whether the process's natural capability is adequate consistently to produce conforming product. Calculate C_p and C_{pk}.
8. If the process is both in control and capable, then the control charts can be used to monitor and adjust the process.

Within an organization committed to Total Quality Management, continuous improvement is a driving force. SPC can form an integral part of this process.

BENCHMARKING

A benchmark is a reference point against which to compare yourself. Leading businesses frequently use benchmarking to compare their performance in key areas against the results achieved by the best companies in the world. Benchmarking provides insight into what's possible, an understanding of how it can be achieved, and a goal to aim for and exceed.

Why Benchmark?

Trying to improve performance is generally difficult. The potential for improvement can be enormous. To restrict yourself to incremental improvements based on existing performance limits your potential achievement. To become a world-class performer, you must adopt world-class techniques. Only benchmarking provides information on what is required for world-class performance.

A study by McKinsey (reported in *McKinsey Quarterly*, 1991, no. 1) suggests that world-class mechanical and electronic companies may introduce new products at less than half the cost, and in less than half the time it takes a typical company.

Data reported by the Massachusetts Institute of Technology and JD Power and Associates (Table 7–1) illustrate the significant differences between Japanese, US, and European car assembly plants. According to this data, US and European car producers have tremendous opportunities for improvement. Incremental improvements in current performance will just not be enough. A 30 percent improvement in productivity might appear to be an ambitious target, but given their current productivity, even this would still leave them a long way behind the best in the world. To survive in today's world markets requires world-class performance.

What Are the Benefits of Benchmarking?

Businesses need to understand the skills and processes that are the keys to their success and to satisfying their customers' requirements. Benchmarking can provide management with the necessary data to enable it to review critically its performance in these key areas against the best in the world. Benchmarking can produce the following benefits if performed effectively:

- An understanding of the activities and processes that are key to the business's success and to satisfying its customers' requirements.

TABLE 7-1
Car Assembly Plant Characteristics—Averages for
Plants in Each Region, in 1989

	Producers			
	Japanese in Japan	*Japanese in the United States*	*Americans in the United States*	*European Producers*
Productivity (hours per vehicle)	16.8	21.2	25.1	36.2
Assembly defects per 100 vehicles	60	65	82	97
Repair area (% of assembly space)	4.1	4.9	12.9	14.4
Stocks (days)*	0.2	1.6	2.9	2.0
Training of new workers (hours)	380	370	46	173
Absenteeism (%)	5.0	4.8	11.7	12.1

Source: Massachusetts Institute of Technology and JD Power & Associates. Reported in *The Economist*, August 10, 1991.

*For eight sample parts.

- Alerting management to what's possible in a world-class organization.
- Setting objective performance standards for key activities to match or surpass the best in the world.
- An insight into how other companies meet world-class standards.

Without benchmarking, a company can become insular and complacent. It may set seemingly aggressive targets based on current performance but may not realize how far behind it's slipping compared with world-beating competitors.

What Can You Benchmark?

Almost any business characteristic can be benchmarked. The range of possibilities includes:

Customer satisfaction	Product conformance to requirements
	Reliability
	On-time delivery
	Lead times
Financial performance	Sales per employee
	Age of debts
	Investment in R&D
Distribution	Cost of distribution activities
	Time in distribution cycle
	Number of levels of distribution
Purchasing	Number of suppliers
	Suppliers per buyer
	Buyers per 1,000 transactions
	Late deliveries
	Rejection rate
	Shortages
Materials management	Warehouse space
	Inventory
	Cycle times
Design	Time to introduce new products
	Number of engineering changes

Another aspect of a business that can be benchmarked is management practice. For example, General Electric's "Best Practices" program found that leading companies tend to focus on how departments work together as they perform processes rather than on how they work in isolation. Its objective is to maximize efficiency as departments interact, leading to reduced lead times for product introduction, partnerships with suppliers, and reduced levels of stock (*Fortune*, August 12, 1991).

Identify key business activities. What are the driving forces behind your business? What activities directly influence customer satisfaction? What activities have an important impact on the bottom line? Which activities account for the largest proportion of your costs? These are all possible candidates for benchmarking.

Determining the key activities is essential because this drives the benchmarking program. The team may identify the key activities using information from a variety of sources. These might include

1. *Customer surveys* carried out by the company to determine its performance and the requirements of its customers, and *industry-*

wide surveys carried out by trade associations, newspapers or magazines may both be of value at this point. Table 7–2 illustrates the sort of information available. Here, the 1991 *Euromoney* Business Travel Survey identifies the parameters people use when choosing airlines and hotels. These results may be used to determine areas where airlines and hotels might benchmark their performance against others.

2. *Functional analysis* identifies the purpose of the business and each of its functions in terms of satisfying external customers' requirements. The key activities identified by this process may be used as a starting point for a benchmarking program.

3. *Financial analysis* indicates the activities that account for a large proportion of costs or where significant nonconformance costs occur. These activities may constitute key targets for benchmarking. Many manufacturing companies today buy components, doing only final assembly in-house. Here the internal value added is relatively small. In this case supply management is a key business activity—it may be more important than the associated in-house manufacturing activity.

Identify key parameters. Once the key business activities have been identified, the team should identify the key parameters driving performance for those activities. These are the parameters that should be benchmarked. In a program described in *The McKinsey Quarterly* (1991, no. 1), one company considered that its purchasing function was a key to its success. It then determined eight key parameters to benchmark:

- Number of suppliers per buyer.
- Vendor lead times.
- Time to place orders.
- Late deliveries.
- Parts shortages.
- Instances of parts rejection.
- Number of joint supplier quality assurance programs to ensure quality of incoming parts.
- Number of buyers per unit value of purchases.

TABLE 7–2
Customer Measures of Performance

	1991	1990
Ranking of Reasons for Choosing an Airline		
Safety	1	1
Punctuality	2	2
Scheduling	3	4
Cabin staff	4	5
Leg room	5	3
Route network	6	6
Price	7	10
Peace and quiet	8	9
Frequent flyers' program	9	8
Connections	10	–
Ranking of Reasons for Choosing a Hotel		
Location	1	1
Quality of service	2	2
Comfort	3	3
Peace and quiet	4	4
Price	5	6
Room size	6	5
Quality of food	7	7
Sport and leisure	8	10
Business facilities	9	9
Prestige value	10	8

Source: *Euromoney* "The 1991 Business Travel Survey."

Once the key parameters have been determined, the company then needs to establish its performance against these parameters. Benchmarking frequently shows that companies don't know how they perform against their key business parameters.

Who Should You Use as a Benchmark?

Benchmarking will frequently incorporate competitor analysis. This involves analyzing a company's performance and products against major competitors. Techniques such as reverse engineering and market analysis may be useful when formulating a product or marketing strategy.

But benchmarking is a much broader concept. It looks at the skills and processes necessary to create world-beating performance. Sophisticated businesses don't restrict their attention to their own industry. They frequently look at other industries where similar processes are employed. This enables you not just to equal your competitors' performance but to leapfrog over them.

A variety of organizations may be used as a benchmark, including

1. *Other parts of your own organization, including other departments, divisions, or companies.* Here information is likely to be accessible, but this may produce insular, unchallenging results.

2. *Competitors.* This is useful because it shows how you're performing against your direct competitors'—the firms your customers could choose to buy from today if you fail to meet their requirements. Competitor analysis is a vital part of any business strategy. Its disadvantage is that it restricts you to performance standards currently achieved in your own industry. It's also generally difficult to get information from your direct competitors unless it's in the public domain.

3. *Other industries.* Companies in different industry sectors than your own may carry out similar activities in a totally different way. For example, a key activity in the fresh food industry is supply management. Here it's vital to ensure the delivery of the correct quantities of food on a daily or hourly basis. Some companies have studied the lessons learned in the fresh food industry to identify techniques to streamline just-in-time manufacturing activities. The main advantage of this approach is that opportunities for dramatic improvement may be available as a result of adopting radically different techniques. It's also generally easier to develop a relationship with non-competitors so that information and visits can be exchanged. But be aware that not all techniques may be transferrable. An open mind is needed to see the possibilities that may be available, but don't underestimate the difficulties that may arise when trying to implement radical new ideas.

How Can You Get Appropriate Information?

Two principal types of information are required for an effective benchmarking program.

1. Who is a world-class performer at the activity you wish to benchmark? This information can be obtained from a number of sources, such as
   a. Customers and suppliers—they'll often have information on your competitors and their performance in certain areas.
   b. Journalists, academics, consultants and stockbrokers—they may often have a wider view of other industries.
   c. Trade associations for your own or other industries.
   d. Your employees—they may well have useful experience, especially of the retail and service industries.
2. How do you get the necessary information to use as a benchmark? In most cases you can only obtain information on what has been achieved by a business. Information isn't readily available to describe how successes have been achieved. Principal sources of information include
   a. Published accounts, market sector reports, and business magazines.
   b. Trade association reports. These are often a useful source of information on competitors who won't exchange information directly.
   c. Customer surveys (by interview or questionnaire).
   d. Approaching companies directly. This may be possible when the company isn't a direct competitor and you can offer information in exchange. This is often the only way to gain data on *how* the performance standard was achieved in practice.

What Have Companies Done in Practice?

Xerox regularly benchmarks a large number of parameters. Its guiding principle is "Anything anyone else can do better, we should aim to do at least equally well." After studying the distribution systems of a number of major companies, Xerox found that

- It held extra stock unnecessarily.
- Information took a day longer than needed to reach the center from the field.
- Other companies improved their warehousing through efficient manual methods, not necessarily through automation.

- Availability of stock in the best warehouses was 90 percent, but in Xerox it was 83 percent.

Xerox uses the results of its benchmarking program to set targets for its Quality Management Program.

ICL regularly compares its performance against that of its 20 leading competitors. This analysis covers a number of criteria relating to product and business performance, such as:

- Outstanding debts as a percentage of revenue.
- Expenditure on R&D as a percentage of revenue.
- Return on capital.
- Revenue per employee.
- Product reliability.
- Delivery time and delivery reliability.

The information obtained for this benchmarking program is analyzed and distributed throughout the company so that everyone is aware of the performance gaps and the needed improvements. (The information on Xerox and ICL used in this chapter is from the DTI booklet "Best Practice Benchmarking").

A Continuous Process: When Should You Use Benchmarks?

Benchmarking can provide valuable information at all stages in the life of a business. One opportunity that's frequently overlooked is at the start of a new venture. At this time key long-term decisions may be taken that influence how the business will develop. Establishing world-class performance measures for key activities at the outset will help to ensure a firm foundation for future operations.

Having completed a benchmarking program, it's important to continue to monitor performance. Benchmarking is a continuous process. Every business seeks to improve its performance. As a result, last year's benchmarks are usually out of date so it's important continuously to

1. Check performance against benchmarks.
2. Update benchmarks for improvements in the performance of your competitors.
3. Review the activities being benchmarked to ensure that they're still key to the success of the business.

4. Seek to identify emerging key parameters that may provide a basis for future benchmarks.

What are the Limitations of Benchmarking?

Benchmarking is only one of a range of tools that can help businesses to remain competitive. It's a very powerful technique for helping identify performance targets for key parameters. But we must understand its principal limitations:

1. Benchmarking alone won't tell you what customers actually want. If your product is obsolete, no amount of improvements in production processes will make it competitive.

2. Benchmarking can lead management to focus attention on existing competitive issues. By the time management has developed a response to these threats, the competition may have moved on. We must not lose sight of the importance of forecasting emerging threats. Look to the future and try to identify the key competitive features that are likely to emerge over the next 5 to 10 years, and establish benchmarks for those activities.

3. Benchmarking is only the first step on the road to improvement. A company will only benefit if it implements improvements.

4. Benchmarking only identifies the performance levels. Little guidance may be given about how to achieve the desired improvements. Management must seek to understand how this level of performance was achieved. It must then try to identify how the same, or better, performance can be achieved in its own business.

How Do You Start?

As with all forms of analysis, it's important to start by planning the program. Because almost any activity can be benchmarked, we must determine the activities that are key to the business's success. Key parameters can then be identified and measured. These are the principal candidates for benchmarking. Then we must find the best available company to act as a benchmark.

A successful benchmarking program can be broken down into a number of key phases:

1. Form a benchmarking team. This should include key decision makers and process specialists. It will probably involve from 6 to 12 people.
2. Determine those activities that are key to the business's success and where improvements need to be made.
3. Establish performance measurements for your own company for these key activities.
4. Identify companies that achieve world-class performance in these areas.
5. Gather information on these companies' performance standards. If possible, arrange to talk with their managers and workers to understand how their performance was achieved.
6. Identify lessons that can be learned from these companies and devise a way to implement them. Implement an improvement program to achieve world-class performance.

The following guidelines are useful in benchmarking:

1. Avoid gathering too much information. This can lead to "analysis paralysis." Focus on a few critical areas rather than too many at once.
2. Benchmarking is expensive. If it's undertaken without an action plan to control, measure, and improve performance, it wastes time and money.
3. Details of how world-class performance has been achieved can only be obtained by talking to the company personnel. A statement that a radical improvement in performance has been achieved by another company is of limited use unless there's accompanying information on how this was achieved. With that data you can determine how these methods can be adapted for use in your company. To this end the basis for comparison must be valid; otherwise the results are only of limited value to your company.
4. It's usually only worth benchmarking those activities that improve customer satisfaction or influence the bottom line.
5. Remember that benchmarking only shows what other companies are already achieving. The important issues change with time. You must devise a forward-looking

program that provides information on the performance standards for the next generation.

QUALITY FUNCTION DEPLOYMENT (QFD)

Quality Function Deployment (QFD) is a planning tool to help businesses focus on their customers' needs when setting design and manufacturing specifications. It draws together marketing, engineering, and manufacturing skills from the moment the project is first conceived and ensures that products are designed to reflect customers' needs and desires.

The principal tool in QFD is the *House of Quality*, a matrix showing the relationship between customer requirements and engineering characteristics (Figure 7–3). Using this tool, companies can reconcile customer needs against design and manufacturing constraints. The model is very flexible and enables a company to record how important each characteristic is to its customers and how difficult it is to modify. This enables the trade-offs between characteristics to be made on the basis of objective criteria.

Who Uses QFD?

QFD was first developed in Japan in 1972 by Mitsubishi for use in its Kobe shipyard. The process has since been developed by Toyota and its suppliers for designing motor cars. Today the technique is used widely in Japan and now being adopted in the United States and Europe by companies such as DEC, Hewlett-Packard, AT&T, Ford, and General Motors.

In Japan, the tool has been used successfully for controlling the design and manufacturing of a wide range of products and services including

- Consumer electronics.
- Cars.
- Domestic appliances.
- Integrated circuits.
- Clothing.
- Local amenities, retail outlets, and housing.

FIGURE 7–3
Basic Outline for the House of Quality

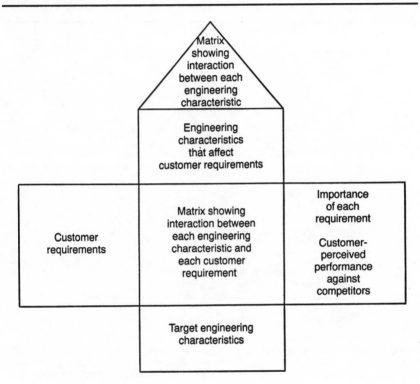

Companies are naturally reluctant to talk about how they utilize QFD in practice because of commercial sensitivity surrounding the product development cycle. Being first in the market with a successful new product provides a significant competitive advantage. Companies are naturally keen to retain this advantage.

What Are the Benefits of QFD?

QFD ensures that a company focuses on understanding the customer's requirements *before* any design work is carried out. This may lengthen the planning phase of design projects, but it generally reduces both the overall length of the design phase and the number of postrelease design changes.

FIGURE 7–4
A Japanese Automaker with QFD Made Fewer Changes than a US Company without QFD

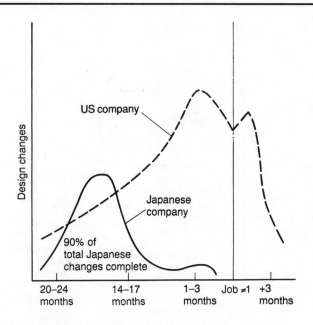

Figure 7–4 shows QFD's tremendous impact on streamlining the introduction of new models. The figure compares the number and phasing of design changes introduced by a Japanese car maker using QFD with those of a US car maker that doesn't use it.

QFD has seven key benefits

1. It focuses the design of new products and services on customer requirements. It ensures that customer requirements are understood and that the design process is driven by objective customer needs rather than by technology.

2. It prioritizes design activities. This ensures that the design process is focused on the most significant customer requirements.

FIGURE 7–5
Start-Up and Preproduction Costs at Toyota Auto Body before and after QFD

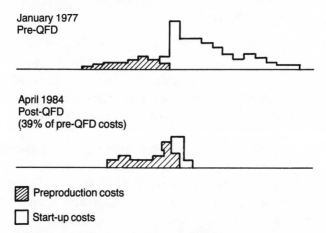

January 1977
Pre-QFD

April 1984
Post-QFD
(39% of pre-QFD costs)

▧ Preproduction costs

☐ Start-up costs

Source: Reprinted by permission of *Harvard Business Review*. An exhibit from "The House of Quality" by John R. Hauser and Don Clausing (May–June 1988). Copyright © 1988 by the President and Fellows of Harvard College; all rights reserved.

3. It analyzes the performance of the company's products against those of its principal competitors for key customer requirements.

4. By focusing the design effort, it reduces the overall length of the design cycle and hence reduces the time to market for new products. Current estimates put this saving at between one-third and one-half of the pre-QFD cycle time.

5. It reduces the number of postrelease design changes by ensuring that focused effort is put into the planning phase. This significantly reduces the cost of introducing new designs. Figure 7–5 shows QFD's impact on start-up and preproduction costs at Toyota Auto Body.

6. It promotes teamwork and breaks down barriers between departments by involving marketing, engineering, and manufacturing from the outset of each project. Each team member is of equal importance and has something to contribute to the process.

7. It provides a means of documenting the process and gives a sound basis on which design decisions can be made. This helps guard the project against unforeseen changes in personnel.

How Does QFD Work?

The simple concept behind QFD represents a commonsense approach to designing new products. In practice it relies on the constructive interaction between design, marketing, production, and engineering departments. It may be necessary to overcome organizational problems in companies that aren't geared up to operate cross-functional teams.

Using the example of one customer attribute for a car door to illustrate the flow of information, QFD works as follows. The flow of information (illustrated in Figure 7–6) was first discussed in "The House of Quality" by John R. Hauser and Don Clausing (*Harvard Business Review*, May–June 1988, pp. 63–72).

1. Details of customer requirements (termed *attributes*) are collected and weighted in terms of importance by the marketing department. The customer attribute here is "Doesn't leak in rain."
2. These customer attributes are translated into key engineering characteristics, such as "water resistance in pounds per square inch (psi)."
3. At this stage we can compare the product's performance against customer preferences, and against competitors' products. This process identifies key areas demanding improvement.
4. We can then assess objectively the impact of engineering changes on customer attributes and other engineering characteristics. For example, increasing the resistance to water penetration may make the door more difficult to close.
5. By assessing factors such as the technical difficulty of introducing engineering changes, the importance of characteristics to customers, and the estimated cost of making the changes, we can determine the target outcome for each engineering characteristic. For example, water resistance has been specified at 70 psi.
6. Engineering characteristics may be translated into a product specification in terms of, for example, the thickness of the weather stripping required around the door (Phase II).

FIGURE 7-6
The Translation of Customer Requirements into Production Planning Using the House of Quality

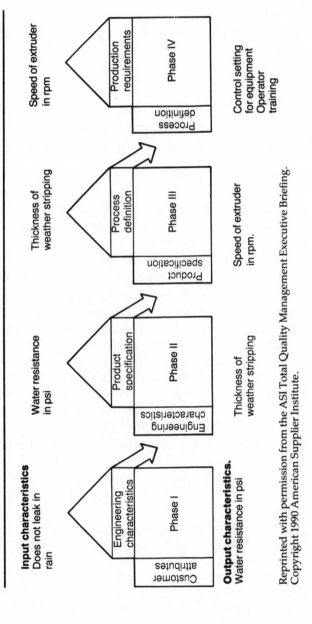

Reprinted with permission from the ASI Total Quality Management Executive Briefing. Copyright 1990 American Supplier Institute.

7. The process requirements for producing the required weather stripping can then be defined (Phase III) in terms of, for example, the speed of the extruder used to make it.

8. Production requirements (such as control settings and operator training) can then be defined (Phase IV).

The House of Quality

The House of Quality is a powerful tool, but it can appear quite complex at first sight. Figure 7–3 shows its basic components.

1. Customer attributes are detailed along the left-hand side of the house.

2. These are then prioritized. The performance of the company and its competitors against these attributes is detailed along the right-hand side of the house.

3. Engineering characteristics that may affect one or more customer attributes are listed along the top of the house.

4. A matrix showing the relationship between the engineering characteristics and the customer requirements completes the body of the house. A number or symbol is used to show the strength of this relationship and whether it's positive or negative. This matrix shows the impact of changes in engineering characteristics on customer attributes. Changing an engineering characteristic may reduce its ability to meet a particular customer attribute (a negative relationship) or it may increase it (a positive relationship).

5. The house's roof shows the interaction between different engineering characteristics. It demonstrates how a change in one characteristic may positively or negatively affect another. Again, a number or symbol is used to show the strength of the relationship.

6. The measured performance of each engineering characteristic of the product is then compared with its principal competitors along the bottom of the matrix. The bottom of the matrix may also be used to list any other information that the team needs to consider when setting targets for engineering characteristics. This might include, for example, the cost to implement changes or the technical difficulty of the change.

7. Finally, the team records the design targets for each engineering characteristic along the bottom of the matrix. This is the result of intensive discussions between the members of the multidisciplinary team.

QFD in practice.   When undertaking a QFD project, more than 100 customer requirements may be identified for an individual product. The QFD matrix enables these requirements and the engineering characteristics that cause them to be met to be displayed in such a way that rational, informed decisions can be taken.

Building a House of Quality.   The following example shows a small part of a QFD matrix. Adapted and reprinted by permission of *Harvard Business Review*, it's an excerpt from "The House of Quality" by John R. Hauser and Don Clausing (May–June 1988; copyright © 1988 by the President and Fellows of Harvard College; all rights reserved).

The following commentary refers to Figure 7–7. Eight steps are necessary to build the House of Quality:

1. The marketing department identifies customer attributes for the product. In this case we're considering five requirements for a car door:

- Is easy to close from outside.
- Stays open on a hill.
- Is easy to open from outside.
- Doesn't leak in the rain.
- Makes no road noise.

These attributes are listed on the left-hand side of the house.

2. The importance of each of these requirements is then assessed. In complex cases, the least important attributes may be excluded from the matrix. The weighting given to attributes may be obtained directly from customers (for example, during surveys) or it may be based on the opinions and experience of the group.

3. Customer perceptions of the relative performance of the company's products, compared with that of its principal competitors, is recorded on the right-hand side of the house. Here we're interested in two competitor products: A and B.

FIGURE 7–7
House of Quality

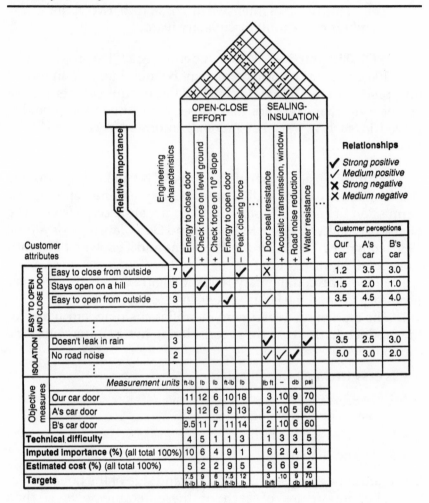

4. The engineering characteristics affecting customer attributes are recorded across the top of the matrix. These characteristics should be capable of being measured (for example, the force required to close a door in foot-pounds or Newtons). Each characteristic is prefixed by a + or − indicating whether an increase or decrease in its value is likely to be desirable. For example, the + in

front of "door seal resistance" indicates that an increase in the value of the seal resistance is likely to be an objective of the team. The – in front of "energy to close door" indicates that reducing the energy required to close the door is likely to be an objective.

5. The team discusses the impact of each engineering characteristic on each customer attribute. The consensus view is marked on the matrix. The strength of the effect and whether it's positive or negative are recorded. In this case, the group decided that the energy required to close the door had a strong positive influence on the customer attribute "easy to close" (meaning a reduction in the energy required to close the door would make it easier to close the door).

The group also decided that "door seal resistance" had a strong negative influence on the ease of closing the door, (meaning an increase in door seal resistance, although it would reduce leakage, would also make it harder to close).

From this example we can begin to see the trade-offs that the group must make when setting design criteria.

6. The group then completes the roof matrix. Here the impact of changing one engineering characteristic on all the other characteristics is recorded. Symbols are again used to indicate the strength of the relationship. In this case, increasing door seal resistance helps to reduce road noise and improve water resistance, but means that more energy is required to close the door.

7. Actual performance for each engineering characteristic is then compared with the product's principal competitors at the base of the house. This part of the house is often customized to give additional information that the team should take into account when making decisions.

In this case the company has recorded measures of the technical difficulty; cost to implement, and importance of making an improvement against each engineering characteristic.

8. Finally the group uses all the information on the matrix, together with its own judgment, to set target values for each characteristic. Here the most important customer attribute was felt to be "easy to close door from the outside." But in this the company's product performs poorly against its competitors'. The group therefore decides to look in detail at improving the door's ability to meet this attribute. Key engineering characteristics

affecting this customer attribute are (a) energy to close door, (b) peak closing force, and (c) door seal resistance.

Both (a) and (b) are positively related to the customer attribute, so the group decides to investigate these further.

The roof of the house indicates that reducing the energy to close the door has a positive effect on door opening energy and peak closing force, but it has a negative effect on check force on level ground, window acoustic transmission, and road noise.

The group then needs to balance the benefits arising from improving the door's ability to close easily with the impact on other customer attributes. The relative importance of the customer attributes as well as current performance against competitors and the cost of making the improvement are all taken into account at this stage.

In this case the group decided that improvements had to be made in the ease of closing the door from outside. Customers perceive this attribute to be important and the company's existing doors perform poorly. Target levels for the key engineering characteristics are then set. Here the target level of energy to close the door is set at 7.5 ft-lb, the aim in this case being to become better than the competitors.

Looking at the customer attribute "doesn't leak in rain," we find that two engineering characteristics have an impact: door seal resistance and water resistance. These are positively related. An improvement in door seal resistance would improve water resistance; and both would improve the door's overall water resistance.

Looking at the roof matrix, however, we see that these engineering characteristics have a strong negative impact on the energy required to open and close the door. Improving door seal resistance and water resistance would make it more difficult to reduce the energy required to open and close the door.

The company's existing door is perceived by customers to have better water resistance than its competitors' so it's decided not to adjust the target for these characteristics because any change would make it harder to close the door.

These examples demonstrate the complex interactions between engineering characteristics and customer attributes. QFD enables all the available information to be presented in a straightforward manner so that the impact of making trade-offs can be determined. This enables sound, complex decisions to be made.

The next steps. Having specified the target engineering characteristics, the team can develop the detailed product specification (Phase II), design the production processes (Phase III), and define the production requirements such as operator training and machine settings (Phase IV).

What Are the Requirements for Carrying Out QFD?

QFD requires commitment from both the project team and management if it's to be successful. Eight key factors help companies to ensure that QFD yields significant results.

1. Most importantly, the project team must have management's demonstrated, active support. QFD is time consuming. But it can become the core of an effective design strategy so the investment can be well rewarded.

2. The team requires time to pull together the necessary information, identify the key parameters, and draw up the House of Quality matrix. An experienced team may take some 16 to 20 hours to draw the first matrix if all the necessary information is available. In companies where this information isn't available, the project will take considerably longer to complete.

Experienced teams may choose to draw up the matrix during a two-day workshop. This may be necessary where team members are located some distance apart and all the information can be made available at one site. If there are no traveling problems, teams tend to meet for a series of two-hour sessions. Each session allows one part of the matrix to be completed, although an extended session may be required for the final decision matrix. This approach allows team members time to think about each part of the matrix and to gather additional information as the house is constructed.

3. Team members should be carefully selected. A representative should be drawn from the marketing, engineering, manufacturing, and quality functions. Team members should be chosen for

their ability to contribute to a team project and their ability to approach new ideas with an open mind.

4. The scope of the project and the team's objective should be clearly defined at the outset.

5. A team leader should be appointed who understands the project and can lead a team. The leader is responsible for ensuring that each team member contributes and that the project meets its objectives.

6. A facilitator who understands the QFD process can help the team to use the House of Quality approach.

7. A relatively easy project should be chosen for the first matrix so the team can learn how to use the House of Quality. A project involving redesigning an existing part may be a good starting point.

8. The team should make a formal presentation of its conclusions to management. A reasoned decision to accept or reject the conclusions should then be made quickly.

Where Does the Customer Information Come From?

QFD is driven by customer requirements so those requirements must be fully understood. In many cases there are a number of customers in a supply chain for any given product or service. A manufacturer may sell to a wholesaler who supplies a number of retail outlets. The retail outlets make sales to the final consumer. Each of these customers is likely to have different requirements.

Take, for example, the case of a kettle. The final customer buys the kettle to boil water. The retailer is likely to be looking for a product that's simple to display, robust during storage and handling and easy to repair. All customers must be identified so that their requirements can be established and taken into account during the design phase.

Companies actively seek customer information through

• Customer surveys and trials.
• Trade surveys and trials.
• Working with selected important customers.
• Competitor analysis.
• Focus groups.

In these cases the company can usually structure the request for information so that it receives the information it wants.

Other sources of information, although not actively sought by the company, have an important bearing on understanding customer requirements. These include

- Customer complaints.
- Legal standards and guidelines.
- Lawsuits against the company or against companies producing similar products or services.
- Informal customer comments and potential customer comments received from sources such as the sales force after customer visits, feedback from other employees, plus comments heard at conferences, training courses, and trade exhibitions.

This information is usually received in a variety of forms. Although it's generally difficult to interpret and use this type of information, it represents a vital source of information on customer requirements.

QUALITY AWARDS

A number of quality awards are made each year around the world. Each award is managed by a different organization using its own judging criteria. The awards generally command a high profile in their own country and sometimes around the world. Award programs can significantly raise the profile of quality in the business community and so may play an important role in a program of continuous quality improvement. In broad terms, the awards have three benefits:

1. They raise the profile of the continuous improvement of quality within the companies that apply for them. Publicizing the award winners and their successful introduction of quality improvements gives an important signal to their customers and employees and may also generate interest in total quality among other companies.

2. The application for an award can add a feeling of excitement to the improvement process. It may also lead to the

recognition of the whole company's achievement if the company wins an award.

3. The award criteria sometimes offer useful guidelines to companies wishing to implement a program of continuous quality improvement. This is particularly true for the Malcolm Baldrige National Quality Award whose application guidelines include detailed selection criteria. (We discuss the Baldrige Award later.)

However it's important to keep the awards' value in perspective. A number of potential pitfalls beset award programs despite the best efforts of the awarding bodies:

1. Companies shouldn't adopt the formal assessment criteria slavishly as a model for success. These criteria may not be appropriate for all businesses. The award criteria should only be used as guidelines, which may be adapted to suit an individual organization.

2. The application for an award should be the result, not the aim, of any continuous improvement program. Companies should focus on continuous improvement, not on winning a quality award. The key reward for a successful program of continuous improvement of quality is commercial success and improved customer satisfaction.

3. The application for an award can be time consuming and expensive. *Fortune* (July 1991) reported that in 1989 Corning's telecommunications division spent some 7,000 labor-hours just applying for the Malcolm Baldrige Award and didn't win! Resources shouldn't be diverted from the program of continuous quality improvement to apply for an award.

In summary, an application for a quality award can provide excitement and renewed focus for an established quality improvement program. The award criteria may also provide useful guidelines to companies that are in the process of introducing or wish to refocus an improvement program. But there's a danger that winning an award can become the goal rather than a consequence of the company's continuous quality improvement program.

Let's look at several specific quality awards.

The Deming Prizes

There are three categories of Deming Prizes open to Japanese individuals and organizations: the Deming Prize awarded to individuals, the Deming Application Prize awarded to companies, and the Deming Factory Prize. These awards have been operated by the Japanese Union of Scientists and Engineers (JUSE) for over 30 years. In 1970, a further award was established: the Japan Quality Control Award to companies demonstrating sustained commitment to Total Quality Control at least five years after receiving a Deming prize.

These awards focus heavily on Statistical Quality Control (i.e., improvement in quality through control of processes) as the basis of a Total Quality Control (TQC) environment. The audit checklist for the Deming prizes covers

- Corporate policy.
- Organization and administration.
- Education.
- Implementation in specific departments.
- Effects of TQC on product quality and other key parameters, such as profits, delivery, safety, and costs.
- How the company intends to carry the TQC program forward.

The Malcolm Baldrige National Quality Award

The Malcolm Baldrige National Quality Award is given for excellence in quality achievement and management. The annual award was established by the US Congress in 1987 to commemorate former Secretary of Commerce Malcolm Baldrige and to encourage quality improvement throughout US industry. The award is funded by application fees, responsibility for the award lies with the US Department of Commerce and it is widely supported by the government.

On the front cover of the 1991 application guidelines for the award, then-President George Bush states, "The improvement of quality in products and the improvement of quality in service—these are national priorities as never before."

Robert Mossbacher during his term as US secretary of commerce
said, "The winners of this award have made quality improvement
a way of life. Quality is their bottom line, and that kind of can-do
attitude makes for world-class products and services."

There are three categories of award: manufacturing industry,
service industry, small business (fewer than 500 employees). Up to
two awards can be made annually in each category. But since 1988,
when the first award was made, only nine awards have been
given.

1988:	Globe Metallurgical Motorola Westinghouse—Commercial Nuclear Fuel Division
1989:	Milliken and Company Xerox Business Products and Systems
1990:	General Motors—Cadillac Motor Car IBM—Rochester Federal Express Corporation Wallace Co Inc
1991:	Solectron Corporation Zytec Corporation Marlow Industries
1992:	AT&T Network Systems Texas Instruments Defense Systems Ritz-Carlton Hotel Granite Rock Company AT&T Universal Cards System

Awards are only open to for-profit organizations in the United
States or its territories.

Administrators of the Baldrige Award issue detailed guidelines
to prospective applicants. In addition to instructions on how to
apply for the award, the guidelines include a comprehensive list of
criteria against which applicants are judged. The company must
address 7 categories and 32 items in its submission. The guidelines
also detail the weightings given to each selection criterion.

To apply for the award, a company must submit a report setting
out its achievements against the award criteria (maximum 75
pages). A panel of judges considers each report and then scores
each item. Scores are then totaled. Companies that score highly on

the written submission are then subject to a three-to-four–day visit by a panel of judges to ensure that the submission is accurate. (Judges receive training on how to assess applicants against the selection criteria. Judges stand for re-election each year.) At the end of the judging process, each company receives a feedback report on its performance.

In addition to capturing business imagination and raising the profile of quality, the major strengths of the Baldrige Award are (1) clear guidelines on continuous improvement and (2) the feedback report that every applicant receives.

There are, however, some potential weaknesses in the system:

1. The whole process takes a lot of time and money. This may divert resources away from the principal objectives of the improvement process itself.

2. Some essential business objectives are missing from the criteria. These include innovation, long-term planning, financial performance, and the ability to change rapidly.

3. The award doesn't seem to focus on profitable businesses. IBM, Motorola, and Xerox have all seen profits fall since winning the award. A brief review of the award winners so far suggests that the award seems to favor blue-chip companies. Perhaps these are the only ones that can afford the necessary time and money to apply for the award?

4. Companies nominate themselves. The award might be more meaningful if companies were nominated by their customers. Customers are usually in the best position to verify the success, or otherwise, of quality improvements made by a supplier.

Baldrige Award criteria. The Baldrige Award's selection criteria provides useful ideas for companies committed to continuous quality improvement although each point's relevance to individual businesses should be assessed. Ten key concepts underlie the Baldrige Award criteria:

1. Quality is defined by the customer.

2. The senior leadership of the business needs to create clear quality values and build the values into the way the company operates.

3. Quality excellence derives from well-designed, well-executed systems and processes.
4. Continuous improvement must be part of the management of all systems and processes.
5. Companies need to develop goals as well as strategic and operational plans to achieve quality leadership.
6. Shortening the response time of all operations and processes of the company needs to be part of the quality improvement effort.
7. Operations and decisions of the company need to be based on facts and data.
8. All employees must be suitably trained, developed, and involved in quality activities.
9. Design quality and defect and error prevention should be major elements of the quality system.
10. Companies need to communicate quality requirements to suppliers and work to elevate supplier quality performance.

These concepts form part of the 1991 award guidelines published by the National Institute of Standards and Technology, a branch of the US Department of Commerce.

The British Quality Award

Founded in 1984, this award is administered by the British Quality Association (BQA), an association of companies committed to quality improvement. One or more awards may be made each year. Special commendations are also made for finalists achieving significant quality improvements.

Entries are judged by a panel of 10 individuals with extensive practical experience in quality management. Selection of these judges appears to be by nomination rather than by open application. No specific training is given to the judges about the selection criteria for the awards.

The BQA's principal criterion in judging the competition is evidence of significant, sustained improvement in quality over a period of at least four years. This improvement can be associated with product design or manufacture, planning or operation of a service, or development or operation of a process.

Judges look for a process of continuous improvement. Key features they seek include

- Satisfying customer requirements at competitive cost.
- Improved product or service performance.
- Technological innovation to improve product quality.
- Measurable commercial and operational success.
- Motivation and education of personnel to improve quality.
- A substantially higher quality standard than that prevalent within the industry as a whole.

No further information has been published to explain these criteria, although it's understood that the BQA is considering issuing guidelines.

A company applies for an award by submitting a report addressing the preceding criteria. The judges study the reports and select approximately a dozen finalists for a site visit. Judges give no feedback to the companies at any stage in the competition (which would be of considerable benefit to applicants). No charge is currently made to applicants.

TEAMWORK FOR QUALITY

The objective of Quality Improvement is to increase the organization's effectiveness and profitability by improving its ability to meet external customers' requirements at minimum cost. This requires (1) clear understanding of external customer requirements and (2) internal processes that work effectively to produce the required output.

A Quality Improvement Program (QIP) is a planned and structured approach to resolving problems causing nonconforming output. Three principal types of teams may be set up to achieve specific objectives as part of a QIP:

1. A Quality Improvement Team plans and directs the QIP.
2. Corrective action task forces resolve complex problems and typically include representatives from a number of departments.

3. Progress groups are small problem solving groups drawn from one department.

Here are further details about the teams' activities plus guidelines for effective teamwork.

Quality Improvement Team (QIT)

In most companies, significant changes are required when implementing a Quality Improvement Program. To plan and direct the program's implementation, most companies form a Quality Improvement Team. This team should be composed of a chairperson, an administrator, and a representative from each department.

Selection of the chairperson and administrator is important since they'll become deeply involved in the program and will direct the running of the Quality Improvement Team. Key requirements for the members of the QIT include

1. The chairperson should be selected by the general manager and management team. Senior management must have confidence in the person chosen.

2. The chairperson should be a senior member of management who understands and enthusiastically supports the need for Quality Improvement and is committed to defect prevention. The chairperson may be from any department within the company. In view of the importance of this role, she needs to be able to devote approximately 20 percent of her time to the QIP. Ideally the chairperson shouldn't be the Quality Manager because this reinforces the myth that quality is really the responsibility of the quality department. Quality is everyone's responsibility!

3. Having been appointed, the chairperson selects the rest of the team in conjunction with the department heads. As all departments are involved in the QIP, they must all be represented on the QIT.

4. The appointment of the administrator generally needs to be approved by the general manager since he'll need to devote approximately 50 percent of his time to the QIP.

5. At the start of the program, it's often useful for the team to consist of the senior management team. This ensures that the QIP receives sufficient management attention to get it off the ground,

and demonstrates senior management's commitment to the QIP. It's not essential for each QIT member to be the head of a department, but all team members must have the full support of their department heads. Each team member represents his department on the team and represents the QIT to the department.

6. In a unionized firm, once the need for a QIP has been accepted by the general manager and management team, union support for the program must be established. It may be desirable to include a union representative on the QIT.

The purpose of the QIT is to plan and direct implementation of the Quality Improvement Program. It's the responsibility of each department head to implement the program in her area.

The QIT should meet regularly. Its first objective is to develop the action plan for the Quality Improvement Program. Once completed, this should be presented to the general manager and management team for approval and support. Firm dates should be set for accomplishing each activity.

The general manager should regularly monitor progress of the QIP with the chairperson and administrator. This helps ensure that the QIP is kept on track and it assures the team that it has the support of the general manager and management team at all times.

Corrective Action Groups

An effective system to recognize and eliminate problems preventing Quality Improvement and performance of error-free work is essential in any QIP. To achieve this, it's generally necessary to consider introducing formal problem solving groups.

Progress groups (also known as quality circles). Progress groups generally include a small number of individuals from within one department who carry out similar work. The group meets regularly to identify, implement, and monitor the progress of actions taken to resolve problems arising within their work area. It may sometimes be necessary to involve other departments in discussions where they're affected by a particular problem.

Members of the progress groups must be trained so they understand QIP objectives and their role in Quality Improvement. Also they must understand how to investigate problems and implement effective solutions. Without adequate training, the group will find it difficult to implement effective solutions. This may well lead to the group losing interest and disbanding.

Unfortunately the concept of quality circles has a poor reputation in the United States and UK. Many quality circle initiatives introduced in the 1970s and 1980s failed—most often because they were introduced as an isolated measure in the hope that they would improve quality. Quality circles were rarely given sufficient authority or training to resolve significant problems. As a result, they were unable to make much impact. Team members lost interest and the teams disbanded.

The key problem here was that management wasn't prepared to invest sufficient resources to make the scheme work. Quality circles don't have the influence to change the culture of a business on their own. That requires the complete commitment of all employees; and the general manager must play a key role in this.

Quality circles do play an important role in businesses. Implemented as one element in a Total Quality Improvement Program, they give employees an active role in resolving the many problems they face on a day-to-day basis.

But quality circles' well-publicized failure in the past may lead to some resistance to their use. This may be overcome by using an alternative name (such as progress group or process action team).

Corrective action task force. Complex problems frequently arise during the course of a Quality Improvement Program. Sometimes these problems are particularly complex or contentious, or may involve a number of departments. To solve these problems it may be necessary to form a corrective action task force. A task force is established with the sole objective of identifying and eliminating the cause of a specific problem. A member from each department affected by the problem is appointed to the team. A task force may involve a substantial commitment from a number of people, so it's essential that only a small number of them operate at any one time. Accordingly, the authority to form a task force is typically restricted to the QIT.

The problem the task force is tasked to resolve should be clearly defined, and progress should be carefully monitored by the QIT. Once the task force's objectives have been achieved, it should be disbanded. Typical problems that may require the setting up of a task force include:

- Problems identified by the management team when formulating the company's strategic business objectives.
- Problems identified during the education sessions.
- Problems identified by progress groups that such groups can't resolve.
- Complex problems identified by the Error Cause Removal system.

Teamwork Methods

Effective teams can develop plans and solutions to problems that couldn't be resolved by individuals working on their own. Managing a team to work effectively and get the best out of each team member can be a complex operation. Its success depends on each individual team member's personal strengths and commitment. This section describes a number of practical ideas to help ensure that teams run smoothly.

Team dynamics. Teams are formed to find solutions to problems. If this simply involved applying problem solving techniques (identifying the problem and potential causes, gathering data, and recommending and implementing a solution), life would be easy. However, when people get into groups, hidden concerns may get in the way of progress and prevent a team from working effectively. If you're aware of the potential pitfalls, these problems may be avoided.

When individuals are chosen to work in a team, they'll inevitably have a number of potential concerns. These may fall into two principal categories:

1. *Identity in the team.* You must help individuals feel that (1) they're an active member of the team who can influence the collective decisions and (2) that all team members are pulling together to find a solution to the common problem.

2. *Identity in the organization.* Individuals will generally retain responsibilities in their departments and will want to know that their duties for the team won't result in any conflict with depart-

mental objectives. Usually it's the team project that suffers if conflict does arise so it's important to ensure that the team objectives don't conflict with team members' departmental objectives.

The team's identity within the organization is also important. For the team to succeed, the team and its objectives must be fully supported by management. This helps to attract people to the team and ensure their commitment to the project. It may also help ensure that the solutions proposed by the team are implemented.

Setting up a successful team. Before the team is set up, it's important to lay the groundwork for success. A team's success or failure can often be determined by the level of preparation before it's established. Key features of a successful team are

- A well-defined objective or purpose.
- Appropriate team members.
- Management support for the team's activities.

Objectives of the team. A formal objective should be established for the team prior to beginning any investigation. The objective may be set by the team itself (in the case of a quality circle) or by management (in the case of a corrective action task force). For example, an accounts department monitoring the time customers take to settle their accounts in order to improve cash flow might set itself the following objective: "To analyze the reasons for the late payment (defined as after 90 days) of accounts by customers and to identify recommended solutions for consideration by the finance director."

Appropriate team members. Team members should be chosen carefully on the basis of the skills and experience they can bring to resolving the problem.

In the case of quality circles, all employees who carry out similar activities in a department should be encouraged to join the team since everyone involved has something to contribute. But if the team gets too large (over 15 people), it may be appropriate to split it into two circles.

Once it's set up, a team may evolve as further issues require consideration. For example, the team set up to resolve the problem of outstanding debts may initially consist only of accounting staff. Once more information is gathered about causes of the problem, it might be necessary to invite personnel from other departments (perhaps sales or service) to join the team.

Teams' principal individuals generally include a leader, a secretary, members, and specialists.

• *Team leader.* The team leader is responsible for the team's smooth running. Her success will generally be measured in terms of the team's success in identifying the problem's cause and implementing an effective solution. The team leader guides the group through the problem solving process, ensuring that appropriate steps are taken and using each member's skills to the fullest. A very difficult role, this requires organizational skill, tact, the ability to get people to work together, and often some inspiration to succeed!

The role of team leader may be rotated among team members in a quality circle. Usually this change in team leader occurs after one problem is solved and the group looks for a new problem to tackle. This avoids disturbing the flow of the problem solving process.

• *Secretary.* The secretary is responsible for the administration relating to the team. This includes notifying members of meetings, preparing minutes and action plans following meetings, and ensuring that assignments are completed according to schedule.

• *Members.* Team members are part of the team because their skills and experience may be necessary to help identify causes of a problem. Their role is to find a solution to the problem and help implement the proposed solution. Individual team members should ensure that their departments understand and support the team's work. They should also keep their departments informed of the team's progress.

• *Specialists.* Specialists attend a limited number of meetings to give the team the benefit of their experience on specific issues.

It is important that at least some members of each team have been trained in problem solving techniques. At a minimum the team leader should be trained in these skills. The team may then provide a means of teaching these problem solving skills to other team members. Chapter 8 highlights problem solving techniques.

Management support.   Management support is critical to a team's success. Before agreeing to set up and lead a problem solving team, the team leader must ensure that the team has management's full support. The level of support necessary depends on the nature of the problem to be resolved. Problems that involve a number of departments and are complex or contentious are likely to require considerable support. These problems are usually addressed by a corrective action task force, which requires the support of the whole Quality Improvement Team to set up. A local team looking at a local problem might only require the support of its departmental manager.

Running a team.   Teams are set up to help resolve problems and effect solutions. As a result, their work is often challenging and may not progress smoothly. Sometimes progress will be rapid; at other times progress may be slow or (hopefully not too often) things will seem to go backward.

A team's success in making progress often has an important impact on morale and hence the smooth running of the team. The team leader must monitor carefully the running of the team and help ensure that all members are working effectively toward the common goal by

- Building a team spirit within the group.
- Ensuring that basic ground rules are established and followed.
- Taking an interest in individual team members.
- Informally helping individual team members to resolve problems.
- Smoothing resistance to suggestions by holding informal discussions between meetings and laying the groundwork for a consensus view.
- Developing a sense of cohesion and common purpose for the team.
- Resolving tensions between group members.
- Ensuring that each member is involved in every meeting and that their views are treated with consideration by the rest of the team.

Running meetings.   During the problem solving process the team may meet many times to discuss the problem and decide on actions necessary to resolve it. The team will spend a lot of time and effort at meetings, so meetings should be run effectively and efficiently. Each team member is responsible for ensuring that meetings are positive and make progress.

At the start of a meeting (especially the first one) the team leader should welcome all the participants and remind them of the meeting's objectives. It's useful to initially ask each team member to introduce themselves and describe their roles. The team leader should then outline the proposed plan to identify and implement a solution to the problem.

Having opened the meeting the team leader is responsible for directing the flow of the meeting. Important points to watch out for are

- Ensure that everyone knows in advance the meeting's purpose and any preparation they're required to do for the meeting.
- Keep the meeting running to schedule.
- Ensure that discussion is focused on the points at issue. It's easy for meetings to be sidetracked and to achieve very little.
- Ensure that basic courtesies are followed and that everyone has the opportunity to express their ideas.
- Dynamize the team if it starts to flag and maintain a positive attitude among members. It's frequently useful to have a board to record ideas and help focus discussion during meetings.
- Ensure that everyone understands and follows the ground rules for meetings.

At the end of a meeting the team leader should summarize the points raised and progress made at the meeting. He should also agree with the secretary on the date when the minutes and action plan will be released. This should be shortly after the meeting, within 48 hours if possible.

Other team members should be prepared to undertake actions between meetings to progress the problem solving activity. Responsibility for specific actions should be recorded in the action plan drawn up by the team secretary.

Ground rules for meetings.   Here are eight useful rules for raising meetings' productivity.

1. Members should attend all meetings if at all possible. The secretary should be informed in advance if a member will be absent from a scheduled meeting. Members shouldn't leave during the meeting.

2. Team meetings should start and end on time. Everyone has other things that need to be done. Arriving late for a meeting wastes everyone's time; it's a cost of nonconformance!

3. The team secretary should find a convenient date for all the members required at the next meeting and then confirm it in a notice stating the date, start time, location, agenda, end time, and details of preparation required of members. It's useful if team members keep the secretary informed of progress in preparing material. The secretary should ensure that all assignments are completed to schedule. Prepared material may be circulated prior to the meeting to enable members to read it in advance, or it may be handed out at the meeting.

4. All meetings should have a stated objective. The team leader's role is to ensure that the objective is met.

5. Each member has an obligation to the rest of the team to contribute to the meeting to the best of his or her ability. All team members should be given the opportunity to express their ideas, which should be treated with respect by the rest of the team.

6. The effectiveness of each meeting should be evaluated to identify any improvements necessary for the next meeting.

7. For future reference a record should be kept of discussions and decisions taken at each meeting.

8. Often a team member must complete assignments between meetings (perhaps gathering or analyzing data or preparing a report on a specific aspect of the problem). The secretary should prepare an action plan following each meeting to record the actions and time scales agreed upon.

Chapter Eight

Problem Solving

WHY PROBLEM SOLVING IS IMPORTANT

A Quality Improvement Program is designed to increase a company's ability to compete in the marketplace. This demands that a company fulfill its customers' needs at minimum cost. This can only be achieved by (1) ensuring that the company understands its customers' needs, (2) ensuring that the company is organized to fulfill those needs, and (3) enabling all individuals within the company to carry out their jobs in the most efficient way possible. This requires the elimination of rework and checking activities and the introduction of means to prevent errors from arising.

One key means of eliminating rework and checking is by tackling all the problems that prevent people from performing their jobs right the first time. Employees' ability to recognize problems, trace their root causes, and implement effective corrective actions is fundamental to the success of a Quality Improvement Program.

Many problems facing modern businesses are complicated or involve more than one group of employees. Design teams should work with marketing teams to develop products that customers will want. They should also work with production to ensure that the product can be produced cost-effectively. The sales and production teams should work together to ensure the right product is delivered to the customer at the right time. In all these tasks, especially where a number of departments are involved, problems may arise that prevent employees from performing every task right the first time. These problems must be tackled and eliminated. Failure to do this may result in dissatisfied customers and increased costs due to excessive aftersale and warranty costs, delayed payment or bad debts, excess inventory, lost customers, or legal action.

To resolve problems effectively, it's generally necessary to set up dedicated groups to investigate and eliminate them. This requires management support to ensure that they have the correct tools and training to enable them to identify the root cause of problems and implement corrective actions to eliminate them.

PROBLEM SOLVING GROUPS

Problems principally arise because of a failure in a process to produce conforming output. Problem solving groups, therefore, focus on analysis and investigation of processes. Problems in business can broadly be divided into two categories: those involving only one department and those affecting more than one department.

As a result, two principal types of problem solving teams may be recognized: *progress groups* (also called *quality circles*) and *corrective action task forces*. A task force is a team formed to solve a particularly difficult problem affecting more than one department. It's disbanded as soon as the problem is solved. Progress groups are formed within a department to solve problems affecting only that department. Progress groups don't generally disband once a problem is resolved but turn their attention to another problem within the department.

PROBLEM SOLVING METHODOLOGY

For a problem solving team to be effective it needs to understand how to investigate a problem, find its root cause, and implement a solution. To do this, groups need to understand a range of problem solving techniques. This chapter describes an effective methodology for solving a problem from identification to the implementation of the final solution. You must understand each problem solving tool and how it can be used in the problem solving process. You must also understand how the tools link together to provide a simple, powerful, proven method for investigating and resolving problems at all levels within an organization.

Figure 8–1's flowchart illustrates the principal steps in this problem solving methodology.

FIGURE 8–1
Flowchart of Problem Solving Methodology

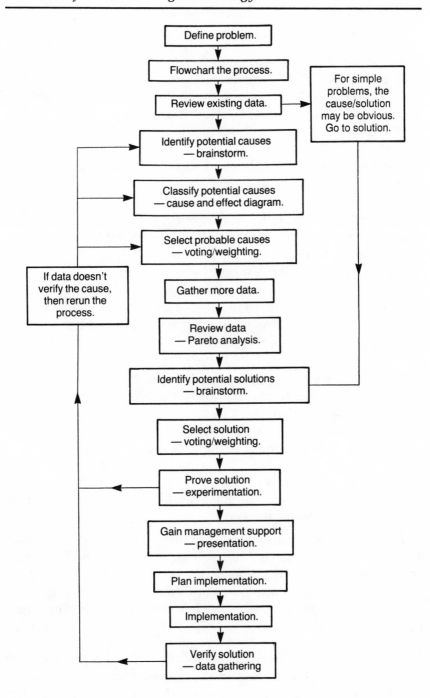

Define the Problem

Before starting to investigate a problem, you must ensure that it's fully understood. This involves defining its symptoms and understanding the process that gives rise to the problem. This helps to avoid wasting effort in the problem solving process. A problem that's fully understood and defined is well on the way to being solved.

The two tools commonly used to help define a problem are checklists and flowcharting.

Checklist method.   Answering the following questions as fully as possible helps to ensure that the problem is thoroughly understood.

What?	What is the problem?
	What has been observed?
Who?	Who's involved in the problem?
	Who's upstream/downstream of the problem?
Where?	Where does it show up?
	Where does it originate?
When?	On what occasion does it appear?
	At what time and for how long does it appear?
How?	How does it show itself?
	How often does it occur?
	How important is the problem—time wasted?
	—cost?
	—frequency?
Why?	Why does the problem occur? This is the key question we seek to answer.

This approach focuses attention on the problem and helps weld together newly formed problem solving groups. At the first meeting, groups often find that they don't know the answers to all these questions. If so, they must find out more about the problem to avoid wasted effort later in the problem solving process. Only then can they try to solve it.

Flowchart method.   Having fully defined a problem, we must understand the process giving rise to it before attempting to identify the cause. Flowcharting provides a means to ensure that every stage in the process and its links to the next stage are understood. A flowchart is basically a picture describing the process as a series of activities, each linked to the next. A problem's cause may lie in any one or more of the activities associated with the process. We must understand the interaction between activities before trying to look for potential causes of the problem. Figure 8–2 shows a simple flowchart describing the process of cashing a check at the bank.

Constructing a flowchart.   When drawing a flowchart the following guidelines are useful:

1. The right people must be involved in drawing the chart. The people involved in the activity, their suppliers, and their customers should generally all be involved. If other people are identified as being involved in the activity when drawing the chart, a decision should be taken as to how these people should be involved in the flowcharting process.

2. All members of the team should be involved in drawing the flowchart. A clear understanding of how the process works is key to the successful resolution of a problem.

3. If the flowchart is prepared at a meeting, it should be visible to all members of the group at all times.

4. Flowcharting usually takes more time than initially anticipated. More than one session is often required. This may be useful as it enables group members to find out more about the process between sessions.

5. Before beginning the flowchart, the group should decide how detailed the flowchart needs to be. A very detailed flowchart is time-consuming to construct and may not always be required.

6. Questions are the key to a successful flowchart. A good team leader will ensure that the group asks questions throughout the process. Useful questions include

   • What is the first thing that happens?
   • What happens next?
   • Where does the service/material come from?
   • How does it get there?
   • When a decision is required within the process, who makes it?

FIGURE 8–2
Simple Flowchart of the Process of Cashing a Check

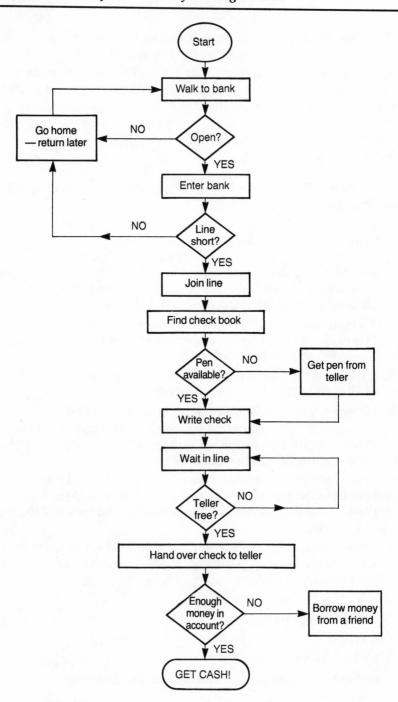

- What happens if the decision is yes/no?
- Where does the product/service go next?
- What tests are performed on the product/service?

Identify and Classify Potential Causes

Once a problem and the process giving rise to it are fully understood and defined, the group must decide on the most likely
cause(s) of the problem. To avoid jumping to conclusions (which
may later prove incorrect), it's necessary to adopt a systematic
approach to first identify all the potential causes and then home
in on the most likely cause. The following steps may be used to
do this:

1. Identify potential causes through
   a. Reviewing existing data.
   b. Brainstorming.
2. Classify and select probable causes by using
   a. Cause and effect diagrams.
   b. Voting and weighting techniques.

Reviewing existing data.   When investigating a problem,
we often find that relevant data already exist within the
organization. We must review this data since they might prove
useful as a guide for subsequent steps in the problem solving
process. Occasionally, for simple problems, existing data may be
sufficient to identify the problem's cause so the group can then
move directly to identifying a solution. But more likely, insufficient
data are available or data aren't directly relevant to enable the
problem's cause to be identified. Perhaps the existing data only
provide circumstantial evidence to indicate potential causes of the
problem. These can be considered during subsequent stages of the
problem solving process.

When reviewing existing data, we should look for threads of
(dis)similarity. Consider the problem of incorrect sales orders. An
analysis of existing data may reveal that

- The problem occurs no matter who enters the order in the sales
  office (similarity).

- It also occurs with orders received from one salesman, Joe, but not from Elizabeth (dissimilarity).

- Errors occur on orders entered directly by the salesperson (who usually uses a printed product listing as a database) but not on orders entered directly by the sales office (which uses an on-line computer database) (dissimilarity).

These data don't identify a definite cause of the problem but they do provide useful information about the potential cause. In this example, analyzing the data in this way would lead you to look more closely at differences between (1) the printed product listing and the computer database and (2) what Elizabeth and Joe do. But it doesn't directly identify the problem's cause. To display the threads of similarity within data it's often useful to use a matrix (Figure 8–3). To get as much information as possible from the data, it's useful to ask the questions detailed in the checklist in the section on defining the problem.

Brainstorming. The objective of brainstorming is to ensure that all potential causes of a problem are identified at the beginning of the problem solving process. It can be used to supplement existing data or to generate ideas when no data are available. It's a creative process that uses all members' knowledge of the problem, their creativity, and any data already available to generate as many ideas as possible about possible causes of the problem. Brainstorming should be fun to do and may be used to build a relaxed and familiar atmosphere within the group right at the start of the project.

Brainstorming is a means of generating as many ideas as possible by allowing the creative thought process of each person in the group to freewheel. It's vital to allow all ideas to come to the surface and be expressed. This will only happen if the atmosphere is relaxed and all ideas are accepted without criticism. To help develop a relaxed atmosphere and keep some structure to such a freewheeling process, six steps should generally be followed:

1. A group leader should be appointed to ensure that everyone understands the problem. She then ensures that (1) all the brainstorming ideas are written down where everyone can see them and (2) the brainstorming rules are followed.

FIGURE 8–3
Matrix for Recording Threads of Similarity Data

	Problem occurs	Problem doesn't occur
Who		
Where		
When		
How		

2. Everyone spends 5 to 10 minutes, in silence, thinking about the problem and jotting down their ideas.

3. Each group member, in turn, then calls out an idea. At this stage all ideas are written down. No comments or criticism are allowed. Only the person calling out the idea and the person writing down the idea should be allowed to speak during this stage.

4. The leader should move quickly from one idea to the next, passing over anyone who's short of a suggestion. All ideas should be welcomed and encouraged.

5. Figure 8–4 shows a typical cycle for the generation of ideas during a brainstorming session. The initial stage where ideas flow thick and fast usually lasts about 20 minutes. Then there's generally a lull, followed by a second peak after about 25 minutes. It's important to continue brainstorming through this lull since the second peak often produces the most creative ideas. These will frequently have been built on ideas generated earlier in the session. For this reason you should keep all the ideas in front of everyone during the brainstorming session.

6. After about 30 minutes, when ideas have started to dry up, the group should review and discuss its list. Duplicated and related ideas can be grouped together and unrealistic ideas can be eliminated. This phase must be handled sensitively to ensure that ideas aren't criticized. The person who proposed the idea may withdraw it, or the group may vote to accept or reject the ideas presented.

Cause and effect diagrams.   Once a list of potential causes has been generated, it's necessary to whittle these down into a working list of probable causes. The "80/20" (Pareto) rule suggests that most of the problem (perhaps 80 percent) will be caused by a few of the causes (perhaps 20 percent). Direct effort at finding these 20 percent so you can maximize the return on effort. Once the most likely causes are identified they may be used to guide the data gathering exercise when you try to prove the actual cause of the problem.

To analyze the ideas generated during brainstorming, it's generally useful to group ideas together under appropriate headings. This can help to identify major potential causes of a problem. A cause and effect diagram (also called an Ishikawa, or fishbone, diagram) is often used at this stage because it provides a clear visual picture of the problem, showing potential causes and links between individual causes.

The following steps describe how to generate a cause and effect diagram:

1. The group agrees on the problem (or effect) being investigated. This is written in the box on the right-hand side of the page. Figure 8–5 shows an outline cause and effect diagram.
2. A long arrow is drawn from left to right. This is the central branch or fishbone.
3. The group identifies the principal categories of potential causes of the problem being investigated. These major cause categories are drawn as arrows pointing toward the main branch. Figure 8–6 illustrates the categories chosen for the problem of persistent car breakdown. If no obvious categories come to mind at this stage, then it's useful to

FIGURE 8–4
Typical Cycle of Ideas Generated During Brainstorming

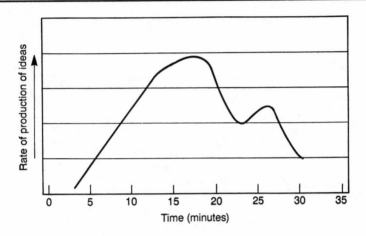

FIGURE 8–5
Outline of a Cause and Effect Diagram

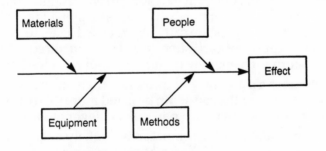

consider the key factors that affect processes, namely machines (equipment), materials, methods (procedures), and people. These are useful general headings to start the process rolling.

FIGURE 8–6
Cause and Effect Diagram to Study the Problem of Car Breakdown

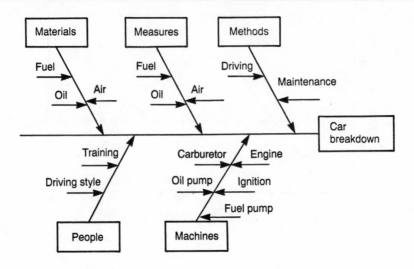

4. The potential causes identified during brainstorming can then be listed under the appropriate headings.

5. In some cases the group may brainstorm directly onto the cause and effect diagram by asking the question, What would contribute to each of the main causes? Having identified subcauses, the question can then be asked again to determine possible causes of each subcause. This structured form of brainstorming generally requires skillful team leading.

6. Sometimes a cause may fit into more than one category. In this case, either the cause can be listed more than once, or the group will vote on which particular category to list it under.

7. The cause and effect diagram can be built up over a number of sessions, especially if the problem is complex.

Figure 8–7 illustrates the potential causes of dissatisfied customers for one company. In this example, the major cause categories are shown together with a more detailed analysis of one of the major categories, service. This shows a number of levels of cause and demonstrates that the diagram can be quite complex when drawn in detail.

FIGURE 8–7
Cause and Effect Diagram Showing Detailed Analysis of One Major Category

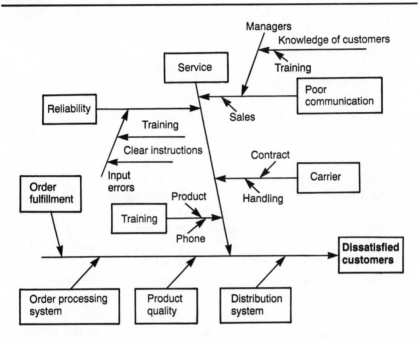

The cause and effect diagram is a powerful, visual means of displaying potential causes of a problem in such a way that related causes are linked together. From this diagram the group may select the most probable causes to guide the data gathering activity.

Voting and weighting. Having identified all potential causes of a problem, the group needs to select probable causes to focus the data gathering exercise. Reviewing the cause and effect diagram directly may lead the group to decide to investigate a particular area further. For example, a cause with a large number of subcauses may well indicate a complex area requiring further investigation. But it's more usual for the group to select the area on which to focus attention as a result of voting on each cause in turn.

Voting. When there are a large number of potential causes, many of these are unlikely to be the real cause of the problem so they can be eliminated fairly quickly and simply by the process of multivoting. This reduces a list of potential causes to a manageable number of likely causes which the group can discuss and analyze more carefully.

Multivoting. This method eliminates the least likely causes without requiring a great deal of discussion and analysis. Each round of multivoting reduces the list by approximately one-half. There are five principal steps:

1. Number each cause.
2. Each member should write down the numbers of the causes that he feels the group should investigate further. Each member should only be allowed to vote for about one-third of the total number of potential causes. For example, if there are 100 potential causes, each individual should have 34 votes. For 48, items each should have 16 votes.
3. The team leader should tally the total number of votes for each choice.
4. Once the voting is complete, those items with fewest votes are eliminated. The size of the group influences the analysis of votes. For groups with fewer than five members, cross off items with fewer than two votes. For groups with 6 to 15 members, eliminate those with fewer than three votes. For groups with more than 15 members, eliminate those with fewer than four votes.
5. Repeat steps 2 through 4, reducing the number of votes each time until 10 or fewer choices remain.

Once the least likely causes have been eliminated, the group can spend more time considering the remaining causes. Because it's difficult for an individual to decide among the remaining 10 possible causes of a problem, a technique such as paired comparison, where only two choices are compared at one time, is frequently used.

Paired comparison. This technique proceeds as follows:

1. List and number the remaining potential causes (10 or fewer).

2. Each member of the group then completes a voting chart (Figure 8–8). Each member compares item 1 with item 2, decides which of the two is the more likely cause of the problem, and circles this number. The process is repeated by comparing item 1 with item 3 through to item 10. Item 2 is then compared with item 3 through to item 10, and so on, until the chart is complete.

3. The number of times a choice has been circled is then tallied for each individual.

4. The scores for each team member are then added together. The choice with the highest score represents the group's consensus view as to the most likely cause of the problem.

Figure 8–9 illustrates the use of the paired comparison technique to identify likely causes of poor telephone answering on a company switchboard. In this case only five choices remain.

Weighting. Another means of selecting the most likely cause of a problem, once the number of potential causes is reduced to 10 or fewer, is for the group to score each potential cause against a number of criteria.

Having decided that each of the remaining causes may contribute toward the problem, now try to determine which contributes the most. For example, each choice may be evaluated and given a score between 1 and 10 against a selection of the following criteria:

Urgency
Frequency of occurrence   Each cause is usually
Risk of nondetection   evaluated against 2 or 3
Importance of the effects   of these criteria.
Influence on CONC

The scores may be selected as follows:

Very low	1–2
Low	3–4
Medium	5–6
High	7–8
Unacceptable	9–10

After we've evaluated each cause against the selected criteria, we multiply the scores together to determine the significance of

FIGURE 8–8
Voting Chart

Choice	Descriptions	Voting chart								
1		1 2	1 3	1 4	1 5	1 6	1 7	1 8	1 9	1 10
2		2 3	2 4	2 5	2 6	2 7	2 8	2 9	2 10	
3		3 4	3 5	3 6	3 7	3 8	3 9	3 10		
4		4 5	4 6	4 7	4 8	4 9	4 10			
5		5 6	5 7	5 8	5 9	5 10				
6		6 7	6 8	6 9	6 10					
7		7 8	7 9	7 10						
8		8 9	8 10							
9		9 10								
10										

FIGURE 8–9
Paired Comparison on Likely Causes of Poor Telephone Answering

						Tally
1	Lack of training	①/2	①/3	①/4	①/5	4
2	Equipment breakdown	2/③	2/④	②/5		1
3	Not enough staff	3/④	③/5			2
4	Poor morale	④/5				3
5	Doing other work					0

(The most likely cause is lack of training.)

FIGURE 8–10
Weighting of Causes

Cause ╲ Criteria	A	B	C
Urgency	4	8	3
Frequency	4	6	8
Risk of nondetection	2	9	6
Total significance	32	432	144

Cause B is selected as the most significant cause. For three criteria,
minimum = 1 × 1 × 1 = 1 and maximum = 10 × 10 × 10 = 1000.

each cause. The most significant cause is the one with the highest score.

Figure 8–10 illustrates the evaluation of three causes (A, B, and C) against three criteria (urgency, frequency, and risk of nondetection). The total significance is calculated for each cause. The one with the highest score (cause B in this example) is the most important potential cause.

Gather the Data

Once the number of potential causes has been narrowed down to the one or two most likely causes of the problem, we must gather data to verify the problem's actual cause.

Data gathering methods. There are a number of standard methods for gathering data. We should ensure that the data gathering methods, in addition to providing relevant and meaningful data, are simple to use, clear, and unambiguous.

Data can generally be gathered in three forms:

1. *A tally sheet or data sheet*. Here data are logged onto a data sheet. Once the data are gathered, further analysis is required before a decision can be made.

FIGURE 8–11
Location Plot Showing Missing Components on a Printed Circuit Board

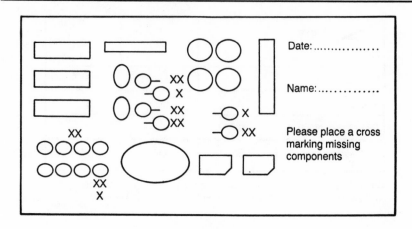

2. *A check sheet.* Here, information collected by the operator is recorded on the sheet in the form of a graph, so that any trends can be assessed directly and decisions can be made without further analysis of the data. This method is widely used in the application of SPC.

3. *A location plot* (sometimes called a *concentration diagram* or *measles chart*). This is a useful, simple method for plotting the location of errors on a chart. Figure 8–11 illustrates a location plot for missing components on a printed circuit board.

The method of recording data depends on (1) the nature and complexity of data being gathered and (2) the degree of analysis required. Data sheets are useful when a lot of complex raw data need to be gathered that may need to be analyzed in a number of ways. Check sheets avoid the need for further analysis. Location plots provide a readily understandable picture of the data, but they only have a limited number of applications (for example, where the location of a defect may be significant).

Before deciding on how to collect data, the following questions must be answered by the group:

1. What's the purpose of collecting the data? What are you trying to prove/disprove?

2. What data need to be collected?

3. Where in the process should data be collected? Try to choose an area that will cause a minimum amount of disruption, provided it will enable you to answer the key questions.

4. Who will collect the data? Select people close to the process who can be trained to collect reliable, unbiased data.

5. When and how much data should be collected? Determine the frequency and duration of data collection.

Having considered all the preceding, the group can decide how the data will be collected. It's then necessary to devise a means to gather the data effectively and reliably. The following steps are a useful guide to setting up the data gathering activity:

1. Write down a clear description of how the data will be gathered. Define what's to be measured or counted, how the measurement/count should be made, how many measurements should be taken, what equipment should be used, what accuracy is required, and what constitutes an error.

2. Devise a clear, simple form on which the information can be recorded.

3. Agree on the contents of the form and the method for gathering data with those who'll actually gather the data, before finalizing them.

4. Once arrangements have been agreed upon by all concerned, train those individuals who'll be gathering the data so they know why the data are being gathered, how to gather and record the data, when the recording will start and end, and how soon the results will be available.

5. Once the data are analyzed, ensure that those who gathered the data are informed of the findings and what will happen next. This enables the data gathering team to understand the significance of its work.

Analyze the Data

It's generally hard to make a decision based on masses of data from tally sheets or tables. It's therefore necessary to analyze raw data and present them in a way that's easy to understand and from which decisions can be made.

FIGURE 8–12
Bar Chart of Power Supply Voltage Output

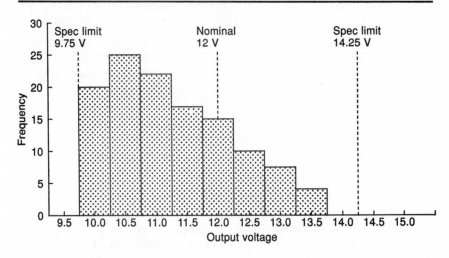

Data may be analyzed and displayed in a number of different ways including bar charts, Pareto analysis, scatter diagrams, and pie charts.

Bar graphs. A bar chart (Figure 8–12) provides a graphic summary of data, making them easy to absorb and understand. The figure shows that, although all the units are within the specification, very few are rated at 12 volts and most are at the lower end of the allowed range, between 9.75 and 11.75 volts. This provides a pointer as to where the problem may lie and where the group should investigate further.

Analyzing data using a bar graph makes patterns easy to spot. Once a pattern can be seen in the data, likely causes may be identified for further investigation.

Pareto analysis. This is another way of looking at data. Problems are frequently the result of a number of factors. Pareto analysis is designed to help identify principal causes of a problem. We can then focus attention on removing these principal causes and have a significant impact on resolving the problem.

This method of analysis is a result of a finding of Italian economist Vilfredo Pareto during the 19th century. He discovered that 80 percent of the wealth in Italy was in the hands of some 20 percent of the population. Looking more broadly, this type of distribution is found to apply to many other situations. For example, 80 percent of the contributions to charity apparently come from some 20 percent of the possible sources: 80 percent of telephone calls made from work typically come from 20 percent of the employees. This principle has become known as the Pareto principle.

In industry, this principle has been applied to help analyze the principal causes of problems. The proposition is as follows: A small number (perhaps 20 percent) of the causes of a problem are likely to account for a large proportion (perhaps 80 percent) of the problem.

If we can identify the principal causes of a problem, we can direct our attention toward removing those causes. This enables us to identify a solution that achieves the maximum impact with the minimum resource. The contribution made by each cause to the overall problem may be analyzed using a variety of measures. Typical measures include

- Frequency of occurrence.
- Length of downtime.
- Cost of nonconformance.
- Measure of customer dissatisfaction.
- Number of defects.

Each factor's contribution is represented on a bar graph by the length of the bar.

Once we've established the appropriate measure to use and gathered the necessary data, the bars should be arranged in descending order from the largest on the left. This form of analysis usually highlights the two or three principal causes of the problem under investigation.

Figure 8–13 shows a typical Pareto chart. Figure 8–14 charts causes of delay in sending a fax.

Multiple levels of Pareto analysis. Sometimes we must use a second level of Pareto analysis to break down a problem into manageable portions before a solution can be readily identified.

FIGURE 8–13
Typical Pareto Chart

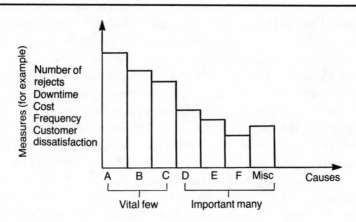

FIGURE 8–14
Pareto Chart of Causes of Delay in Sending a Fax

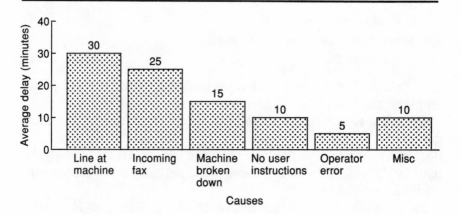

For example, a finance department trying to reduce the time debtors take to settle their accounts (measured as debtor days) identified the causes put forward to explain why customers took over 120 days to pay their accounts (Figure 8–15). From this analysis, it was decided to gather data on the reasons for incorrect invoices. The second Pareto chart is illustrated in Figure 8–16.

On the basis of this information, it was discovered that the person responsible for raising the invoices didn't always have access to all the information required to enable correct invoicing. The information came from a variety of sources. No one source contained all the necessary information. This problem was solved by changing the method of raising invoices and holding a training session for the employees concerned.

Monitoring improvements using Pareto analysis. Pareto analysis is a very useful means for monitoring improvements resulting from corrective actions. Data can be compared before and after implementation to identify corrective actions' impact.

Scatter diagrams. Scatter diagrams are a simple means for comparing two characteristics to see if a relationship exists. For example, we can assess whether the number of typing errors made by a secretary might be related to the backlog of work. Figure 8–17 illustrates a series of data tending to support this suggestion.

The independent variable (backlog of work) is drawn along the x-axis and the alleged dependent variable (the error rate measured as errors per page) is plotted along the y-axis. For each measurement, a cross is marked on the graph where the x and y values meet. For example, point A shows that when the secretary had 32 hours' backlog, the typing error rate was nine per page. Completing the diagram, we see a positive relationship between backlog and typing errors in this case. The longer the backlog, the greater the number of typing errors. In some cases the relationship might be inverse (as, for example, the relationship between the shelf life for dairy products and temperature). Or there may be no relationship at all.

But scatter diagrams suffer from two principal drawbacks. A fairly large amount of data is required before a meaningful diagram can be drawn; and scatter diagrams can suggest a correlation between two parameters even if they aren't related. One well-known example of a spurious relationship is between the level of Lake Superior and the Dow Jones index! A scatter diagram of these

FIGURE 8–15
Pareto Chart of Causes of Excess Debtor Days

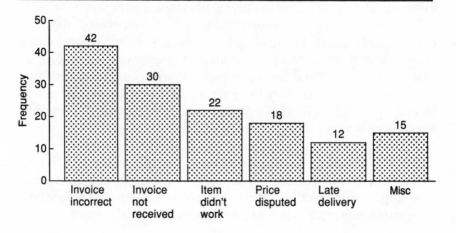

FIGURE 8–16
Pareto Chart of Causes of Incorrect Invoices of Figure 8–15

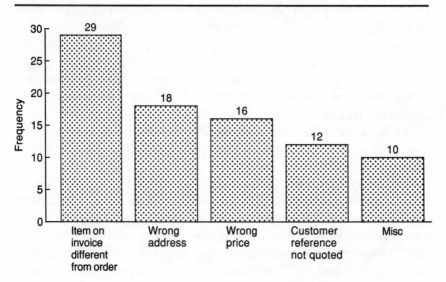

FIGURE 8–17
Scatter Diagram Showing Relationship Between Typing Error Rate and Work Backlog

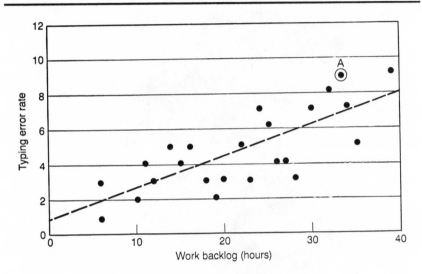

shows that as the level of the lake rises, so does the Dow Jones index. It's therefore important to screen results to ensure that such spurious relationships are eliminated before implementing potential solutions based on this type of analysis.

But be aware that, although a simple scatter diagram may provide some useful indicative evidence, it's not sufficient to support quantitative conclusions. Regression analysis can be used to identify the line that provides the best fit for the data in a scatter diagram, but it's a complex technique and requires expert input.

Pie charts. Pie charts take the form of a round chart, or pie, in which each cause of a problem is shown as a slice. The size of each slice represents the proportion that the cause contributes to the problem.

A pie chart is particularly useful for illustrating data for presentations. Pie charts aren't so useful for analyzing data as the methods described previously, although they provide a clear visual picture

FIGURE 8–18
Pie Chart Showing Causes of Delay in Sending Faxes

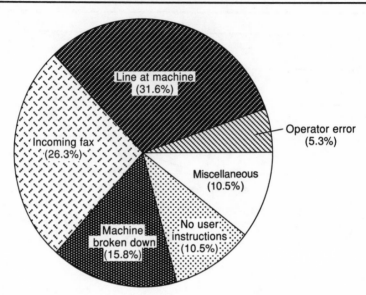

to aid the understanding of data, and they demonstrate particular points.

Figure 8–14's data on causes of delay in sending faxes is shown in Figure 8–18 in the form of a pie chart.

Establish the Root Cause of the Problem

Having reached this stage in the process, we must step back and assess whether the root cause of the problem has been identified. Implementing a solution may be expensive in terms of both management time and necessary resources. If we haven't eliminated the root cause of the problem, our efforts will be an expensive mistake. It's therefore worth critically reassessing the previous steps' results to get to the root cause of the problem. This is particularly important if the problem is complex and involves a number of departments. The following errors may be identified thanks to a critical reevaluation of the results of the previous steps:

1. The cause identified wasn't the root cause. With complex problems, especially where only limited data are available, it's often hard to identify the root cause at the first attempt. You may need to repeat the data gathering process to identify the cause of the cause. This is rather like peeling layers and layers of skin from an onion.

2. The probable cause turns out not to be the real one. In this case you must go back to the cause and effect diagram and see if an alternative cause can be identified. You may have to rerun the brainstorming activity.

3. There's insufficient data to enable a cause to be identified. Deciding on the appropriate data to gather is a skilled task that takes experience. With new or inexperienced problem solving teams, there may be insufficient data to enable the root cause to be identified. In this case, you must repeat the data gathering exercise.

Choose a Solution

Once the root cause of a problem has been identified you must identify, gain support for, and implement a solution that eliminates it once and for all. In practice more than one potential solution might be proposed. It's then necessary to identify the most cost-effective solution with the best chance of succeeding. The solution must also prevent the problem from recurring. To introduce inspection and correction activities would merely add to the company's costs and not solve the root cause of the problem.

The following steps provide a useful practical approach to choosing a cost-effective corrective action.

Devise potential solutions. By this time you should know a great deal about the problem and its causes. This accumulated knowledge will often enable a number of potential solutions to be identified.

It's frequently useful to hold a brainstorming session to identify all of the possible solutions, particularly if there are only a few obvious alternatives. Recording some basic information on each solution at this stage (Figure 8–19 is a useful outline for this) will form a useful basis for the selection process.

FIGURE 8–19
Table to Analyze Possible Solutions

PROBLEM:

Possible solutions	Resources to implement	Cost to implement	Reduction in CONC if implemented	Time to achieve results	Probability of achieving result	Comments

At this stage you should take account of the whole range of possible solutions and avoid the danger of jumping to one superficially attractive solution. All potential solutions should be ruled out unless they're prevention activities designed to eliminate the cause of the problem once and for all. A short-term inspection and rectification activity should only be considered as an interim measure pending implementation of a final solution. The danger of pursuing this course of action is that the interim solution may become a permanent fixture!

Select one solution. Once a number of potential solutions have been proposed, you select one solution to implement. A number of selection criteria may be important when evaluating each solution:

1. *Costs of implementation.* The costs of implementing a solution can be calculated. These include the one time only start-up costs (such as training personnel and writing procedures) and the additional ongoing operating costs (equipment, materials, and labor) resulting from changes in procedures.

2. *Reduction in the cost of nonconformance (CONC).* Each solution may resolve the whole problem or only part of the problem. The problem is likely to cause some nonconformance costs associated with errors and rectification. These costs can be estimated. The reduction in the CONC can be measured for each proposed solution. It's often useful to compare the cost of implementation and the reduction in CONC in terms of a cost benefit analysis. For each solution the ratio of benefits to costs can be calculated.

3. *Time taken to implement the solution and achieve the results.* In some cases, you must implement a solution fairly rapidly so it may be important to know how long each of the proposed solutions will take to yield results. In some cases, especially if the existing CONC is high, it might be appropriate to implement a quick interim solution followed by a more permanent solution at a later date.

4. *Risk of solution not being effective through lack of support.* However beneficial a solution might appear, it won't succeed unless it's supported by the people who have to implement it. Sometimes a financially less attractive solution may actually yield a better result because it's more likely to be accepted by the organization. Be aware of the forces working for and against each solution before making a selection. This will help when selecting and implementing the optimum solution.

The ideal solution is one that:

- Fully eliminates the root cause of the problem.
- Is most cost-effective.
- Has the support of everyone.
- Is certain to succeed.
- Takes only a short time to implement.

Seldom will a solution meet all these criteria so alternative solutions' relative merits should be compared and the most appropriate solution should be selected. There are a number of approaches to assessing the relative merits of alternative solutions. Now let's look at one important technique.

Often we can split the selection criteria into two types: those that the solution *must* meet and those that the group *wants* the solution to meet. For any given problem the musts and wants will differ. For instance, in a company where cash flow is tight, it may be necessary to limit the cash outlay for implementing the solution. ("It must cost less than $10,000 to implement in the first year.") In another company other criteria might assume greater importance. ("It must be implemented within three months, before peak production starts.")

Each solution can be evaluated according to the musts. Any solution that doesn't meet these key criteria is eliminated. The remaining solutions can then be assessed against the wants. Wants may be weighted according to their importance as the following example shows.

1. The group may consider it important that the solution is widely supported within a number of departments or it just won't work. This criterion might be given a weighting of 9.
2. The group might consider it important that the solution is implemented quickly. If the solution isn't implemented before the beginning of the busy season (in four months time), then it won't be implemented this year. As a result, the group assigns a weighting of 7 to this criterion.
3. The group wants the solution to be cheap to implement. This is given a weighting of 6.

The potential solutions should then be evaluated according to these predetermined criteria. Figure 8–20 illustrates the weighted evaluation of the following three potential solutions to a given problem. Solution A is quick to implement, is well supported, but is expensive; solution B is cheap and quick to implement, but isn't well supported; and solution C is well supported, but will take a long time to implement and is expensive.

The higher the score, the more closely the potential solution meets the selection criteria. In this case, solution A is selected as it meets the selection criteria most closely.

FIGURE 8–20
Weighting Solutions

Solutions / Criteria + weighting	A Score	A Score × Weight	B Score	B Score × Weight	C Score	C Score × Weight
Well supported 9	8	72	2	18	8	72
Quick to implement 7	9	63	9	63	2	14
Cheap to implement 6	3	18	8	48	3	18
Total	153		129		104	

Address Internal Obstacles to Change

At this stage you must ensure that any forces acting against the solution are addressed and appropriate action is taken to ensure the problem is effectively resolved.

A useful technique to assist in this process is force field analysis. Here the solution is drawn in a box on the right-hand side of a piece of paper (Figure 8–21). The forces helping the solution to succeed are drawn below the line pointing upward. These are known as driving forces. Forces working against the solution are drawn pointing downward to the line. These are restraining forces. The length of the line, or the thickness of the line, indicates the size of the force.

Restraining forces may include factions, rivalries, or vested interests, increased complexity of a process, or inertia. Restraining forces must be addressed as part of any plan for implementing potential solutions to the problem. These forces might be so

FIGURE 8–21
Diagram of Force Field Analysis

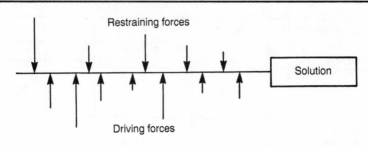

powerful that they influence the group against a given solution, or it may be possible to overcome them by appropriate action when implementing a solution.

Experiment

Once a solution has been chosen, you must verify that it eliminates the problem when implemented. It's also important that the solution doesn't cause new problems to arise, or just cause the old problem to reappear elsewhere in the process. It's frequently useful to carry out a series of experiments to demonstrate this. If the experiments yield satisfactory results, then it's time to gain management approval to implement the solution.

Gain Support

Once a solution is chosen and proven, you must convince management to give its authority to implement the solution. This may require a formal presentation to the Quality Improvement Team or an informal presentation to the department manager, depending on the nature of the problem. In either case this represents a milestone in the group's efforts and is very important. The team's presentation should include (supported by data and diagrams to stress important points)

- The team objective.
- The original problem.
- The investigation carried out by the group.
- The cause of the problem supported by the data gathered.
- The proposed solution.
- The expected results and a description of how they'll be measured.
- The proposed plan to implement the solution and achieve the results.

A formal presentation may typically last about 30 minutes, and the group will be closely questioned on the data gathered and their decisions. In addition to the material presented, the group may need to refer to additional data to support their case and answer questions.

The aim during the presentation is to persuade the audience to commit its support to implementing the proposed solution. The team leader should ensure that a decision is made before the meeting is closed.

Implement the Solution

Once the solution has been agreed upon and the team has been given the go-ahead to implement it, it's important to plan thoroughly the implementation before proceeding. In most cases it's advisable first to implement a pilot scheme to prove the solution and the implementation plan. Where possible, the pilot should be restricted to a small part of the business (such as one product line or one secretary) and strictly controlled by the group. The pilot scheme demonstrates whether the solution is feasible and eliminates the problem. It also enables the group to determine if any changes are necessary before full-scale implementation of the solution.

The following guidelines are helpful when planning to implement a solution:

1. Define the sequence of key steps required to implement the solution. Then break this down into substeps.
2. Define who'll be directly involved in each step, who'll be affected, and who must be consulted.

3. Define the changes that will be required in work methods. How will these be documented? What training will be required and who'll carry this out?

4. Determine how long it will take to implement each step.

5. Determine (1) how you'll know when each step is complete and (2) what milestones will be used to measure progress.

6. Decide (1) how you'll check the success in implementing the solution and (2) what data will need to be gathered.

At this stage it's frequently useful to draw a GANTT chart (Figure 8–22) to plan and monitor progress. This is a time chart showing the proposed start and finish date for each of the necessary actions. Progress can be monitored against this plan and actions taken if the schedule slips. Other techniques, such as PERT, may be employed if the solution is complex or will take a long time to implement.

Having planned the implementation phase, the team can then go ahead. Possibly the most important aspect of implementation is communicating what's going on to everyone affected by the changes. You must gain their support and incorporate their suggestions where possible. Useful groundwork for this should have been laid down during the data gathering phase. If people were consulted and involved then, they'll be more likely to accept changes now.

Once the procedures have been written, the training carried out, and the solution implemented, you should gather data to ensure that the problem has been eliminated and doesn't recur.

Generalize the Solution

Once the solution has been implemented and proven to work, you must see if it can be applied elsewhere in the organization. This can be done in a number of ways:

1. The method used to resolve the problem and identify the solution should be documented. This material can be made available to other problem solving groups that may find it useful.

2. The group's success should be publicized throughout the organization to encourage other people to (1) become

FIGURE 8–22
GANTT Chart

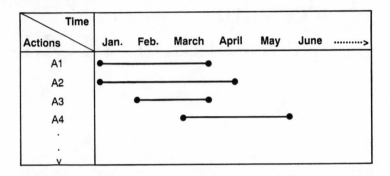

involved in problem solving and (2) identify problems in their own area where the solution could be applied.

3. The group might be tasked with looking for other areas where the solution might be applied (other product lines, departments, or sites, for example).

Chapter Nine

Successful Implementation of TQM

Now let's look at how organizations can successfully implement TQM. First we'll read about a high tech company's achievements. Then we'll examine the quality revolution in retail banking with brief discussions of two specific banks.

THE ICL EXPERIENCE

ICL was formed in 1968 as a result of the merger of two leading British computer suppliers: English Electric Computers and ICT. In 1984, ICL was acquired by STC. In November 1990, the Japanese company Fujitsu took an 80 percent shareholding in ICL.

Following its merger with Nokia Data Systems, ICL has some 26,000 employees in over 70 countries. ICL concentrates on providing information systems and services in four key market segments: retailing, manufacturing, financial services, and public administration.

ICL develops, manufactures, sells, and supports products ranging from notebooks to mainframes. It provides customers with a complete range of related services, including hardware maintenance, systems design, software design, and customer training and consultancy services. Table 9–1 summarizes the group's 1986–90 financial results.

Product development takes place in Bracknell, Manchester, Reading, and Stevenage in the UK and in Santa Clara, California. Manufacturing takes place primarily in Kidsgrove (printed circuit board production) and Ashton-under-Lyne (product assembly) in the UK as well as in Denmark (UNIX systems) and Irvine, California (retail and office systems).

TABLE 9-1
Summary of ICL Results, 1986–90

	1986	1987	1988	1989	1990
Turnover	1,194.2	1,307.6	1,353.1	1,632.3	1,611.8
Pretax profit	81.2	112.2	139.0	148.6	110.1
(All figures in £ Million)					

The Decision for Total Quality

In the mid-1980s, ICL undertook a complete overhaul of its business strategy. It set its objective as becoming customer-driven, focusing on providing systems, products, and services that meet customer requirements in its four key markets.

This mission relies on getting close to customers (1) to understand their wants and requirements and (2) to understand how current performance levels could be improved. To support this change in the company's culture, Chief Executive Peter Bonfield and the board decided in 1986 to implement a program of continuous quality improvement. This program is designed to ensure that all employees recognize and fulfill their role in providing outstanding customer service. Employees are responsible for understanding their customers' needs and ensuring that those needs are satisfied. The voice of the customer must drive every activity at every level within ICL.

To underline senior management's commitment to the Improvement Program, and to ensure that all employees recognize its importance to the success of the group as a whole, Joe Goasdoué was appointed to the Main Board as director of quality. This commitment is also demonstrated by the investment, in terms of both time and money, in the program. ICL estimates that it spends £1 million each year to ensure the success of its improvement program. In excess of 100,000 labor-days have been invested so far in the training program.

Implementing Total Quality

The steps ICL took illustrate how one company has achieved considerable success as a result of implementing a program of continuous quality improvement. Implementation occurred in six phases.

Phase 1: Planning. ICL recognized early on that planning is one of the keys to success in the drive for the continuous improvement of quality. Its first action was to form a central team, chaired by the quality director, to investigate the methodologies available, generate ideas about how to implement the program at ICL, and formulate its basic strategy. This team started with some 30 members and stayed together (with the number of members gradually diminishing) for almost 12 months. This team developed the blueprint for quality improvement within ICL, known as "Quality—The ICL Way," which would be followed by each Quality Improvement Team throughout ICL. Responsibility for implementing the program, within the blueprint, lies with each unit's management.

To focus attention on the Quality Improvement Program's key objectives, the central team stresses four underlying principles (which are basically the "four absolutes" propounded by Philip Crosby):

1. Quality is defined as conformance to requirements.
2. The system for causing quality is prevention.
3. The performance standard is Zero Defects.
4. The measurement of quality is the price of nonconformance.

To ensure that each employee understands the company's commitment to these principles, the board adopted the following statement of its quality policy, setting out the key objectives of the group in relation to its service to customers:

> To provide competitive systems, products and services which fully meet the customers' requirements first time, on time and every time.

To translate these basic principles into practice, the team produced a step-by-step guide for use by the Quality Improvement Team (QIT) in each operating unit. The QIT handbook sets out the quality blueprint to be implemented by the QIT; each step is described in terms of the objectives, the benefits, and who needs to be involved, with guidelines on how it can be implemented. The

QIT then adapts each step to fit its own organization before implementation. The handbook provides structure and commonality to the program without restricting each unit's creativity. Each unit is responsible for implementing a program that fits its organization. This is felt to be particularly important in such a diverse, multinational organization.

Phase 2: Identifying quality costs. When persuading management and employees that the "right first time" approach is in their interests and the company's interests, a key element is to calculate what it costs the company to keep doing things wrong and then correct them afterward (the price of nonconformance).

Rather than collect the price of nonconformance (PONC) for every activity, ICL decided to nominate eight key areas, the "Big Eight," for which the PONC would be collected throughout the group. Although by no means the only areas in which improvements could be made, they were areas where a reduction in PONC would significantly improve business performance. The Big Eight (support, bug fixing, avoidable service visits, rework, performance concessions, overdue accounts, delivery to time/spec, and inventory) were identified following the review of the total PONC for a pilot site. The Big Eight were those areas with the highest PONC during the pilot study.

This illustrates ICL's intensely pragmatic approach to improving quality. It hasn't become bogged down in detailed calculations of PONC for all activities at the start of the program. Instead it focused on the areas giving rise to the largest PONC. This has enabled it to gather the necessary information quickly and set improvement targets.

The real significance of the QIP to ICL's success was underlined in 1987 when it was announced that the total PONC in the Big Eight for the group as a whole amounted to some £160 million (13 percent of turnover). In the same year ICL achieved a pre-tax profit of £112.2 million! By tolerating nonconformance, ICL severely impaired its ability to compete effectively in an ever more competitive market.

As a result of this study, ICL determined to eliminate nonconformance in the Big Eight areas over a five-year period. Let's look at the means utilized to achieve this ambitious objective.

Phase 3: Training and communication. At ICL (as at most companies) implementing a program of continuous quality improvement meant a permanent change in how the company is run.

A key to making the necessary changes lies in educating all employees throughout the company. By starting at the top and then working down and across the organization, the training message cascades through the company. The objective is to teach management and employees that errors and problems aren't a fact of life. By insisting that errors and problems be eliminated at their source, once and for all, it becomes unnecessary to work around them by providing temporary fixes. Employees are also encouraged to plan to do all their work right the first time and to try to find means of preventing errors and problems once they've been identified.

To date, 22,000 employees have attended a basic quality training course. A further 1,500 have attended additional specialist courses. In total, more than 100,000 labor-days have been invested so far in the training program.

This type of comprehensive training program has two goals: (1) to lay the foundations necessary to enable every employee to fulfill her commitment to Total Quality and change the way the company operates, and (2) to indicate to every employee the importance of TQM and the company's commitment to ensuring its success.

Phase 4: Measuring success. When introducing the continuous quality improvement program, ICL decided to measure its overall success in three key areas:

1. Improvement in the opinions held by customers about the quality of the overall service provided by ICL and its ability to satisfy its customers' requirements.
2. Improvement in (1) ICL employees' opinions of the quality of the service provided by ICL to its customers and (2) their satisfaction with the company as an employer.
3. Reduction in the PONC.

Customer opinion. A business's ability to meet its customers' requirements better than its competitors is the only reason a company survives and prospers. To survive in today's market, businesses must understand their customers' requirements, how well these requirements are being met by the company, how well they're being met by competitors, and how the business can improve its performance in key service areas.

ICL has been careful to avoid falling into the potential trap of becoming introspective and concentrating so much on improving internal processes, procedures, and practices in an effort to reduce PONC, that external customers' needs are forgotten. External customers are the ones who pay the bills. All improvement activities at ICL are designed to improve the company's ability to meet its customers' needs. This element of the program can't be overemphasized.

Since introducing the continuous quality improvement program, ICL has monitored its customers' opinions directly and by means of independent surveys to gauge the program's success.

A survey carried out by Datapro in France showed that the ICL mainframe series 39 gave the greatest overall level of customer satisfaction of any comparable mainframe product. It was rated top in 8 of the 12 categories surveyed.

ICL's own surveys show a significant change in customers' perception of the quality of service provided by ICL. Since implementing the continuous quality improvement program, ICL is perceived as a company committed to quality improvement and to meeting its customers' requirements.

Employee opinion. ICL surveys its employees annually to determine their views on how well the company is run, how well each individual is treated, and their opportunities to develop within the company. Table 9–2 shows key results from the 1987 and 1989 surveys. The data illustrate the improvement in employees' perception since the continuous quality improvement program was launched. Employees are generally much happier in their work, the company, and their development within the company. A common finding among companies that are serious about quality improvement, this has important implications for staff recruitment and retention.

The price of nonconformance. In 1987 it was estimated that the annual PONC for the Big Eight areas amounted to £160 million.

TABLE 9–2
Results of Employee Survey

	1987	1989
View of your work	24.4%	18.7%
Objectives and performance appraisal	21.4	17.0
Training and career development	40.3	29.5
Planning	39.8	32.4
Organization style and standards	25.8	16.6
Communication	30.2	20.1
Pay, benefits, conditions, and work environment	21.4	21.2
Quality	29.8	18.5
Overall satisfaction with ICL	31.4	21.4

To reduce this tremendous burden, each operating unit was allocated target savings required over the next five years. ICL has since tracked the reduction in the PONC by measuring the savings achieved by each operating unit. Provided they deliver the savings, they've met their PONC targets. ICL chose this method rather than to rerun the PONC calculation annually.

One key success achieved by ICL is the £160 million savings targeted in 1987 in the first five years of the program.

The group has continued to set demanding targets for reducing waste as a result of the quality improvement program. Overall the group seeks to save £25 million yearly. To achieve this, each operating unit is allocated a proportion of the target for the year. Management's ability to achieve the required savings and other quality improvement goals is an important part in the performance appraisal for each unit and its senior management at the end of each year. These criteria are taken into account in the management bonus scheme.

Phase 5: Prevention and improvement. ICL has implemented a comprehensive program of prevention and improvement to ensure that it continues to become more competitive. Key features of this program are:

1. *Setting goals for improvement.* The key financial goals targeted have already been discussed. The group also targets

operational goals. Benchmarking (one of the keys to the successes) is discussed in an upcoming section.

2. *Corrective action teams and quality circles.* In the five years since the program of continuous quality improvement was implemented within ICL, several hundred corrective action teams have been formed to tackle specific problems affecting a large number of people or departments. Members of these teams are drawn from the affected departments. On the other hand, quality circles are formed to tackle quality problems that only affect a specific work area.

Benchmarking. ICL makes extensive use of benchmarking techniques. As part of the training process, every employee is encouraged to examine critically how activities are currently performed and suggest how these can be improved. This informal benchmarking is encouraged throughout the company at every level and for every activity. Formal benchmarking teams are set up periodically to identify the best practices in particular activities throughout the world. ICL then examines the techniques to identify whether they can be adapted for use within ICL to improve performance and competitiveness. Here are three examples of parameters ICL has chosen to benchmark.

1. The time it took to get a personal computer from the feasibility study to launch was a problem. A comparison with the best in the market showed that ICL was taking too long to be competitive. As a result of the benchmarking study, a time to market target of nine months was set. The ICL DRS model 95 beat the target with an eight-month time to market.
2. The ICL distribution activity was benchmarked against those of Harrods and Marks and Spencer (companies for whom distribution is one of the keys to survival).
3. ICL is now benchmarking its level of overheads.

The ability to study the best in the world, understand how their performance is achieved, and then take the lessons on board and apply them within ICL is a key feature of ICL's competitive strategy.

Phase 6: Recognition. Implementing a program of continuous quality improvement requires the commitment of all

TABLE 9–3
Quality Involvement at the Ashton Manufacturing Facility

	1988	1989
Measurement		
Charts in use		214
Charts with goals		137
Charts with PONC		54
Big 8 PONC (£ million)		4.24
Forecast PONC saving (£ thousand)		400
Corrective Action		
ECRs raised	178	445
ECRs cleared	16	325
Corrective action teams (CAT)	3	32
Quality circle teams (QC)	15	34
Recognition		
Number of awards	17	69
Employee Involvement		
Number in QCs or CATs	124	385
% in QCs or CATs	20	63

employees. The excerpt from the Quality Improvement Status Report for the Ashton manufacturing plant (Table 9–3) illustrates how employees have become involved at one ICL facility. Out of a total work force of some 610 people, over 60 percent were involved directly in Corrective Action Teams (CATS) or quality circles in 1989.

Active involvement in TQM gives employees the ability to change how things are done, utilizes more of their skills, and makes them feel more involved in how the company is run. This in turn frequently improves morale and loyalty to the company. This can have a significant impact on employees' performar.ce and, as a result, the performance of the business as a whole.

In view of the extra efforts required from employees, management must consider means of rewarding exceptional performance. At the Ashton plant, quality awards were made to some 69 employees in 1989; this demonstrates the level of commitment made by employees.

Reaping the Rewards

In the five years since ICL became committed to continuous improvement of quality, it has made significant improvements to its business. The following key performance indicators illustrate its success.

1. It has eliminated £160 million in wasted time, effort, and other resources. In some instances this has resulted in direct savings and improved the bottom line. An example is the reduction of inventory. In other cases it has released time to enable individuals to improve both their own personal performance and company performance.

2. It has significantly improved its level of customer service. ICL is now perceived as a company committed to quality and to satisfying customer needs.

3. Commitment to the continuous improvement of quality has taken hold throughout the organization. Over 60 Quality Improvement Teams and several hundred corrective action teams and quality circles have been formed. Examples of improvements achieved by these groups are given at the end of this section.

4. ICL won National Training Awards for its quality training in both 1988 and 1989.

5. ICL's factory at Ashton-under-Lyne was chosen as one of the five Best British Factories in 1989 judged by *Management Today* and A. T. Kearney, consultants, against quality, productivity, cost, and customer satisfaction criteria.

6. ICL won one of only three British Quality Awards presented by the British Quality Association in 1990. The association looks for evidence of the total commitment to quality throughout an organization over a number of years, resulting in sustained improvement in quality across all activities.

Examples of Improvement Achieved by ICL

Here are six examples of improvements ICL has made since 1987.

1. The worldwide spares organization addressed reasons for the large number of complaints about deliveries of spare parts. Many deliveries were late, included the wrong items, or were badly packaged. To gauge the scope of the problem,

ICL encouraged customers to record errors and complaints on a standard form that was analyzed by the group. Applying problem solving techniques to complaints, the group defines the problem, responds to the customer, and arranges a replacement of the part within 24 hours. The group then seeks to identify the root cause of the problem and introduce corrective action. This program is saving £500,000 a year.

2. The ICL Services Division calculated that the annual cost associated with people not turning up at training courses or canceling at short notice amounted to £650,000. A corrective action team introduced a central tracking system and improved the processes for booking, confirmation, waitlisting, canceling, and informing attendees of courses' benefits. The result is savings of £580,000 per year.

3. A corrective action team was formed by a number of secretaries to look at how they could save the time and effort associated with looking for standard information. Time wasted was estimated at an hour a day per secretary and equated with some £1 million per year. An information file has been introduced for every secretary which contains the most frequently used information.

4. In December 1989 a team was formed to improve the time taken to repair client equipment. At that time, the call-to-fix time was 13 hours. During 1990 this was reduced to five hours by measuring the call-to-fix times for each repair and implementing corrective actions in all areas where this exceeded five hours. One reason for the long call-to-fix times was the number of wasted service visits. These might result from the operator's failure to read the manual or the service engineer's not having the correct parts when making a site visit. A range of corrective actions was introduced to reduce the number of these visits. Figure 9–1 shows these measures' success.

5. At the Ashton facility, over 90 percent of product cost is represented by materials. Effective management of materials is therefore a key to the business's success. With a manu-facturing program that can change significantly each month, manufacturing flexibility must be achieved with the minimum investment in inventory. The materials manage-ment activity is responsible for ensuring that the right materials are in the right place at the right time. This requires

FIGURE 9–1

Reduction in Costs of Unnecessary Service Visits

accurate data on inventory levels and production requirements. The materials management department undertook the following steps to introduce a just-in-time (JIT) method of working to improve its performance: by thoroughly re-examining its role, it determined the key service measures to enable it to achieve maximum flexibility and service to the customer while, at the same time, minimizing inventory levels. It then introduced actions to improve performance in all areas. The success of the measures undertaken at Ashton is shown in Table 9–4.

6. In 1985 the purchasing department's approach was to buy on price. It would be prepared to switch suppliers frequently and accept any supplier that came close enough to the required quality standards. As a result of the change to a JIT method of material control, the purchasing department recognized that it needed to change its buying philosophy and relationship with suppliers. It implemented a policy focusing on long-term partnerships with suppliers. Before entering into this commitment, it had to ensure that every supplier was world-class in terms of quality, service, and total cost. This meant taking account of the overall service from a supplier, and not just the price of goods purchased. To achieve these improvements, the following series of measures was introduced:

TABLE 9–4
Improvement in Materials Management, 1980–89

	1980	1985	1986	1987	1988	1989
Program cycle time (days)	50	40	30	26	15	14
Goods receiving process time (hours)	60	40	16	8	2	0.5
Manufacturing cycle time (days)	50	40	29	22	15	13
Automatic data capture (%)	0	0	5	10	60	80
Stock service level (%)	90	92	95	98	99	99
Data accuracy (%)	90	90	94	98	99	99
Output service level (%)	93	94	94	95	95	96
Inventory turns (number)	2.5	3.2	6.6	7.1	11.2	12.2

- By agreeing to a specific time slot for deliveries by major suppliers, ICL can ensure delivery of goods to the production line and minimize inventory levels. This is one feature of a just-in-time regime.

- The Ashton plant regularly reports on the quality of incoming materials to the supplier. This has a salutary effect on the conformance of these goods to requirements.

- Ashton regularly reviews the procedures, methods, and performance of each supplier and agrees on quality improvement targets in these areas. The resulting improvement in quality has enabled a significant reduction in the level of goods-inwards inspection, and an increase in the number of suppliers on "ship-to-stock" rating. This initiative has developed into a formal vendor rating system, and Ashton makes awards to suppliers who achieve consistent high levels of performance quality, delivery, and service.

- On-site inspection is carried out at the supplier's premises by Ashton employees before shipment of any new part is permitted. This ensures that (1) the supplier remains responsible for any nonconforming products and is made aware of the importance Ashton attaches to quality and (2)

TABLE 9–5
Improvement in Supplier Management

	1985	1989
Number of suppliers	180	240
Number of parts	1,500	4,000
Orders per month	1,000	2,500
95% requisition clearance	20 days	8 days
Lead times less than 6 weeks	10%	60%
Daily deliveries	None	60%
Daily pickup	None	20%
EDI—suppliers	None	50 (12.5% of total)
EDI—parts	None	1500 (35% of total)

enables the Ashton goods-inwards inspection facility to be minimized.

- The purchasing department organizes periodic conferences with suppliers to discuss improvements that could be made on both sides to improve supplier performance.

Table 9–5 shows these measures' significant impact on the purchasing department at Ashton.

A QUALITY REVOLUTION IN RETAIL BANKING

The market for retail banking services is becoming ever more competitive. In this environment, the quality of customer service grows increasingly important in attracting and retaining customers. Competition for services traditionally offered by banks is rising rapidly from a number of directions:

- A multitude of businesses and societies are offering credit cards.
- Oil companies and department stores offer their own credit cards.
- Bank mergers and failures are rampant.

- Speciality financial services (such as mortgage companies and credit card services) are nibbling away at core services.

In view of the increasingly competitive nature of the retail banking market, banks must continuously improve the quality of their service to customers. They must identify their customers' requirements and provide a service that satisfies those requirements the first time every time. Each individual bank must develop a strategy to take account of its strengths and weaknesses. Banks must

- Develop a strategy to enable penetration into selected markets in which the bank may trade profitably.
- Develop a strategy to gain access to customers in the market sectors chosen for penetration. A comprehensive retail banking operation requires an extensive network of branches or offices. Other services, such as consumer credit services, don't require an extensive branch network and so can be established without the same level of capital expenditure.
- Identify and pursue opportunities for establishing relationships with foreign banks where these are advantageous.

Bank Products and Services

Retail banks' wide range of services to customers includes checking accounts, credit cards, deposit accounts, retirement accounts, loans for major purchases (such as cars and houses), and other miscellaneous services such as brokerage services, trust services, foreign exchange, and safety deposit boxes. For each of these services, customers have a number of key requirements. Customers' decisions on whether to do business with a particular bank are based on

- *Products:* the terms attached to the checking account, deposit account, loan, credit card, trust, and other services banks provide for customers.
- *Customer service:* the additional help banks provide their customers including account and other enquiries, customer references, and resolving problems.

- *Service facilities:* the physical environment banks provide for customers to access the bank's services, including the branch network, automatic teller machines (ATM), and electronic banking facilities.
- *Service manner:* the behavior of the bank's personnel toward customers when they visit or telephone the branch. Considerations include friendliness, courtesy, promptness, and patience.

What Are the Key Objectives for a Successful Retail Bank?

The key objective of any business is to maximize its profitability. For a successful retail bank, this strategy may be achieved by

- Retaining existing profitable business from existing customers.
- Cross-selling products to existing customers.
- Winning profitable business from new customers.

Although customers are becoming increasingly sophisticated, these objectives are unlikely to change. But banks are likely to find that customers are growing more discerning and will shop around for the best deal when entering major transactions such as home loans. Additionally, customers with large amounts on deposit are frequently willing to turn over the account to maximize interest income, adding to the overall market instability.

How Do Banks Win New Customers?

Until recently, customers have frequently only held accounts with one bank. In many cases, customers open their first account when they start work or college. As a result, they may only take a short-term view about the services they require from their bank.

In practice, customers may not invest much time deciding with whom they'll open their first bank account. They often open an account with their parents' bank, the bank around the corner because it's convenient, or a bank recommended by a friend.

Having chosen a bank, customers may be reluctant to change to another, although they may change branches. This isn't necessarily because they have a great loyalty to the bank or believe they get a better service than they would elsewhere. A principal reason for not changing banks is the hassle associated with the change. Barriers confronting customers who seek to change their bank include

- Surveying the market for a better package deal.
- Closing the existing account and canceling existing arrangements.
- Negotiating new loan and overdraft arrangements.
- Opening a new account.
- Reinstating direct debit arrangements.
- Informing employers and other interested parties of the change.

As a rule, people don't generally change banks unless they've suffered a poor level of service or if they can secure a better package deal from another bank for the services they require. If a bank could reduce the effort required to move bank accounts, then it might receive an increased inflow of customers, provided it offered a better overall service level.

Once a bank has secured a new customer, it has traditionally been quite difficult for another bank to attract her away. But a number of customers now hold more than one account. As customers grow more sophisticated and discerning about the quality of service they require, they may become more inclined to change banks if they aren't satisfied with their existing bank's service. As a result, banks must work increasingly hard to keep their existing customers. Providing the services their existing customers require is the key to success. Servicing their existing customers and attracting profitable new lines of business from them may well represent the best source of business for many banks. The Maryland National Bank, for example, increased its retention rate by 4 percent and saw a corresponding profit increase of 10 percent during 1990. (Neil Loghachan, "Customer Retention, Overlooked Profits," *Oeyer's Office Dealer*, vol. 155, no. 9, September 1990).

Banks must also try to attract profitable new business from new customers. There are two means to do so:

- Attracting new customers who've never previously held a bank account.
- Attracting customers who are dissatisfied with other banks.

The most effective form of communication with potential new customers is through an existing customer. Word of mouth communications are more likely to increase bank patronage than an advertisement (Skern and Gould, "The Consumer as Financial Leader," *Journal of Retail Banking*, vol. 10, no. 2, 1988). A positive message will only be given if the customer receives outstanding service from his bank. Advertising may be useful for bolstering corporate image, but its effect on sales is unclear or slight.

What Do Customers Look for in a Retail Bank?

(Information in this section is drawn from "Customer Service Strategies in Financial Retailing" by Su Mon Wong and Chad Perry, *International Journal of Bank Marketing*, vol. 9, no. 3, 1991.

The factors customers consider important in choosing a bank have changed in recent years. In the 1970s convenient access to a branch was the single most important factor (Meidan, *Bank Marketing Management*. London: Macmillan, 1984). Although still important to customers, the competitive advantage of location has now largely been lost with the expansion of the branch networks of most major banks.

In the retail banking market, development of new products doesn't appear to play a significant role at present. Competitive advantage from new products usually only lasts up to six months. For example, the Bank of Melbourne introduced a check book for left-handed individuals, but this type of new product is easy to copy, so the competitive advantage is rapidly eroded.

The key to marketing in the financial services industry now is customer service (Lewis, "Service Quality in the Financial Sector," *International Journal of Bank Marketing*, vol. 7, no. 5, 1989). One US survey of 1,500 customers found that 44 percent rated "ease of doing business" as the principal factor in choosing a financial institution, while 28 percent rated "quality of personal service" as the principal factor. These two service-related factors clearly were more important than other factors such as location (Skern and Gould, "The Consumer as Financial Leader," *Journal of Retail Banking*, vol. 10, no. 2, 1988).

Why Do Customers Change the Banks They Do Business With?

Two-thirds of the customers who stop doing business with a particular organization do so because they've received poor service (LeBoeuf, *How to Win Customers and Keep Them for Life*, Piatkus, 1990). A study of the factors influencing the decision to switch financial institutions provides an interesting insight into customers' requirements. The five principal factors affecting the decision to switch were convenience of branch location, poor counter service, disrespectful staff attitudes, excessive questioning and hassles by staff, and "nickel-and-dime" penalties and charges. Customers are now increasingly looking for high-quality service from their bank. Table 9–6 shows the core qualities of a high-quality banking service.

What Are the Implications for Retail Banks?

Attracting a new customer to replace a lost one takes five times as much effort, time, and money as it would have taken to keep an existing one (Seller, "Getting Customers to Love You," *Fortune*, March 13, 1989). One dissatisfied customer will tell 25 other people. Thus 25 dissatisfied customers per month will tell as many as 7,500 other people a year about the poor service they received (Gattorna, "Customer Service, Cliche or Clincher?" *Marketing*, February/March 1987). These comments may discourage the listeners from becoming customers. They may even encourage existing customers to seek a new bank if the comments reinforce a poor impression already held by the listener.

How Can Banks Achieve a High Level of Service?

A business will only achieve outstanding customer service if there's demonstrable commitment to this objective throughout the organization, starting from the top.

Although driven from the top, a high quality of service can only be achieved if all employees are involved. The key employees are those who are in day-to-day contact with customers. Here are seven elements of service excellence:

TABLE 9–6
Core Qualities of a High-Quality Banking Service

Core Value	Operational Response
Be responsive.	Identify customer requirements and take account of them when developing new services or improving existing services.
	Reply to requests for new services (such as loans) sympathetically and promptly. If it's not possible to grant a loan or overdraft extension, then ensure the customer isn't given the impression that it will be granted until a firm decision has been taken.
Be accessible.	Incoming calls should be routed directly to the appropriate employee who has responsibility for handling the enquiry.
	Incoming calls should be answered promptly, perhaps by the fourth ring.
	If a customer leaves a message, this should be answered on the same working day.
Be credible.	Don't promise more than you can deliver.
Be courteous.	Don't keep customers waiting for meetings, for delivery of services (e.g., for replies to requests for a loan, a new check book, or for bank statements), at the counter, or at automatic teller machines.
	The bank premises should be kept clean and tidy.
	Employees should always look neat and be considerate to customers and fellow employees.
Be competent.	Employees should know your products.
	Employees should be trained so that they can deal with customer enquiries effectively and promptly.
Understand your customers.	Employees should take time to learn your customers' requirements.
	Services should be developed that respond to customer requirements.
Be reliable.	Do every job right the first time.
Be reasonable.	Consider the overall business with each customer when assessing charges for facilities such as very short term overdrafts of a few days.
Communicate.	Be able to explain services to different customers in language that they can understand.
	Don't overburden customers with details of services they aren't interested in when sending them letters. Consider sending a brief guide to the range of services you offer. Customers can then request details of services they're interested in.

Source: Adapted from R. Eric Reidenbach and M. Ray Grubbs, "A cultural approach to developing service quality," Reprinted from *Bankers Magazine*, New York: Warren, Gorham & Lamont. © 1989 Research Institute of America, Inc. Used with permission.

- New employees are thoroughly coached and trained in customer service and satisfaction.
- Supervisors are aware of employees' day-to-day problems, assist in solving them, and indeed view their job as providing service to employee "customers."
- Management empowers supervisors and employees so that problems may be resolved satisfactorily at the lowest possible management level.
- The physical environment is pleasant and conducive to efficient work habits.
- Management by crisis is minimized.
- Internal customers are recognized as well as external ones.
- The bank ensures that it understands its customers' ever-changing needs and expectations.

What Factors Should Banks Consider Measuring and Monitoring?

Having identified their key customers' key service requirements, banks must measure their performance against key service criteria. Banks may then determine targets for performance. Improvements can be measured against such objective criteria as

- Time customers spend in line at the counter at peak times and on average.
- Time customers spend in line at ATMs at peak times and on average.
- Convenient access to ATMs on inclement days, in terms of room to form a line without hindering others, and in terms of proximity to shopping areas.
- The time taken to respond to customers' letters and telephone requests.
- The number of errors made in processing checks.
- The number of accounts closed at each branch each week or month.
- The number of customer complaints received each month.

- The number of customer complaints resolved satisfactorily each month. (This may require a supervisor or an independent agent.)

How Are Banks Improving the Quality of Their Services?

First Wachovia. First Wachovia (a regional bank based in Winston-Salem, North Carolina) conducts business in the North Carolina and Georgia areas. First Wachovia has elected to be the low-cost provider of high-quality services. To do so, it has established a "Personal Banker" program. Instead of a customer becoming familiar with a particular branch, a customer has a single point of contact for all of her banking needs. There are four ranks to the personal banker program. The lowest level handles around 2,000 ordinary customers, while the highest levels handle a few wealthy individuals or corporate accounts.

Personal bankers aren't glorified tellers. They're decision makers. They approve loans, open accounts, and are well placed to make sensible recommendations since they can see the customer's entire banking picture. Selling additional products is made easier because the personal banker can identify gaps in client portfolios and make suggestions. By tying salary of the personal bankers to their customer accounts' size and quality (analyzing such factors as growth rates, yields, and default rates), a blending of banker and seller occurs that results in a high-quality service to the customer ("Mix and Match: State Street and Wachovia Are Two Making the Future Work," *The Economist*, April 7, 1990).

First Wachovia's percentage of nonperforming assets to total loans is significantly below that of most other regional banks its size (in one recent year 0.37 percent of the total compared to the national average of 1.22 percent). First Wachovia was second in market capitalization-to-asset ratio. Over a 10-year period (1979–89), total return for shareholders was 20.4 percent, compared with 14.9 percent for the Standard & Poor 500 index ("Medlin Reveals His Secrets," *United States Banker*, Vol. 100, August 1990, p. 26).

But this success didn't come without a price. An expensive, extensive customized computerization effort had to be made, along with intensive software training for the staff. Such customized software is costly to develop and maintain. Data for the files weren't cheap either. The "customer information files" forming the backbone of the data for the system have taken years to collect and perfect. This high barrier has prevented most other banks from following suit. The system is now so sophisticated that customers can obtain certain account information over the phone via voice recognition technology—which had to be adapted to account for the local southern accent. This unusual service is a popular edge over the competition.

State Street—Bank and Trust. Boston-based State Street Bank and Trust Company has assets of around $7 billion. But is it a bank? State Street would seem to be a medium-sized regional bank, but it has closed or sold some 90 percent of its branches. It makes few or no student loans (a way to gain tomorrow's customer) and makes few mortgages or car loans. State Street customers are institutions with large sums of money to invest.

Why do they choose State Street? Because of its nearly unique service ability in tracking and reporting on securities portfolios. Due to reporting requirements, keeping track of the thousands of shareholders (many with multiple holdings with one institution) is a daunting task. Thus State Street looks more like a data-processing and bookkeeping company than a conventional retail bank.

State Street's strategic move into a narrow, definable service-driven niche has enabled it to capture 10 percent of the world's securities market, worth over $625 billion. In custody of the assets of mutual funds, State Street tops the list at 41 percent market share; the next competitor has a 12 percent share. The reason few others can match this is the computerization involved. Not content to rest, however, State Street continuously upgrades its computer technology, ensuring its domination in the field. (Thomas D. Steiner and Diogo B. Teixeira, *Technology in Banking*. Homewood, IL: Business One Irwin, 1990)

What Are the Features of a Successful Guarantee?

For a service guarantee to attract customers, it should be

1. *Unconditional—or its conditions should be simple.* A five-minute waiting pledge might require that customers wait for no more than five minutes during normal business hours.
2. *Easy to understand.* The guarantee should be specific and clear so both employees and customers know what to expect. A promise that service will be provided in five minutes can be monitored. A promise of prompt service can't.
3. *Meaningful.* Maryland National Bank's Performance Guarantee is an example of the sort of terms customers expect from a bank that cares about its customers. This guarantee provides that if the bank makes a mistake in a customer's account, it will give the customer $10, absorb any overdraft charges, apologize in writing to the customer, and apologize in writing to any third party affected by the mistake.
4. *Easily invoked.* If a customer has suffered from poor service, then complex complaint procedures will only exacerbate the problem and may result in the loss of the customer. An unsatisfactory, complicated procedure will likely also lead the aggrieved customer to complain to friends and colleagues.
5. *Easily fulfilled.* If a customer invokes a guarantee, then immediate corrective action may produce a statisfied customer.

A guarantee that's severely limited in scope and difficult to use is unlikely to be effective. Guarantees that offer recompense only if the customer closes his account do nothing to improve the bank's service, retain the customer's business, or minimize damage to the bank's reputation in the event of an error.

The provision of service guarantees isn't very widespread at present. But they do represent an effective means of demonstrating to customers and employees the bank's commitment to service quality. Banks that promise perfect service don't appear to have been excessively hard hit by guarantee payouts. Offering this type of guarantee is unlikely to be expensive for a bank that already achieves a high level of service quality. But such a guarantee may be costly for a bank providing poor service to customers. Principal benefits of a service guarantee include

1. It demonstrates a commitment to customers that the bank will strive to provide a service that meets certain

predetermined criteria. If these criteria aren't met, then the bank will make some form of restitution to the customer.

2. It focuses all employees' attention on the continuous improvement of service quality.

3. It encourages management to identify customers' key service requirements. Performance to meet these criteria is likely to be the most effective means of satisfying customers.

The prospect of offering a service guarantee may be daunting for banks. But guarantees may provide a clear competitive advantage if employed effectively. They can also provide a focus for a strategy directed toward providing outstanding customer service. (Based on Christopher W. L. Hart, "An Objective Look at Unconditional Service Guarantees." Reprinted from *Bankers Magazine*. New York: Warren, Gorham & Lamont © 1990 Warren Gorham Lamont. Used with permission.)

LESSONS LEARNED FROM TQM IMPLEMENTATION

Every organization is unique and needs to tailor the continuous improvement process to its own organization, culture, constraints, and marketplace. As TQM programs have been implemented and have prospered, a number of important lessons have been learned. Any organization planning to implement a continuous improvement program can benefit from the experiences of organizations that have done one already.

Here are 10 key points to remember in implementing TQM.

1. The culture of an organization must be respected when implementing a Quality Improvement Program. Individuals must be actively involved in improvement, rather than driven or threatened by it.

2. Management at all levels must be committed to Quality Improvement and must communicate this commitment to the entire work force. This commitment must be visible and active every day and in every activity.

3. Quality Improvement will take years, not just one quarter. Quality Improvement requires careful planning to ensure a

long-term strategic focus coupled with short-term action-oriented performance goals.

4. The Quality Improvement Program should focus on understanding and meeting external customers' needs at minimum cost to the organization. It's easy to become internally focused (concentrating on improving the business processes) and forget that the business only survives through meeting external customer requirements.

5. Training is essential to transform an organization and ensure that Quality Improvement is successful. Quality Improvement can only be achieved through the involvement of individuals. Individuals will only become involved if they understand why Quality Improvement is necessary and how they can become involved and contribute. This is achieved by training. One of the most powerful forms of training is employees training other employees. This creates a powerful framework for teamwork within the organization.

6. Account for the cost of quality at the beginning of the program so that improvement can be subsequently monitored. This should be done, not as a grand top-level accounting exercise, but as a means of identifying and tabulating the quality costs of the individuals in the organization. Quality costs will only be reduced if they can be understood, owned and targeted by individuals or groups. If quality costs are identified in this way at the beginning of the program, improvements can be identified in terms of their impact on the bottom line, and Quality Improvement should lead to improved profitability.

7. Quality Improvement requires a business to change, but it's important that the change is managed. The change needn't be chaotic and take on a life of its own. This will only be achieved if Quality Improvement becomes part of the normal business activity and is managed through the normal management channels.

8. Like any other significant activity undertaken by the business, Quality Improvement must be planned, managed, monitored, reviewed, and updated as the marketplace and business evolve. Quality Improvement must be part of the strategic business plan for the organization.

9. Communication, both written and verbal, is vital to the process. Employees must understand the need for change and how it

will affect them, and they must be regularly updated on progress against the improvement plan. Without this, Quality Improvement will just wither and die. Consider lack of communication to be the buildup within a pipe or artery that eventually blocks off the flow and endangers the system.

10. Beware of TQM being seen by the work force as "just the latest fad." So many fads have been forced on employees over the years that they will be understandably wary of any new program and will resist it for a long time, believing it will "go away" if they can avoid it long enough. Both management and employees need to understand that Quality Improvement isn't just another fad, nor is it a tool or technique that can be implemented and then forgotten about. Management must demonstrate that TQM is much more than that—it's a long-term strategic commitment that involves everyone in the organization and is a new way of corporate life.

Chapter Ten

What Can We Learn from the Quality Gurus?*

Total Quality is a systematic approach to quality planning and the management of activities. The underlying concepts were first conceived in the United States in the late 1940s by quality practitioners, such as W. Edwards Deming and Joseph Juran. After the second World War, these principles were rapidly embraced by Japan in rebuilding its industry. In those years a number of American *quality gurus* spent considerable time in Japan teaching the philosophy and techniques of quality control.

During that period, consumer demand in the West was so great that product quality didn't seem particularly important so it wasn't clearly addressed by industry. But in the 1960s and 1970s, US industry increasingly began to focus attention on quality. The drive for this quality revolution stemmed primarily from demands of the military and related customers. Only later did the principles percolate through to consumer products.

WORK OF THE QUALITY GURUS

A relatively small group of American and Japanese quality experts have developed a number of concepts and methodologies that have profoundly impacted how companies approach and manage quality. These experts are frequently referred to as quality gurus.

* The authors thank Professor Tony Bendell, East Midlands Electricity Professor of Quality Management and director of the Quality Unit at Nottingham Polytechnic for permission to quote from "The Quality Gurus; What Can They Do for Your Company?" (a booklet he prepared for the Department of Trade and Industry's "Managing into the 90's" program on behalf of Services Ltd., Nottingham).

Besides developing their own quality philosophy, many of the gurus are charismatic individuals who generate excitement and enthusiasm for quality.

Each expert has a different perspective and approach to quality, which depends in part on his business or professional background. Although there are differences in approach, there's also much common ground between their approaches. The gurus' common commitments include

1. Quality is the key to a successful business. Inadequate attention to quality will lead to the business's failure in the long run.

2. Quality improvements require management's full commitment to succeed. This commitment to quality must be continuous. Once made, it will quickly be seen to be worthless if, for example, product is shipped although it doesn't conform to requirements.

3. Quality improvement is hard work. There are no short cuts or quick fixes. Successful quality improvement frequently requires a change in culture for the whole organization.

4. Quality improvement always requires extensive training.

5. Successful quality improvement requires all employees' active involvement and senior management's absolute commitment.

Most of the gurus' methodologies focus on a basic underlying philosophy together with tools and actions to effect quality improvement. Some experts focus on particular tools for quality improvement in specific areas, while others consider the business as a whole.

Each guru can provide an important insight into how to tackle problems and implement quality improvement in practice. Some philosophies are more accessible than others. Perhaps the most accessible guru worldwide is Philip Crosby. Crosby has written a number of books on quality management. He has also founded Crosby Associates, a worldwide quality consultancy specializing in the practical implementation of quality improvement methods. Although Crosby Associates follows the Crosby methodology, it tailors the implementation of quality improvement programs to ensure that its clients take ownership of them.

Other gurus, such as Deming, have written extensively on quality issues, give talks, and lead training seminars. But Deming doesn't have an associated consultancy with a standard methodology to implement. The Deming approach appears to be that there's no methodology to install; the only way to succeed is for the company to work out an approach that fits the organization's own culture and language.

For most companies the most appropriate approach is to take account of the gurus' ideas and adapt these to suit the organization's culture. Companies frequently find it helpful to take advice from external quality consultants during the implementation process. But a business can only obtain a long-term benefit if it takes ownership of the Quality Improvement Program. This approach may take longer and require greater perseverance and experimentation to implement successfully, than to rely on the approach put forward by any one of the gurus in isolation.

The remainder of this chapter describes briefly the key principal gurus' key ideas and their practical application. One short chapter can't fully describe these gurus' contributions. A number of books cover each of the gurus in depth.

PHILIP CROSBY

Crosby's quality experience was gained through working on a number of US missile projects and from 14 years' experience as ITT's corporate vice president responsible for quality.

His philosophy is underpinned by four *"absolutes of quality"* that answer fundamental questions:

1. What is quality?
2. What system is needed to cause quality?
3. What performance standard should be used?
4. What measurement system is required?

The four absolutes are

1. Quality has to be defined as conformance to requirements, not as goodness or excellence.
2. The system for causing quality is prevention, not appraisal.

3. The performance standard must be Zero Defects, not "that's close enough."

4. The measurement of quality is the price of nonconformance, not indexes.

These concepts have a wide range of supporters, although many people have difficulty accepting the concept of Zero Defects. It's sometimes portrayed as simplistic and unrealistic to expect individuals to perform every activity perfectly. It just won't happen. Crosby's explanation of Zero Defects is that it's not an exhortation to the work force to do better, but it's a management performance target. It's not meant to imply that errors will never happen, but that they shouldn't be expected to happen. When errors do occur, they shouldn't be accepted as inevitable. Prevention activities should be introduced to ensure that errors don't occur.

Crosby believes that management is the cause of at least 80 percent of the quality problems within an organization. The only way to improve is through the leadership of management. To eliminate the many nonconformances in an organization, Crosby recommends administering a *quality vaccine*.

The Quality Vaccine

This consists of three components administered in equal measure:

1. *Determination*: management's recognizing that its action is the only tool that will change the organization's profile.

2. *Education*: helping all employees develop a common language of quality and understand their individual roles in the quality improvement process.

3. *Implementation*: guiding the improvement program.

Crosby's 14 Steps to Quality Improvement

Building on the philosophy of the four absolutes and the components of the quality vaccine, Crosby recommends 14 steps that any organization can follow to achieve continuous quality improvement:

1. Management commitment.

2. A quality improvement team to pilot the improvement process.

3. Measurement of quality throughout the organization.
4. Cost of quality analysis throughout the organization.
5. Quality awareness of all employees.
6. Corrective action implementation.
7. Zero Defects program planning to plan the commitment to Zero Defects.
8. Employee education.
9. Zero Defects day to make the Zero Defects commitment.
10. Goal setting to target improvements.
11. Error cause removal to highlight and fix problems causing nonconformances.
12. Recognition of those who make an outstanding contribution.
13. Quality councils to coordinate improvement and share ideas across sites/divisions.
14. Do it all over again.

W. EDWARDS DEMING

Dr Deming is perhaps the most widely known quality guru. After graduating as a doctor of physics, he spent his early years as a US government employee—mostly with the Department of Agriculture and Bureau of the Census, where he specialized in statistical techniques.

Following World War II, the US government played a significant role in rebuilding Japanese industry. Here Dr Deming first became involved in Japanese quality. Following his introduction of the concept of statistical quality control into Japan, the Japanese Union of Scientists and Engineers (JUSE) held a number of seminars to spread this knowledge throughout Japanese industry. Dr Deming was invited to participate in this lecture tour. This led to his long-term involvement in the development of Japanese management thinking on quality.

Statistical quality control methods have been widely adopted throughout Japan and taken up with great enthusiasm by the work force. In the early days Deming focused on statistical quality control methods. In later years he developed the concept of quality as a management activity.

Dr Deming has been recognized by the Japanese as making an outstanding contribution to quality in Japan. In 1960, he was awarded Japan's highest imperial honor, the Second Order of the Sacred Treasure. Even today, Dr Deming's contribution is recognized in the annual awards made for outstanding application of statistical quality control throughout industry, the Deming Prizes.

Deming's major philosophy is that quality improvement is achieved through the statistical control of all processes (not just those involved with the product) and the reduction in variability of these processes. He emphasizes that this can only happen if management allows it to happen by encouraging employee participation, and if employees are able to contribute through understanding processes and how they can be improved.

This management requirement is embodied in Deming's 14 points for management.

Deming's 14 Points for Management

1. Create constancy of purpose to improve product and service.
2. Adopt new philosophy. Management must accept responsibility and lead the change process.
3. Cease dependence on inspection; build quality into the product.
4. End the awarding of business on price. Instead minimize total cost of ownership.
5. Improve constantly and forever the system of production and service.
6. Institute training on the job.
7. Institute leadership and supervision of workers.
8. Drive out fear to improve the effectiveness of all employees.
9. Break down barriers between departments; all departments must work together to achieve results.
10. Eliminate slogans, exhortations, and numerical targets.
11. Eliminate quotas or work standards as well as management by objectives or numerical goals.
12. Remove barriers that rob people of their right to pride of workmanship.

13. Institute a vigorous education and self-improvement program.
14. Put everyone in the company to work to accomplish the change in how the company works.

These 14 steps summarize the management goals. Dr Deming has been highly critical of Western managers, viewing the way they work as totally counterproductive to quality improvement through employee involvement. He calls the key weaknesses in Western management style the "Deadly Diseases." These include

1. Lack of constancy of purpose.
2. Emphasis on short-term goals (especially profits).
3. Evaluation of performance, merit rating, or annual review.
4. Mobility of management.
5. Management only by the use of visible figures with no consideration for unknown figures.

To overcome the Deadly Diseases, Dr Deming proposed an action plan for management:

1. Management must understand and accept the 14 points and the undesirability of the Deadly Diseases. It must then formulate an action plan for change.
2. Management takes pride in having taken this decision and develops courage to follow the new direction.
3. Management explains to everyone in the company why change is required.
4. Every activity within the company is divided into stages. The customers and suppliers of each stage are identified. Each stage should be improved continually and each stage should work together.
5. An organization should be put together to guide quality improvement. Deming advocates the Plan, Do, Check, Action cycle when introducing any improvement.
6. Every employee can take part in a team to improve.
7. An organization for quality is required. (This requires the participation of statisticians to guide process improvement.)

Dr Deming has written a number of books on his philosophy and methods. The only way to decide whether Dr Deming's philosophy has something to offer a company is to invest time in seriously investigating and understanding his philosophy and how it can be applied.

JOSEPH JURAN

Joseph Juran is another guru of long standing. Like Deming, Juran was part of the early quality movement in Japan and participated in the lecture tours organized by JUSE. Unlike Deming's, Juran's focus is on the management of quality. He believes that quality control is an integral part of management control. His view in the early 1950s was that the technical control of quality was well developed but that there was no knowledge of how quality should be managed. The Juran approach therefore focuses on top and middle managers. He believes that the vast majority of quality problems are caused by management, and that the only way to improve quality is through management's participation.

Juran, like Deming, made an important contribution to the development of quality in Japan. This was recognized by the award of the Second Order of the Sacred Treasure by the emperor of Japan.

In 1951 Juran drew together many of his ideas on the management of quality, together with information on the technical control of quality, into what's probably the best-known quality book so far published, *The Quality Control Handbook*. New editions of this book are still regularly published. For many years it was regarded by many practitioners as the "Quality Bible." Later Juran publications have focused on the planning and management of quality, rather than on technical quality control. This reflects Juran's ever increasing commitment to the view that quality is an essential management discipline and that quality doesn't just happen—it must be planned. Quality control is important but it's only part of total quality improvement. Juran puts forward his "quality trilogy" for total quality improvement: quality planning, quality control, and quality improvement.

Overall improvement requires the implementation of each part of the trilogy. Juran proposes key activities for each part of the trilogy, particularly in the areas of quality planning and quality improvement.

His proposals for quality planning are

1. Identify customers and their needs. This includes internal and external customers.
2. Translate the customer needs into the language of the company.
3. Set quality goals based on these needs.
4. Develop and optimize the product/service to meet those needs.
5. Develop and optimize the process that produces the product/service.

Having understood its customers' requirements, the organization must continuously improve its ability to meet their current and future needs. To do so, Juran recommends 10 steps to quality improvement:

Juran's 10 Steps to Quality Improvement

1. Ensure that all employees are aware of the need for quality improvement. This requires management leadership.
2. Set specific goals for the continuous improvement of quality in all activities.
3. Establish an organization to ensure that goals are set and that a process for achieving them is established.
4. Ensure that all employees are trained to understand their role in quality improvement. This must include upper management since it's the cause of most quality problems.
5. Ensure that problems preventing quality improvement are eliminated by setting up problem solving project teams.
6. Ensure that quality improvement progress is monitored.
7. Ensure that outstanding contributions to quality improvement are recognized.
8. Ensure that progress and outstanding contributions are publicized.
9. Measure all processes and improvements.
10. Make sure that the continuous improvement of quality and the setting of new quality goals are incorporated into the company's management systems. Make sure that rewards are based on the results achieved.

Obviously the three principal Total Quality gurus have many ideas in common. But they also have differences in approach so each guru has something special to offer. Every company needs to identify the most appropriate approach for it. Each company is unique so each improvement program needs to be individually tailored. There's no one right way to succeed with continuous quality improvement.

THE JAPANESE QUALITY GURUS

Three Japanese gurus have made significant contributions to quality improvement in Japan. Certain of their ideas have also spread to the Western world and are applied in specific areas. These gurus have developed techniques to effect quality improvements in specific applications. They haven't generally developed a comprehensive program of continuous quality improvement.

Shigeo Shingo

A graduate mechanical engineer, Shingo (born in 1909) has spent time in industry, including the Taipei railway factory, Toyota, and Mitsubishi shipbuilding.

Shingo has focused on the control of production quality rather than the management of quality. Initially he concentrated on statistical process control. Later he developed the Zero Defects or poka-yoke concept. This concept is based on the theory that each process may be continuously monitored at the point where potential errors could occur. Once an error has been identified, the process is stopped until the source of the error is identified and corrected. In this way, Shingo claims that errors can be prevented from becoming defects so defect-free processes can be developed. The difference between poka-yoke and statistical process control is that poka-yoke monitors process parameters rather than the output of the process. In a poka-yoke system, instrumentation (not humans) is generally used to monitor the potential sources of error since it's less fallible than humans. Human skill is used to identify potential sources of error and determine the best instrumentation to use to monitor these sources.

Kaoru Ishikawa

Born in 1915, Ishikawa is a graduate in applied chemistry and a doctor of engineering. He has spent his working life as an academic at Tokyo University, with much of this time devoted to writing and working with Japanese industry on the introduction of quality control techniques.

The main focus of Ishikawa's work has been to make available statistical techniques for improving quality to grassroot workers within Japanese industry. Perhaps his greatest achievement was the successful introduction of quality circles into Japan. The quality circle movement's success in Japan was greatly influenced by the user-friendly problem solving techniques that Ishikawa introduced. These enabled quality circles effectively to investigate problems, collect good data to identify their cause, and implement solutions to eliminate them and lead to improved quality. He also developed the cause-and-effect (or Ishikawa) diagram for use by quality circles. This is a diagram used to identify, sort and document potential causes of a problem so that relationships between causes can be identified.

Genichi Taguchi

Born in 1924, Taguchi gained his early experience in the Ministry of Health, Ministry of Education, and Institute of Statistical Mathematics. He later joined Nippon Telephone and Telegraph Corporation where he began to apply statistical techniques to improve the productivity of the R&D process. The publication of a number of books, the support of a number of well-respected American statisticians, and visits to the United States have led to the application of Taguchi methods in American companies such as Ford, Xerox, ITT, and Bell Laboratories. To date, his methods have made little impact in Europe.

Taguchi has developed three key ideas that have proven controversial in the West:

1. The quadratic loss function.
2. Parameter design.
3. Statistically planned experiments.

Quadratic loss function. Taguchi has developed a unique definition of quality that underpins the rest of his philosophy. He defines quality as "the loss imparted to society from the time a product is shipped." This includes the loss to the company and the total loss to society caused by the product. This loss is defined mathematically as a quadratic loss function around the target value for the characteristic concerned. The minimum loss occurs at the target value, and the loss increases quadratically with variation from this target. This loss is minimized, and quality is optimized, when variation is minimized and the product is manufactured to the target value. Any item that varies from the target value may cause some problems and loss to the customer or society.

This differs from the traditional concept underlying quality management in the West, which holds that anything within the specification limits is equally acceptable to the customer whereas anything outside the limits is unacceptable. Taguchi has realized that, in reality, the further away the product is from the target value, the less acceptable it is. The specification limit is just the cutoff point at which the product becomes totally unacceptable.

This philosophy produces the same results as an SPC environment in which the objective is to reduce variability in output, as a result of controlling all processes.

Parameter design. Taguchi considers that the reduction in variability of output is best achieved by optimizing product and process specifications during the design stage rather than through quality control methods such as inspection or SPC.

Careful design of the product, the parts used to produce the product, the processes, the equipment and settings used to produce the product, and the tolerances of both the parts and the process settings should ensure a robust product and process that are little affected by changes in external conditions. This is achieved by assessing each parameter's susceptibility to external factors: its signal-to-noise ratio. The signal represents the required output from the process, and the noise represents how much the output is affected by external factors. Parameters and processes with the highest signal-to-noise ratio should then be selected as they produce the most robust designs.

Statistically planned experiments. A process that produces a part often has many parameters that can be varied. Changing any of the settings will affect the product. Experimentation to determine the correct setting for each parameter to optimize output can be an expensive and time-consuming task because many combinations may need to be considered. The Taguchi methodology, "Orthogonal Arrays," is a mathematical technique that minimizes the number of combinations and consequently the number of experiments that have to be carried out.

Although the Japanese gurus have a number of ideas to offer companies in specific areas of quality improvement, their beliefs aren't so accessible as the ideas of their Western counterparts. Companies should consider the Japanese gurus' ideas. But only those techniques that fit the organization and have the potential for significant benefits should be adopted.

Index

Other books of interest to you from Irwin Professional Publishing . . .

MANAGEMENT OF QUALITY
Strategies to Improve Quality and the Bottom Line
Jack Hagan
Co-published with ASQC Quality Press

Presents core concepts of quality improvement in a language any manager can
understand: the language of business. Jack Hagan examines the true state of
quality today and shows you how to link its basic principles to your company's
business strategy—including its profit-oriented objectives. (163 pages)
ISBN: 1–55623–924–6

WHY TQM FAILS AND WHAT TO DO ABOUT IT
Mark Graham Brown, Darcy E. Hitchcock, and Marsha L. Willard
Co-published with the Association for Quality and Participation

Offers a way out of the frustration, wasted energy, and endless waiting that has
recently stigmatized the quality movement! Readers will uncover the root causes for
the collapse and failure of total quality and will find practical advice for correcting and
preventing them. (285 pages).
ISBN: 0–7863–0140–6

GLOBAL QUALITY
A Synthesis of the World's Best Management Methods
Richard Tabor Greene
Co-published with ASQC Quality Press

Finally, a book that organizes the chaos of quality improvement techniques so you
can select the most appropriate system for your organization. Inside you'll find 24
quality approaches used worldwide, essentials of process reengineering, software
(groupware) techniques, and much more. Also reveals what the top 1% of quality
professionals are doing to advance quality, including 7 new quality improvement
techniques being tested in Japan! (784 pages)
ISBN: 1–55623–915–7

CORPORATE QUALITY UNIVERSITIES
Lessons in Building a World-Class Work Force
Jeanne C. Meister
Co-published with the American Society for Training and Development
A Fortune Book® Club Alternate Selection!
Discover the country's best training practices and then put them to work in your training program. This book profiles 30 innovative training programs at Motorola, General Electric, and others, giving you strategies your work force can use to become more productive. *Includes a networking guide to these 30 world-class training programs!* (275 pages)
ISBN: 1-55623-790-1

Available at fine bookstores and libraries everywhere.